# STORMIE OMARTIAN

# Stormie

**HARVEST HOUSE PUBLISHERS**
Eugene, Oregon 97402

## STORMIE

*This book is dedicated to the three most important men in my life. The first one is my dad, Mr. Dick Sherk, who is one of the greatest men who ever lived. I regret that it took me so many years to recognize that fact. The second man is my husband, Michael, whose unwavering love and support was instrumental in my becoming the whole person I am today. The third person is my beloved pastor and spiritual father, Pastor Jack Hayford. He introduced me to Jesus and over the years taught me to know and love God more each day.*

# CONTENTS

# ACKNOWLEDGMENTS

Thank you, Diane Kendrick, Constance Zachman, Dick and Margo Salsbury, Terry Harriton, Tami Pelikan, Anna Krausse, and Andrea Mejia for your long labor as my dedicated prayer partners. I pray that the blessings you have given me through your ongoing prayers will be heaped a hundredfold back upon you, but then again I don't want to limit God!

Thank you, Janet Southwell, my secretary and friend, for your belief in this project and for your willingness to stand with me in the struggle to triumph over my word processor. Without you I would still be typing and crying.

Thank you to my son, Christopher, and daughter, Amanda, for loving your imperfect mom and showing it so often. I prayed that God would cover for my failings and help me raise you. He is doing that, and I am thankful for His mercy and so very proud of you.

Thank you to my wonderful editors, Bill Jensen, Eileen Mason, Al Janssen, and Ray Oehm, for their invaluable contributions and their dedication in seeing that this book is all that God wants it to be.

# PREFACE

For awhile I believed no one had more emotional scars than I did. Now I know I was not alone. We have all had times of failure and pain. Even people who experienced a wonderful childhood are often scarred later in life by bad choices, a painful marriage, or tragedies of one kind or another. Little by little, pieces of our lives are chipped away and restoration is needed.

This is the story of my struggle to overcome the emotional damage of child abuse and the heartbreak of being a potential child-abuser. It has never been my intention to blame anyone else for what happened in my past. It's too easy to point out someone else's faults, since we all have them. And because no parent is perfect, it is cruel and unfair to hold them forever accountable for mistakes they have made. It is my goal to instead point the reader toward the One who forgives all mistakes and restores any damage that has been done.

There are countless numbers of people who experienced similar or far worse treatment than I did, and many who have given up hope for ever being healed. I am telling my story so that they will find their way out of the pit that was dug in their past and onto the path of healing and wholeness that God has ordained for them. I needed restoration and I found it. If I can find it, others can too.

I have prayed continually that this book would bring God's healing, deliverance, and restoration to anyone who desires to receive it. May God so bless each reader.

—Stormie Omartian

# Stormie

*Let the redeemed of the Lord
say so, whom He has redeemed from
the hand of the enemy.*

—Psalm 107:2

# ALIGNED WITH EVIL

I woke up late. It was ten A.M. and sunlight blazed through the cracks in the window shades. My head throbbed as I opened my eyes. The stifling air plus my sweat-encased body indicated that already the day was hot. Long into a California heat wave typical of August, my tiny two-room apartment never cooled down much. There was no air conditioning, and it was dangerous to leave the windows open at night. Sitting up abruptly in my single-sized daybed, I groaned, then fell back on the pillow. Exhausted from the fitful night's sleep, I was too groggy to get up.

I had found another rose on my front door handle when I arrived home around midnight. This made the tenth consecutive rose placed there every evening after dark. It was beginning to bother me. What at first appeared to be a flattering gesture by a secret admirer was now becoming strange. Only someone with a sick mind would continue this odd ritual day after day without identifying himself. I had a longtime problem with insomnia anyway, and this wasn't helping.

I had worked late last night taping another television segment of the Glen Campbell Show. Hired three years before as one of Glen's regular "on-camera-blonde-blue-eyed-size-eight-singer-dancers," I had become the resident actress as well. Playing dumb blonde comedienne roles, I worked with a different guest star each week. Adjusting to a new temperament every seven days was a challenge. There never seemed to be enough rehearsal time, and I suffered from chronic doubt about my abilities. Taping day, which began before dawn and lasted long into the night, had once been very exciting, but lately all I felt was exhaustion.

I sat up again, slowly this time, leaned across the bed, and turned on the television. I wasn't much for watching TV because I was afraid it would make my mind irreversibly numb. However, this morning, for no apparent reason, I turned it on.

Immediately on the screen was a full news report detailing the grisly stabbing deaths of actress Sharon Tate and four others in Benedict Canyon. That was not far from my apartment! Horror gripped me as the details of what happened unfolded. I didn't know Sharon Tate and her friends personally, but I knew who they were. Hollywood is a small town. They lived close to me and I traveled through their neighborhood frequently. The slaughter would horrify anyone, but what I began to feel was beyond horror. It was growing inside me to a paralyzing terror.

It was the knives. Sharon Tate was stabbed! I had always had an unreasonable fear of knives. For as long as I could remember, I had suffered from recurring nightmares in which I was stabbed repeatedly. The mere thought of knives made me deathly afraid.

The ring of my phone temporarily broke through the grip of fear that kept me riveted to the TV. "Did you hear about Sharon Tate and the others?" inquired a friend on the other end of the line. Many similar calls followed. No one could believe what had happened or could understand why. There seemed to be no motive for the murders.

That evening I went out to a restaurant with friends, and the Sharon Tate murders were the main topic of conversation. We all agreed that the heat wave made people crazy and that the flourishing psychedelic drug scene of the sixties had brought with it a kind of evil madness that pervaded everything.

When I returned to my apartment about 11 P.M. there was another rose draped across the door handle. I shuddered as I suddenly realized a pattern to this madness. The roses had started out as tiny buds. Gradually they had gotten bigger each night. And now they were beginning to open. What would happen, I wondered, when the roses were in full bloom? I hurried into the apartment, bolted the door, and went to bed in fear.

The next morning I immediately turned on the TV to see if there was further news about the Sharon Tate case. Desire to understand what happened and why filled my mind with the frustration of unanswered questions. Much to my horror, during the night there had been two more stabbing murders. A husband and wife by the name of LaBianca were butchered. The details matched those of Sharon Tate, and the police suspected that the murders were done by the same people.

Fear immediately spread all over town. The rich put up security fences, installed burglar alarms, and purchased guard dogs. The poor bolted their doors and windows and did not open them for anyone. I couldn't stand being alone, and my boyfriend, Rick, was out of town. The apartment was too small to have people over, so I went out with friends again that night, as I desperately needed to be with someone.

When I returned to my apartment at around two A.M. there was another rose on the door handle. This one was beginning to blossom. I quickly threw it into the bushes, ran inside, and slammed the door.

As I dressed for bed, my mind sorted through the macabre details of the stabbing death of Sharon Tate. Here was a beautiful, wealthy, young woman, nine months pregnant, living in a big house with burglar alarms and an electronic fence. She was totally protected yet totally vulnerable. She, and the others murdered with her, were not the type of people to be involved in the occult practices implied by certain news reports. They were also not the type of people you would ever think could end up murdered. If Sharon Tate could have the sanctity of her home invaded in that way, then what protection was there for me? And the knives—I couldn't even bear to think of the knives.

There was something more that bothered me. Something about the *spirit* of what had gone on there that was familiar. It was like meeting someone you know you've met before, but you can't seem to place him.

I had been heavily involved in the occult for years. It started with Ouija boards and horoscopes. Then headlong into astral projection and seances to summon the dead. Numerology fascinated me so much that I considered changing my name when I learned that if the letters in your name added up to a certain number, you could become successful, beautiful, and fulfilled. However, I knew of a promising young actress who paid a numerologist to devise a new name for her. She changed her name legally, moved to New York City to begin her life of success, and was never heard from again. A numerologist sending me into obscurity was not what I had in mind, so I decided to go on to other things.

I took hypnotism classes which were very popular in the entertainment industry. I frequently went into a trancelike state and told myself things I wanted to hear. "Stormie," I would say, "you are beautiful, successful, and a wonderful person. You can talk, sing, and act, and you are not afraid." But, like all other things I had tried, the help was only temporary, and afterwards I was worse off than before.

Next I threw myself into Science of Mind. It seemed perfectly logical to believe that there was no evil in the world except what existed in a person's mind. And if you could control your mind, you could control the amount of negative experiences you would have. I bought every book available on the subject and read each one thoroughly. I associated with other Science of Mind advocates, which wasn't hard to do because so many of the Hollywood show-business people, especially actresses, were into it. Unfortunately, the help I so desperately sought was only temporary.

I became involved in anything that told me I was worth something and that there could be a life without pain in my future. I frequently visited mediums hoping that they could give me good news. Sometimes they did and I was elated. When they didn't, I was despairing. I rode an emotional roller coaster and there was no balance to my life.

Devoting myself to Eastern religions, I began meditating daily. However, the God I searched for so diligently was distant and cold, and peace eluded me. Once, when I was in the middle of meditation, I opened my eyes to find that I was looking at my body lying on the couch across the room. This was the out-of-body experience I had read about and desired, but it didn't bring the "oneness with the universe" I had hoped. Instead it brought fear. The more involved I became, the more I saw strange things—odd beings and forms floating in front of my eyes. I didn't understand what was happening or why.

Despite the frightening aspects of the occult, I was irresistibly drawn to it. I knew there was a real spirit world because I had seen it. And the books promised that by pursuing these methods I would find God and eternal peace. Why did it seem to have the opposite effect on me? Yet because I was desperate for anything that could possibly fill my emptiness inside, soothe the intense emotional pain I felt constantly, and quell the unreasonable fear that threatened to control my mind, I continued my search. There had to be an answer for me, and I was going to find it.

Something about my occult practices reminded me of the Sharon Tate murders. I felt I was a part of what happened even though I knew I wasn't. Remembering the old adage "You always recognize your own," I found the events all too familiar. Somehow I was aligned; I could feel it. I feared that if I continued the path I was on, what happened to Sharon Tate could happen to me. Yet, I felt powerless to stop it.

"I can't think about it anymore," I said to myself as I slipped into a thin summer nightgown and headed into the bathroom to wash my face. I flipped on the light switch and was startled by the sight of hundreds of large cockroaches scurrying everywhere on the tile floor. I had lived there for more than a year and had never seen a single cockroach before.

I dashed into the kitchen for a can of pesticide and sprayed the bathroom ruthlessly until every bug was dead. The thought of sleeping there with even one living cockroach drove me on. When there was no sign of life, I finally stopped. By then the smell of poison was deathly strong. In my tiny place I knew that I couldn't stay in those fumes for long, yet at two o'clock in the morning it was too late to go anywhere else. I threw open the bathroom window as wide as it would go to try and air out the room and hopefully the whole apartment.

I went to my closet just outside the bathroom and began to hang up the clothes I had tossed there. As I put the last garment in place, I heard a rustling of leaves through the opened window. My apartment building was located in the hills surrounded by trees and bushes and often there were small furry animals that scampered about.

I held very still and listened for more sounds. The rustling came closer and sounded more like footsteps than small animals. They stopped directly under the window and I heard something slide slowly up the wall. When I saw what I thought was a hand grab the top of the windowsill, I was terrified. Having no place to hide, I screamed with every bit of bodily strength I could muster and ran for the front door. Thoughts of Sharon Tate, the LaBiancas, and bloody knives raced through my mind. The way the apartments were situated on the hillside, each one was isolated in a checkerboard effect with bushes and trees in between. For me to try and run to someone else's apartment would be risky, especially if no one was home. Once outside, I stopped screaming and hid in the thick bushes.

I hardly let myself breathe. My heart nearly pounded out of my chest. I stayed like that for what must have been close to a minute. Then I heard movement again, this time on the roof of the apartment closest to me. That apartment was situated above mine and nestled into the hillside so a person could hop on the roof easily from the road above it. I peered through the bushes, and there was a man's form coming cautiously over the roof. He held a flashlight and shined it to and fro on the ground just in front of me. In back of him I perceived another form. The glare of the flashlight made it difficult to see clearly, but it appeared that there were two men dressed in black. One man yelled in my direction.

"Is anyone down there?"

I was silent.

He shouted it again with more conviction. I held my breath. The third time he yelled, he turned in such a way that I caught a glimpse of a gun in its holster and what looked like a policeman's hat. From the bushes I called, "Yes. I'm down here. Who are you?"

"We're the police. Come out where we can see you."

"Thank God!" I cried as I moved cautiously from my hiding place. "Someone tried to come in my bathroom window. I screamed and ran outside and hid here in the bushes."

"We heard the screams from our police car as we were patrolling the neighborhood. You stay right here. We'll check around back and see if we find anything."

I was filled with relief that they had providentially arrived in perfect time, but I didn't want them to leave me alone. I hid in the bushes again as they made their search. It was only a minute or two before they came back and said, "Whoever was here is gone now. Your screams probably scared him away."

They escorted me back inside the apartment and searched it thoroughly to make sure no one was there. The apartment was so tiny it took all of 30 seconds to check the kitchen, under the bed in the main room, the closet, and the shower. There was no place else to look. They could have just passed it off as nothing but a petty burglar, but I could tell that because of the Tate-LaBianca murders they were taking this event seriously. I desperately wanted them to stay, for I was still afraid. Instead, I thanked them profusely, bid them goodnight, and locked the door and the bathroom window. After they were gone, I suddenly realized that in my fright I had not mentioned the roses to them.

I went to bed but tossed and turned. With every noise my body stiffened and my heart pounded. I could hardly breathe from the heat, and sleep eluded me.

The next day my boyfriend, Rick, called. He was back in town after a long tour with his band. We had sung together in the same group for several years and then started dating. I told him about all the events of the night before, as well as about the roses, and of course we talked about the Tate-LaBianca murders.

We went out that night, and on the way back home we drove over the canyon near Sharon Tate's house. It was a direct route from Beverly Hills to my apartment and one we traveled frequently. The road was deserted and appeared unusually dark. Terror crept over my back, inside my chest, and up into my throat until I nearly convulsed with fright. The fear was so strong that if someone had touched me at that point I'm sure my heart would have stopped. I tried desperately to pull myself together so Rick wouldn't notice what was going on inside me. Keeping up a good front was very important. No one must ever learn that I wasn't totally together.

Rick walked me up the long winding stairs to my door, and there, draped over the door handle, lay another rose. He picked it up. The beautiful red velvet petals were unfolding.

"Stormie!" A young woman's voice penetrated our intense silence. It was my friend Holly, who lived a few apartments down the hill. She was just coming in with her boyfriend.

I grabbed the rose and ran down the stairs. "Holly, look! Another rose! They keep getting bigger, and I'm afraid that whoever is leaving them might be planning to do something terrible."

Holly was concerned as well. This had all started as a joke, and we had laughed over it just the week before. But now it wasn't funny anymore.

"I have an idea," said Holly. "Let's wait out in the bushes tomorrow night and see if we can discover who it is."

"Are you serious?" My voice betrayed my fear.

"Don't worry. He'll never see us. We figure he comes around ten every evening, right? Let's meet here at nine." Rick and Holly's boyfriend agreed to watch with us.

When the time came, we positioned ourselves in four strategic places, hidden in the bushes outside of my apartment. In order to get to my front door, the rose man would have to go by one or all of us.

We waited.

No one came.

We were silent except for a brief exchange at about 11 concerning whether we should stop at midnight or continue on. Midnight came and still no one showed up. Finally we were tired and aching from staying cramped for so long and decided to call it quits.

Holly and her boyfriend went home. Rick walked me to my apartment, came in for a drink, then left around 12:30 A.M. I readied myself for bed, then went to the front door to make sure it was locked securely. As I opened the door to slam it tightly shut, a bright, beautiful rose, almost in full bloom, fell at my feet.

I gasped and my heart started to pound. Quickly I slammed the door shut. My mind raced. Always before the roses had come around ten P.M., never at one A.M. The only answer was that the rose man had been watching me. He knew we were waiting in the bushes. He knew that Rick was in my apartment. He knew when Rick left. He had been watching.

I quickly called Rick who had just arrived home. Without giving him a chance to speak I told him what happened. "Obviously we were observed," he stated. "Perhaps it's someone in the apartment complex."

I called Holly and she suggested that the two of us go door-to-door in the morning, telling our neighbors about the roses and the near break-in, and asking questions. Maybe someone had seen or heard something.

The next morning we started knocking on doors. *No one* had heard the screaming of two nights before even though two policemen driving by had heard it from inside their car. No one had seen anyone suspicious. But, yes, they would tell us if they did.

The last apartment we checked belonged to a large, dark-haired, mustached man named Leo. He was in his mid-twenties and a would-be actor like every other male in town. We had talked briefly several times and each time he had asked me to go out with him. I always assured him I was steadily and seriously dating someone else and he always backed off. I tried to maintain a friendly but distant relationship with him because something about him was strange.

When we questioned Leo he said he had heard the screaming. This was odd because other people who were home the night of the attempted break-in, and whose apartments were closer to mine, had *not* heard it. I was amazed that he heard me cry for help but never even checked to see what was wrong. I told him about the roses and he said he had seen no one suspicious.

"I'm concerned," I said. "Anyone who would leave a rose on my door handle 14 days in a row without identifying himself has got to be a weirdo with a sick mind."

The moment I said the words "weirdo with a sick mind" I saw Leo's eyes wince and his expression darken. It was ever so subtle and only for a moment, but his look was exactly what one would expect if I had said that about *him*. In that very instant, I knew it *was* him. I had wounded him with what I said and now I was even more afraid. Politely I thanked him and we left quickly.

I knew I had to get out of my apartment so I made plans to move immediately. I found a place away from the hills and moved quietly and secretly early the next morning while it was still dark. Because I had few belongings, the move was easy. I left no forwarding address.

Afraid that the rose man would find out where I lived and follow me, my first few nights alone in the new apartment were filled with tension. The Tate-LaBianca murderers were still at large and, as far as I was concerned, so was he.

But nothing happened. The roses stopped. Only the fear remained.

# CHAPTER TWO
## Stormie

# ESCAPE INTO MARRIAGE

I rushed past the guard at the entrance to the giant CBS building on Beverly Boulevard. Having seen me almost daily for four years, he didn't question my identity but waved me on through. Up the elevator and down the hall to the enormous sound stage where the Glen Campbell Show was being filmed that day, I practically collided with the director.

"Sorry I'm late, Jack," I apologized, as I had done countless times before.

"You're working yourself too hard, Stormie," he reprimanded in his stern but kind voice. He knew that I was filming another local TV program on the three days away from the Campbell Show, which meant no time off whatsoever. The look on his face questioned my sanity.

Unable to confess that I was too insecure to turn down any work, I joked, "They're hounding me, Jack. Dumb blondes are the rage this year, you know."

He gave me a fatherly hug and said, "Get to makeup quick. Cher is sick and can't do one of the skits with Glen. You're going to do it."

"What!" I exclaimed with surprise on my face and terror in my heart.

"You're exactly the same size, so her costume will fit," he assured me. "A quick study like you will have no problem with the lines. Besides, you've watched them rehearsing all week, so you'll remember the blocking."

I was constantly amazed at Jack's faith in me. "What about

my own skit with Glen?'' I questioned.

"You'll be able to do both. Cher's costume lady will help you with the fast changes. I'll send someone to run over your lines with you right after makeup.''

I ran straight to the makeup room and collapsed in a chair in front of the head man. "I need a miracle, Ben. They're making me a star today, and you've got to make me beautiful,'' I joked.

Ben Nye was an expert, so I didn't have to worry about what he was going to do. I closed my eyes and tried to breathe calmly and pull myself together. It was only eight in the morning and already I was exhausted. In the months following the Sharon Tate murders I had filled my life with work. Not only did I have two TV series a week, but I also crammed every spare hour with recording sessions and commercials. I was obsessed with working. It helped minimize my deep feelings of inadequacy and keep a tighter rein on the depression and fear that always threatened to control my life.

Depression was something I dealt with daily. For most of my life, at least as far back as 13 years old, I awakened every morning to the thought "Should I kill myself now or can I make it through one more day?'' When my alarm sounded at five this morning, I lay frozen in bed, trying to decide what to do. "You've got an important job to do today,'' I had told myself. "You're doing a great skit with Glen Campbell. Rehearsal has gone well.

"No, I can't kill myself today,'' I'd finally decided. "If this part I'm doing turns out great, I might be recognized as an important talent. Then everyone will love me and I won't feel any more pain.'' It had taken only a few minutes to get myself out of bed this morning; some days it took hours. Unfortunately, I believed I was only as good as my last performance, so when a job was over so were my good feelings about myself.

"You're gorgeous!'' said Ben as he put the finishing touches of mascara on my false eyelashes.

"You're a genius Ben,'' I smiled and ran off to Cher's dressing room. It was the fancy one with the big star. The crew had taken down her name and put up mine in their own crude handwriting.

It made me laugh, and I appreciated their constant support. I admired Cher and thought she was one of the most beautiful stars I had ever worked with. I was sorry she was sick, yet thrilled to fill in for her.

"Hi, Maggie," I greeted the costume lady.

"Stormie, we're late," she said, concerned for me as well as herself. Jack ran a tight schedule, and wardrobe people were responsible for having the star dressed and in the proper place at the proper time. An aide came by with my lines, and Maggie helped me dress as I quickly studied them.

"All cast for the opening scene on stage immediately," boomed the assistant director over the loudspeaker just as Maggie zipped up the back of my costume. "It fits perfectly," she beamed.

Off I ran to take my place in front of the camera on the mark designated by a little piece of blue tape on the floor.

Glen Campbell came in and gave me a big hug. "How're you doing this morning, lady?" he smiled.

"Great!" I lied. "Do I look enough like Cher?" I joked nervously, running my hands through my long blonde hair and blinking my blue eyes. Compared with Cher's dark-eyed, black-haired beauty, I felt terribly inadequate.

"You look sensational!" Glen stated in his usual sweet, encouraging manner. He was a wonderful employer, and besides admiring his talent, I loved him as a person.

"Cameras are rolling! 5-4-3-2-1 action!"

I remembered all the blocking, and with the help of cue cards I got through all the lines without a mistake.

"Great!" boomed Jack's voice over the P.A. system. "Let's run it one more time and I think we have it. Good job, Stormie— I knew you could do it!" I was elated to hear that encouragement, and wondered why I myself could never feel that good about anything I did.

On my way back to the dressing room after the scene was over, one of the pretty blonde singers said, "The costume looks great, Stormie. Too bad you don't have Cher's voice."

"Yes, and her money too," I laughed.

Although I'm sure the comment was spoken innocently, it

triggered a memory from far back in my past. Immediately
unreasonable fear gripped my chest and unbearable pain from
deep within my gut rose up into my throat and made it difficult
to speak. Breathing became labored and I felt like I was suffocat-
ing. I had to get to a bathroom, dressing room, or empty rehearsal
hall as soon as possible.

"I'll be right back, Maggie," I said breathlessly as I ran past
her into the cast bathroom. "Just give me a few moments."

Once inside, I locked the door, braced myself against the wall,
and tried to stifle the convulsive sobs that were just beneath the
surface. The pain in my gut was so intense that I wanted to die.
When I contained myself enough to return to work, I acted as
if nothing happened. Keeping up a good front for others was
a constant requirement for me.

"You okay, honey?"

"Sure, Maggie—just a minor emergency," I laughed. "Help
me out of this costume."

I breathed a shaky sigh of relief. Once again no one suspected
anything about my anxiety attacks. Because of them I didn't allow
relationships to get too close, for I would never be able to explain
my actions to someone else when I didn't even understand them
myself. I assumed that I had these attacks because I was
strange—a misfit. If I let someone get too close, they might figure
that out, and I couldn't bear the thought of rejection. Besides,
in my eyes everyone else was perfect, and I fell short by comparison. The closer I got to other people, the more intense the
comparison became and the more aware I was of all my short-
comings. It was better to remain at a distance.

The taping day ended a success and I was relieved. "Great
job, Stormie—I knew you'd do it!" beamed Jack as he left the
sound booth to go home. "See you in a couple weeks."

"A couple weeks?" I questioned. Then before he could answer
I said, "Oh, of course, the two-week hiatus while Glen's out of
town. Sure, see you then." My heart sank. Since my other TV
show had just ended its 13-week season, that meant no work at
all for two weeks. The thought terrified me. When I wasn't
working, I lived in the throes of constant depression. I did find

that drugs helped and because it was the late 60's, they were everywhere. In fact, they were almost difficult to avoid. Psychedelic
drugs were used commonly too, but people were freaking out
from them all the time and ending up in a mental hospital. I
wasn't about to drop any acid. I was too close to ending up in
a mental hospital as it was. Simple marijuana was good enough
for me.

I found that as long as I was either working or stoned I could
survive life, but I was careful not to combine the two. Work meant
too much to me to jeopardize that. Even though I was into health
food and exercise in the extreme, I still smoked and drank, and
marijuana was a part of every gathering.

That night I took some downers and went to sleep dreading
the next day. As expected, I woke at midmorning thinking,
"You're no good. Why don't you kill yourself?

"You did well yesterday, but yesterday is gone and you won't
do anything good again.

"You'll never amount to anything.

"Who are you kidding? Everyone knows you don't have it.

"You're a nobody."

Slowly and steadily depression sank on me like a thick, still
blanket. When I couldn't withstand the force of it any longer,
I knew I was entering one of my "blackouts."

For the next two weeks I could barely function. I lay in bed
unable to read or even watch TV, getting up to do only the
minimum requirements for life. The only thing that could have
lifted the "blackout" was a call for work. But no one called.

When the Glen Campbell Show resumed, I returned to CBS
with the usual mixed emotions. I was eager to work yet always
fearful that someone would find out about my lack of ability
and my intense fear. I waved to the guard at the gate. "Did you
have a nice vacation, Stormie?" he yelled.

"Great!" I called back. "Not long enough, though."

"I know what you mean," he laughed. I laughed with him and
perfectly masked the person I was.

● ● ●

As helpful as it always seemed, I did recognize that marijuana was becoming a problem for me. One night before a trip to Las Vegas to work with Glen Campbell in the main showroom of the MGM Grand Hotel, I stayed up late getting stoned with friends. I slept a few hours, then left at six A.M. for the airport, not realizing that I was still under the influence of the drugs from the night before. Traveling down the main boulevard to the freeway, I didn't hear an ambulance coming full speed in the opposite direction until it came over a rise in the road. We were inches from a head-on collision. I jerked to the right as he swerved left. We were so close as he sped by that the air between us jostled my car. As I braked to a stop to catch my breath, I realized that everyone else on the road had already pulled to the side. They had heard the sirens; I hadn't heard a thing. I knew then that I was going to kill myself if I didn't back off from the drinking and drugs.

A few weeks later at Rick's house, I baked a pan of brownies with a large amount of marijuana in it. Rick ate a few pieces and I nearly finished off the rest of the pan by myself. I had an uncontrollable chocolate habit, and once I started eating it I couldn't stop until it was gone.

It takes longer to get high from eating marijuana than smoking it, but once the high happens it doesn't wear off for a long time. I didn't pay attention to the amount I had eaten. At first I got giddy and silly, then dizzy and numb. Suddenly I realized that I had eaten way too much, for a crushing heaviness settled in my body and I felt like I was going to pass out.

"I've got to lie down," I said breathlessly to Rick as I stumbled to the couch and fell facedown. I hung on tightly to the cushion as the room began spinning so fast I thought I would disintegrate. Soon I couldn't move. I was paralyzed. My body felt dead, but inside I was still very much alive, trapped and unable to escape.

*Where was Rick? Why wasn't he helping me?* I called his name. Or at least I thought I did. But there was no answer.

Six hours later I finally managed to lift my head. I could see Rick in the bedroom asleep. It took another two hours to force my body to the kitchen, where I washed my face with cold water and got something to drink.

*What a stupid move!* Had I almost killed myself again because of drugs? I knew I had to take action to correct my lifestyle or I was going to self-destruct, but I felt powerless to do it. Something inside was driving me to keep making bad choices—choices for death—over and over. Half of me wanted to die, and the other half wanted to live but didn't know how to.

In the months that followed the Tate-LaBianca murders, the mystery surrounding them began to unfold. A group heavily involved in the occult and drugs was responsible. *I* was involved in the occult and drugs too. Was that where I was going to end up—with my mind so fried that I didn't even know right from wrong or life from death? Fear engulfed me more than ever now—fear of death, fear of rejection, fear of failure. I wished desperately that I didn't have to live alone.

One morning about 4:30 as I slept soundly in my apartment, my bed began to shake violently and a loud overwhelming rumble from the bowels of the earth convinced me that I was in the middle of an earthquake. Instantly I knew it was a bad one, certainly the most violent shaking I'd ever experienced. I thought the walls and ceiling were going to cave in and I would die a painful death—crushed, maimed, and all alone. The quake was violent enough to frighten anyone, and since my normal state was one of fear, this made me hysterical.

I ran for the door of my bedroom; the force of the shaking threw me against the wall. Groping for the doorpost in the pitch black of the room, I used it to pull myself into the hallway. I was thrown from side to side against the walls of the short and narrow hall, then out into the living room, where I landed hard against the coffee table.

I grabbed the phone and stumbled back to the doorjamb of the hallway, where I knew I was safest. Falling to the floor, I tried to dial the phone, but the tremors were so violent that my fingers couldn't rest on the dial. I tried three or four times before I realized the phone was dead. All power was off. There were no street lights. In the total darkness I dropped the phone, grabbed the doorjamb, and hung on tightly to keep from being thrown against the walls. "God help me!" I pleaded. "God, please help me!"

All around I could hear the crashing of dishes falling out of the cupboards, paintings dropping off the walls, and lamps shattering against the floor. The enormous roar of the earth rumbled so loud that I could barely hear my own screams.

What lasted only a few moments seemed like eternity. Finally the rumbling and shaking stopped. The sun was just beginning to rise, but I hung onto the doorpost until I could see enough to get to the bedroom, throw on jeans and a T-shirt, grab my purse, and get out. I didn't check the damage. That was the last thing that concerned me. Earthquakes that violent would have aftershocks that could bring the roof down. I was terrified of dying alone.

Once outside, I ran to my car and sped off quickly to Rick's house. Broken glass and fallen trees were everywhere. While I was driving, the first aftershock hit, and immediately I pulled to a stop away from power lines to wait it out. The highway rolled and rippled like it was made of rubber. I had visions of the earth opening up and swallowing me so that I would never be heard from again. When it was over I made my way cautiously.

During the drive to Rick's place I resolved that I couldn't live alone any longer. I wasn't brave enough to live openly with a man, and I couldn't live with a girlfriend because I desperately needed a man's affection. Besides, my steady stream of boyfriends was enough to irritate even the most patient of women.

Marriage was the answer, and Rick was the most likely candidate. I had known him the longest of all the fellows I was dating. We were somewhat compatible. Beyond eating together and having sex, what else was there to any relationship? Besides, Rick was one of the few men I was dating who was not married. I was forever ending up with some guy who had just freshly separated from his wife—or intending to as I would later find out. They were not good candidates for the security in marriage I needed. Even if Rick wasn't the greatest partner, I decided that I would rather have a two-year marriage with a nice friendly divorce than live alone.

Over the next few weeks I set about to manipulate Rick into asking me to marry him. I cajoled, pleaded, threatened, sulked, and stomped. I told him I didn't want to live alone, and we must either make plans to be married or the relationship was over. Finally one night he said, "Okay, I'll marry you. But it's got to be 50-50 financially. I'll make a down payment on a house if you pay the monthly payments and all the rest of the bills."

I said, "Okay," but I would have agreed to anything.

After Rick put the down payment on the house we were to live in, we made plans to get married right away. His family was Catholic, and although I had never heard him mention God, he insisted on a Catholic wedding. What did I care? A Buddhist wedding would have been fine with me. I just wanted a male roommate.

Four weeks before the wedding, a young singer friend of mine named Terry Stilwell called to ask me to sing on a Christian recording session. The leader of that session was Jimmy Owens who with his wife Carol was recording a musical that they had written called "Show Me." It was a full three days of work, and I was eager to do it.

From the start this recording session was peaceful and pleasant, in direct contrast to the stress and pressure of the Hollywood recording business. I didn't know any of the people in the studio except Terry, who informed me that everyone there was a Christian. She never mentioned the fact that I wasn't.

I watched each person carefully. Christians to me had always fallen into two categories. Either they were insensitive and obnoxious, trying to beat you over the head with their Bibles, or else they were bland, boring, uninteresting, and without any known personality.

The Christians on this recording session were different. In some ways they *were* boring because nobody drank, smoked, did drugs, told dirty jokes, or swore. So when I was with them I felt I shouldn't do those things either. I wondered what they did for excitement. Yet there was a very appealing and clean quality about them. They were genuinely caring, and when I was around them I felt comforted and peaceful. They treated me like someone special as opposed to the outsider that I felt I was.

On our first break of the first day, Terry introduced me to a young man she had been telling me about for weeks. I gathered she thought we would be perfect for each other, so I was somewhat wary but curious at the same time. The minute I saw him, however, all doubts were dispelled. He was the cutest guy I'd ever seen. He had thick, dark, curly hair, beautiful olive skin, and large, expressive brown eyes that confirmed his Armenian heritage. He had an intensity about him and a sense of purpose that was very attractive to me. I was smitten the minute I saw him.

"Stormie, I want you to meet Michael Omartian," Terry said and left us alone to talk. Michael was warm and friendly, and I enjoyed his company immensely. As we talked I heard violins and saw hearts. I was transported into another realm where no one else existed except us.

We were together every spare minute over the next few days, never running out of things to say. During one break, everyone except Michael and me left the studio to go for coffee. Michael sat down at the piano to play while I leaned across the side of it to watch his hands and listen intently.

When he finished the song I said in amazement, "Michael, you're one of the greatest piano players I've ever heard."

He smiled, looked down at the keyboard, and shook his head. "That's nice of you, but it hasn't been easy finding work." I heard the frustrated musician in his voice.

"It's only a matter of time for you, Michael. You're a major talent, and it won't be long before other people recognize it." I had been around Hollywood long enough to be certain that what I was telling him was true and not just flattery.

"It just depends on what the Lord wants," he stated.

"The Lord?" I questioned. "What does the Lord have to do with it?"

"Do you know anything about Jesus?" he questioned.

"Sure, Science of Mind teaches that He was a good man. Play me another one of your songs," I quickly changed the subject.

He complied and I studied his intensity as he played. I was attracted to him in a profound way. He had a confidence and an energy that I found irresistible. The more my attraction for him increased, the more my confusion also increased. I thought about Rick and our plans to be married. "What am I doing?" I asked myself. I had no answers, so I kept silent.

At the end of the third day I invited Michael to my apartment for a "health drink." He had been sick for weeks, he told me, and was unable to shake the congestion in his head. Having been into health foods for some time, I had a combination of things I knew would help.

"Hi, Michael," I smiled with enthusiasm as I opened the door. I was eager to be with him again.

"Hello," he said coolly. I was taken back by his sudden change from the warm person I met at the studio.

There was little conversation as I mixed up a concoction of brewer's yeast, wheat germ, lecithin granules, vitamin C, acidophilus, and more into a glass of grape juice. As he drank it, I could tell he thought it might kill him. However, my credibility was saved when in 20 minutes his head started to clear.

We made small talk quietly and with great hesitation on his part. There was something different about him now. He had been friendly at the studio, but now he was cool. I didn't understand it. Perhaps I had misread his friendliness. Or maybe he felt uncomfortable about being in my apartment late at night. After all, he was one of those Christians. Or maybe he saw through me and found many things he didn't like.

When he left I was painfully sad. I had felt so good being with him at the studio, and now this encounter was so strained. It reaffirmed my beliefs that there were no good relationships, only tolerable ones. You just had to grab a tolerable one and get all the life you could out of it until it was time to go on to the next. I was getting married because I couldn't take living alone and Rick was the most tolerable of all the relationships. We would do well if we could stand living together for more than two years.

Even though I accepted the fact that what seemed like a potentially fantastic relationship had fizzled, I couldn't get Michael out of my mind. There was a quality in him that I loved. Something beyond just physical, although that was certainly there too. I couldn't give it a name, but it was the same dynamic of life that I recognized in my friend Terry.

Two weeks later Terry asked me to go with her to visit her friend Paul Johnson, a well-known Christian musician. Michael was one of his two roommates. They lived up in the hills of Sherman Oaks in a large, modern house with enormous windows that overlooked the city. The view was tremendous. The view inside was even better with these three good-looking fellows. All of them had clean, healthy, vital good looks plus that sweet, loving, irresistible quality that I still couldn't put into words.

When I saw Michael again he wasn't cold this time—only tentative and cautious. Like before, I was caught up somewhere between heaven and earth as we talked about one thing after another. He asked me out for dinner the following night, and I accepted.

At the restaurant our conversation began to move beyond things, places, and people to the deeper topic of feelings. He explained that the reason he turned suddenly cool at my apartment was because Terry revealed to him my plans to be married. He was confused and baffled. "Terry thinks you're making a big mistake, Stormie," he said emphatically, "and so do I."

"I know I'm making a mistake, but I can't do anything about it. The whole thing is set in motion and I can't stop it." I swallowed hard to fight back tears.

I couldn't tell him I was terrified to live alone, that I didn't deserve anything better, and that if anyone were to find out what I was really like he wouldn't want me. How could I share that I believed there were no good relationships, at least not for me?

I saw Michael every night for the ten nights before my wedding date. Rick never questioned where I was. One night Michael came to pick me up and Rick dropped by for a few minutes. I introduced them. Rick left immediately and never at any time asked for an explanation. The incident was indicative of our nebulous relationship.

It was obvious that Rick and I had no basis for a marriage.

We barely saw each other for the two weeks before the wedding. It was insane. I knew Michael thought I would call it off, but my life was out of control. It was spiraling downward at a horrifying rate and I thought getting married would keep me from hitting rock bottom.

The night before the wedding, Michael and I saw each other to say goodbye. He picked me up at my apartment and we went for a drive. I was so depressed I could hardly speak because I knew we would not see each other again.

"What are you doing, Stormie?" Michael asked, his voice intense with frustration. "You're marrying a man you don't love. Everyone thinks you're making a big mistake, and I *know* you're making a big mistake. You can stop this now, so why won't you call it off?"

"I can't, Michael," I pleaded, wishing he could understand. But no one understood, not even me. "I know it doesn't make any sense, but I can't stop it." My fear and my intense emotional needs were making my decisions for me. The self-doubt was greater than my ability to do what was sensible.

Michael pulled to the side of the road, took my hand, and said, "You know I love you very much."

"I love you too," I said as I fell into his arms and began to cry. "I love you more than I've ever loved anybody."

"Then why won't you call this whole thing off?" His voice betrayed anger.

"I can't," I sobbed. "I just can't."

It must have confused him terribly. No normal person would have behaved that way. No one was forcing me to get married. I was choosing this myself.

Weeks earlier, when Michael had briefly tried to talk to me about Jesus, I had wanted no part of it. I had assumed it would mean intellectual suicide to identify with Christianity, and I just plain didn't want to hear about it. Now I wished I had listened a little more, but it was too late. Even though I found it difficult to let go of the purity and cleanness of our relationship, I knew I had to forget Michael and get on with the problem of survival.

We said goodbye and I went to bed and cried myself to sleep with the kind of tears that mourn a death.

The next morning I awoke with my usual depression and suicidal thoughts. The sense of futility was greater than ever. I was getting married. This was the only feasible alternative for my life, and it felt like I was headed for hell.

I worked through the morning depression by convincing myself that this marriage would be better than living alone. For a moment I thought of Michael. "Once he learned what I was really like, he would surely have rejected me," I thought. That would have been devastating. I had to settle for some security and a reprieve from my intense loneliness and fear. I needed a place to belong, no matter what the conditions.

In an unimpassioned state, I went through the motions as Rick and I were married. My descent into hell began immediately.

# THE EDGE OF BREAKDOWN

"Rick, would you please rinse the breakfast dishes for me? I'll wash them when I get home tonight," I yelled as I was about to leave for my eight A.M. appointment with the speech coach.

"That's not my job," Rick snapped.

"Well, what exactly *is* your job?" I insensitively retorted. "During the last year-and-a-half since we've been married you've worked exactly four days. At least you could stop watching TV for an hour or stay away from your mother's house one evening and help me with some of this housework. I can't do everything."

From the beginning I knew that Rick was unnaturally devoted to his mother and loved her far more than he could ever love me. He wanted me to be like her, and I did my best to imitate her many good qualities. But I could never measure up. He used criticism to try to mold me into an acceptable human being. I didn't respond well to it, however, and withdrew.

"The insurance on the cars is due today," he admonished me, completely ignoring all that I had said about helping me with housework.

"Oh, no, that's over 600 dollars! Can't you pay half of it?" I pleaded.

"That's not our agreement. I made the down payment for the house. You pay for everything else," he boldly reminded me.

It didn't take me long to see that our financial agreement was an unfair arrangement. But I *had* agreed to it and there was no turning back.

I went out and slammed the door. Through the window I could

see Rick return to his TV where he would spend the rest of the day while the dirty dishes sat on the counter. "It's obvious that this marriage arrangement is not working out as I'd planned," I thought as I drove to my speech coach.

Living with a male roommate was definitely not what I'd expected. My loneliness had increased, and my fear and self-doubt had mounted. I began to feel that I was better off single. At least then I only had to support and clean up after one person. With my busy schedule and Rick doing nothing at home to help, I was constantly angry with him. There was no communication between us, and although we had a sexual relationship, there was no affection or tenderness outside of that. I needed more from him than he could give, and I resented him for not being able to give it. Silently I demanded that he love and adore me, but he couldn't. He had his own problems, his own depression, and I was so steeped in mine that I couldn't begin to understand his. I had no idea what he wanted out of our relationship, but I was sure he wasn't finding it.

As I drove along Benedict Canyon I passed Cielo Drive, the street where Sharon Tate had lived and the house where she and her friends were murdered. I shuddered. Even in the daytime I was afraid to drive there, but my speech coach was just down the canyon, so this was the most direct route from my house.

"Hi, Gloria, sorry I'm late," I mumbled as I walked past my speech coach into the warm, rustic living room typical of many canyon homes in Beverly Hills.

"You look very tired. And why are you mumbling?" She showed her displeasure.

"I *am* tired and I just had a fight with Rick." I tried to speak slowly and remember all she had taught me.

For years I had studied with different voice therapists to try and overcome a speech impediment I'd had since childhood. Hours and hours of tedious, boring exercises resulted in only minimal improvement month after month. As a child I tried to hide the problem by either being quiet or carefully rehearsing what I had to say. That's why acting appealed to me. I could practice lines over and over, work them out with my speech coach, then say them without shame. Gloria had helped me tremendously. Besides regular speech therapy two times a week, I sought her expertise with every acting part I received. On this particular morning she was going to help me learn to speak my lines correctly before I went to the studio at ten.

"Slow down—you're talking too fast!" she said as I started. "You're slurring your words."

I tried again. "No! It's too nasal," she said. "Start over."

A minute later she interrupted again. "You're retaining too much tension in the throat. Practice these lines with a wine cork between your teeth." I dutifully opened my mouth so she could place the cork. "Now speak from the diaphragm, not the throat."

Over and over I rehearsed the lines. Changing incorrect speech habits had to be far more difficult than learning how to speak correctly in the first place. We worked for a solid hour, and by the end I was exhausted and starting to shake. I knew that the depression and growing bitterness toward Rick was taking its toll on my body. I was frequently ill and I felt ugly and old. I was dying inside. All the choices I had made for my life that I thought would save it were killing me. At times I felt like there were other beings living inside me and I wasn't in control of them. Perhaps this was because of all the drugs I had taken over the years, or maybe the dabbling in out-of-body experiences.

As I paid Gloria and left, she looked at me with that same expression I had seen on so many people. It was an expression that seemed to say, "Stormie's such a nice girl with so much potential. I wonder what her problem is."

I drove to CBS eager for work but, as always, afraid of it at the same time. Because of my unhappiness at home, I threw myself into work more than ever. The Glen Campbell Show was just beginning another season and I had a great part on the very first segment. Besides that series I was doing every possible record session, commercial, or movie background date that I could fit into my schedule. As more acting parts came my way, I lived to do them. CBS felt more like home to me than my own house in Benedict Canyon.

That night I arrived home from the CBS studio earlier than

usual. Rick was watching TV. "I'm exhausted," I said and headed upstairs for a nap. "Wake me up at eight and I'll fix us some dinner."

I climbed into bed and pulled the covers up over my face to shut out the daylight. The next thing I remember was Rick pulling the blanket off my face. My eyes were open and staring at the top of the wall. He called my name but I saw and heard nothing.

When he reached down and shook me, I was startled to consciousness in a fit of hysteria as I realized what had just happened. It was as if my spirit had left my body and had gone to a place of extreme torment. For a moment, I felt as if I had lost control over part of my being and might never get it back. It was frightening, and I sobbed uncontrollably.

Trying to calm me, Rick said, "Let me get you some water," and began to walk away.

"No, no! Don't leave me here alone!" I pleaded. "Please. I'll come with you."

He put his arm around my shoulder, helped me downstairs, and sat me on the two steps of the entryway leading into the sunken den. As I put my face in my hands and cried, I didn't see him leave to go into the kitchen. When I heard the sound of footsteps down the hall, I looked up to see a dark form coming toward me. It looked like my mother carrying a knife and I feared she was going to kill me! "Help me! Someone help me!" I went out of control with hysterical screaming.

Sensing that I was hallucinating, Rick grabbed me by the shoulder and shook me hard. "Stormie, it's me! Rick!" he yelled in my face.

I looked at him in total surprise. "Rick," I sobbed. "Oh, Rick, I thought it was. . . ." My voice stopped. Apparently the glass of water he was carrying must have reflected light in a way that made it look like a knife. But I couldn't tell him. . . I had never told anyone about that. ". . . I don't know what I thought it was," I mumbled as I began to shake.

After that experience I was afraid to be alone even in the daytime. As for Rick, he never mentioned the incident again. Maybe he thought I was nuts, or perhaps he was too passive to take much notice. He never talked much about anything.

A few days later I began to develop painful sores in my mouth. I could hardly eat or swallow. When I finally consulted a doctor, he told me I had a severe vitamin B deficiency.

"I don't know what your lifestyle is," he said, "but you're under way too much stress."

"But I eat healthy food and I exercise," I protested.

"Healthful food and exercise are good, but they won't balance out against too much stress. You'd better see about resting more and working less. And get rid of whatever is causing you stress. You're only 28—much too young to be having these problems. The older you get the more serious this will become. In the meantime, I'm going to give you shots of vitamin B three times a week until you're better."

That afternoon I went home and looked in the mirror. My face was deeply lined around the eyes, the mouth, and the forehead. My hair was dull and lifeless; it had been falling out for some time. My skin color was a yellowish gray. My body was chronically fatigued and my figure misshapen. The pain inside me was unbearable. I felt old and washed up, and as far as I knew it was a permanent condition that could never be repaired. I sank into a depression that overtook all depressions I had ever suffered before. Once again I thought seriously about suicide, and planned it out in detail in my mind.

I never talked with anyone concerning what was going on inside of me, but on a record date with my Christian friend, Terry, I shared about my out-of-body experience and how it frightened me. She advised me to speak the name of Jesus over and over when I got scared. "It will take the fear away," she told me.

I thought it was an odd piece of advice; nevertheless, at the first sign of fear I did what she said and the feeling lifted. I was surprised.

The name of Jesus had no special meaning for me, but if it had some kind of special power, then why not use it? At least this time it helped.

My emotional affliction was severely affecting my work. I began losing concentration, and my voice failed because of tension in my throat. One evening a friend called to give me the name of a psychiatrist. "Why don't you give him a call?" she suggested. "He has helped me a lot and I know he could do the same for you."

"Is this a doctor who will *talk* to me?" I questioned, remembering all the money I'd wasted on doctors I felt needed help more than I did. "I don't need any more psychiatrists who make me do all the talking and then sit there looking either bored or like they think I'm crazy."

"This doctor talks," my friend assured me. "And he gives good advice."

With that assurance, and the hope that he might help me control my emotional pain and cope with depression, I made an appointment for the following week.

At my first meeting with Dr. Foreman I found him a very likeable, polite gentleman. He was a distinguished, mid-fifties, gray-haired man who was five times more expensive than any other doctor I'd ever been to. But if he was going to be five times more personable, it would be well worth it. Right away he treated me as if I were an intelligent person and not insane. This impressed me so much that I was immediately at ease. He motioned me to sit in the chair across the desk from him.

"What's been troubling you, young friend?" he said with a warm smile.

"I live in constant fear, Dr. Foreman. And I'm not even sure what it is I'm afraid of. I'm surrounded by people, yet the loneliness I feel is unbearable. I suffer with debilitating depressions and anxiety attacks that make me feel like I'm dying. I have emotional pain all the time and I don't know what to do about it. I thought getting married would relieve some of this, but it has only made it much worse."

I couldn't believe I was blurting out all that information to this man, but I couldn't hold it in any longer. Dr. Foreman laughed an accepting laugh, leaned across the desk, and patted my hands reassuringly. "Don't look so worried," he said. "These sound like symptoms of something deep inside that you have probably hidden away. It's as if you were a child and you locked what you thought was a lion in the closet because he frightened you. Through the years as you grew up, you often thought about that lion and how scary he was. But if, as a full-grown adult, you were to go back to that closet and let out the lion, you would probably discover that he was actually only a kitten. He seemed large to you as a little girl, but he is nothing to be afraid of anymore. What we need to do is open a few doors from your past and let you see that what was once so frightening no longer poses any threat to you now.''

With Dr. Foreman's calm, reassuring words, I knew that I was finally going to tell someone my story—things I had never before told *anyone*. I took a deep breath and slowly began with my earliest recollection.

# CHAPTER FOUR

# FOUNDATION FOR BROKENNESS

I sat cross-legged on top of the large laundry basket that was filled to overflowing with dirty clothes. The musty smell of my dad's soiled shirts was comforting as I waited in the darkness of the small closet underneath the stairway. The old two-story ranch house was so tiny I could hear exactly where my mother was most of the time. At the moment she was coming out of the single small bedroom on the second floor, and I could hear her shoes on the hardwood as she came down the stairs.

I held my breath as she approached the closet.

"Maybe she's coming to let me out," I thought. "Or am I going to get another spanking?"

Instead, she walked right by my door and into the kitchen. "I think she's forgotten me," I began to cry silently. "How long will I have to be in here this time?" I wondered.

My only light source inside the cramped closet came from a small crack at the bottom of the door. I dared not get down from my position on the laundry basket to peek through it because of the mice that frequently scurried across the floor. I was afraid they would jump on me. Once I had found a large snake in the small room off the kitchen, and the possibility of another one joining me in the closet was very real. I made sure my feet never touched the floor.

"Why was Mother always angry at me?" I wondered in the silence. "All I did was ask her for a glass of water, and she turned and yelled, 'Get in the closet until I can stand to see your face!'" I learned at an early age that if I cried or protested I got beaten and then put in the closet, so I never resisted. The force of my mother's personality was so strong that even my father seemed powerless against it, for he always let her do as she pleased.

I saw her shadow pass the door once more and I could hear her muttering to herself as she headed into the living room. She had entered her dream world again, and it would be hours before Dad came home and she returned to reality.

I pictured Dad laboring outside in the hot sun. He was a tall, quiet, even-tempered man with a square jaw and large hands who always worked long, hard hours just to eke out a living. When he wasn't working he was "dead tired," as he always phrased it. Today he had gone to haul lumber for another rancher. Though he had much work to do here, we needed extra money to make ends meet. I wished he was home more. Mother didn't make me stay in the closet when Dad was home. Once I tried to tell Dad about having to go into the closet, but Mother had called me a liar and I'd gotten a spanking. I never tried that again.

Hot tears began trickling down my face. Why was Mother always mad at me? Did all children have to spend time in dark, stuffy closets? I didn't know any other children, for we lived on a small cattle ranch in Wyoming, 18 miles from the nearest town and several miles from our closest neighbor. We had no radio or telephone, and apart from occasional visiting relatives we were isolated from the rest of the world.

Visits by our relatives were the highlight of my life. Mother was a different person around them. She was cheerful, giving, outgoing, the life of the party. Her ice-blue eyes sparkled as she played the piano and sang while everyone gathered around to join in on the choruses. I admired her beautiful voice and pretty smile. I had heard my mother's older sister, Aunt Delores, say that Mom's tall, dark-haired beauty reminded her of actress Vivien Leigh, star of the movie "Gone with the Wind." I hoped someday I could see that movie.

My mother's good-humored younger sister, Jean, whom I adored, usually visited along with Aunt Delores, Uncle Mark, and their three children. When we were all together I was in ecstasy. It was like death the day they left, for all the happiness went out of my life. We all hugged each other and said good-bye, but as soon as their car left the driveway I fought back tears as Mother began her typical stream of critical remarks. "Nothing but a bunch of leeches," she grumbled as she turned and marched into the house. "All they want is free food and lodging. They have no consideration for our lives." Dad made no reply and headed out to the barn. Within a day I knew I would probably be back in the closet.

One time my mother's dad came to live with us for awhile. Pappy, as he was called, became my best friend, and life was good as long as he was around. Pappy and mother argued continually, but she never laid a hand on me while he was present. I missed him terribly when he left. He was a wonderful reprieve from my miserable existence.

Mother had two distinct personalities, and it was the bad one that she reserved for me when we were alone. Then she was critical, cold, and unpredictable. Her bitter anger could flare up instantly, and it frightened me. I had many nightmares about her. When people were around, Mother was highly concerned about making a good impression on them. It was very important for her to appear perfect. In fact she often said to me, "I am perfect. I have never done anything wrong."

"Never?" I questioned in disbelief.

"Never," she stated with such emphasis that I knew I would always fall short of her perfection. In fact she often told me I was ugly and stupid, and would never amount to anything.

I soon accepted the fact that I was not only a very unimportant person, but also rather undesirable. Helplessness, hopelessness, futility, rejection, abandonment, sadness, fear, and self-hatred were words too big for me to verbalize, but they were feelings I experienced every day.

The hours passed slowly on this muggy day in the closet. The still, stale air made me sleepy and I dozed for awhile. I awoke to hear Mother head into the kitchen to start dinner. A few minutes later she opened the door and I scrambled out, so grateful to be free that I didn't complain. Dad arrived home shortly after that and collapsed on the couch, saying, "I'm dead tired tonight."

He was not gruff, yet it was obvious that he would not have time for me today. There were so many times when I wished Mom or Dad would give me a big hug or kiss, but I never remember them doing that.

Mother called us to dinner. We ate in silence except for Dad's statement that he would be hauling lumber for the next couple of days at a neighbor's ranch. When he finished, he said, "I'd better go feed the cows," and he was out the door.

I was afraid of the dark, and there was no electricity on the ranch. When I went to bed, it was pitch-black except for the light I could see coming from the kitchen. I pulled the covers over my head and didn't move. I awoke with a start a short while later, full of fear. I must have had a nightmare. I slipped out of bed and headed to the kitchen for a drink of water. Mother was still there and I nearly collided with her as I entered. In terror I saw that she was clutching a large butcher knife. The upraised steel blade gleamed in the dim light. A sinister smile crossed her face as she stared at me with her cold, steel-blue eyes. As I backed away, she began to laugh. It became a wild, howling cackle as I tore back up the stairs to my room and fell shaking into my bed. It was a while before I slipped into a fitful sleep.

I awoke as dawn was beginning to break and thought of Mother poised with the knife as if she fully intended to stab me. The memory of that moment of terror never left my mind. I repeatedly had nightmares about my mother in the kitchen with the upraised knife, laughing at my fear.

● ● ●

Shortly before my sixth birthday we moved to a small farm 18 miles from town. Like the ranch, there were no modern conveniences. No indoor plumbing—only a foul-smelling outhouse. No running water or bathtub. No phone or radio. There were electric lights, but no heating system except for a potbellied stove in the dining room. Life was hard there; nothing came easy. The bright spots were the many nice neighbors who lived within a few miles of the farm. They didn't stop by often, but when they did, Mother was cordial.

That winter I had a sore throat that swelled painfully, to the point where I was unable to swallow food. Even drinking was unbearable. My nasal passages filled with a thick, rope-like material that the doctor pulled out daily with a special instrument. As with everything else in that small town, the hospital was overcrowded and didn't have a bed for me. We had to make the long trip to town every day through the snow so the doctor could give me a shot and pull the diseased material from my nose. The whole treatment was painful, but I endured it, hoping I would soon be well enough to eat again.

After a few weeks in this condition, the doctor became disturbed that I was losing weight and getting weaker. He decided to send a sample of the nasal material, along with blood and urine samples, to a special clinic to find out what was wrong. We drove home to wait for the results.

That night a blizzard hit, and for the next few days we were snowed in. As the storm worsened, Mother made a bed for me in the dining room next to the potbellied stove. Temperatures were below zero, and because there was no indoor plumbing, I had to go to the bathroom in a big metal pot that was kept under my cot. Despite the odor, the weather was too cold to permit emptying it more than every few days.

It was hard for me to breathe, and I was so weak that often during the long, cold days I felt that death would be a pleasant relief. In the midst of my misery I sensed a concern in my mother that I had never seen before. Frequently she tried to give me something to drink, but I could stand only two or three swallows before the pain became unbearable.

A week after the doctor took the tests we still had heard nothing. The snowstorm made it impossible to go to town, and we had no way to contact him. Dad spent most of the day trying to get hay to livestock trapped in the fields.

One afternoon there was a knock on our front door. I was too weak to care who it was or to recognize how unusual it was to have a visitor in such severe weather. My mother gasped as she opened the door. It was the doctor, snow caked over his heavy coat, hat, boots, and gloves.

"I had to come immediately," the doctor said as he removed his coat. "I drove as far as I could, then walked the last few miles. Your daughter could die at any time if she doesn't have this medicine."

My young heart marveled, "This man came all the way out here to save my life!"

As the doctor removed his suit coat and rolled up his sleeves, he told my mother that I had "nasal diptheria." After a quick examination, he plunged a needle into what little flesh I had left on my bottom.

I went to sleep immediately after the doctor left, and when I woke up hours later I could see the sun setting as it reflected through the bottles of cream soda on the dining room table. My throat was much improved, and for the first time in many weeks I asked for something to eat.

Mother seemed overjoyed, and when Dad came home she welcomed him with the good news of what the doctor had done. Dad in his usual quiet manner didn't say much, but I could tell that his smile was a sign of relief.

It was a slow recovery, but Mother's behavior made me want to stay in bed even longer. There were no harsh words now. She often smiled cheerfully, played the piano, and sang pretty songs. It was as if this near-tragedy had given her a new perspective on life.

As the snow melted and we saw the first signs of spring, I thought that perhaps life would be different. No longer would I experience Mother's harshness. We would be a happy family all the time. Unfortunately, that hope was short-lived. Gradually she drifted back into her unseen world. The period of my recovery was the last time I remember her being truly happy.

•  •  •

It was a warm morning, yet I ran to the roadside shivering at the prospect of another school day. The imposing yellow bus stopped in front of me and opened its yawning door. When I hesitated, the driver, with a wave of his hand, said "C'mon, we don't have all day." The first few times he had seemed sympathetic about my fears; now he only expressed irritation. I was one of many stops on the hour-long trip into town.

I hurried aboard and slid into the second seat behind the driver. I practically mashed myself against the window, hoping no one would notice me. As more students boarded, the noise level grew. Everyone seemed to know everyone else, and their lively talk frightened me. I sat motionless and stared out the window, hoping no one would notice I was alive. I got my wish; no one did.

When the bus finally parked in front of the school, I had survived another trip without anyone speaking to me.

School was even more terrifying than the bus ride. Because of my long illness, I was starting first grade as the oldest and tallest person in my class. I didn't have nice clothes like the rest of the girls. They had beautiful shiny hair; mine looked like tangled straw. My one haven was the classroom itself. There I felt safe. I never uttered a sound unless spoken to, and I obeyed every command and rule. The work was not too difficult; I studied hard and got straight A's as a result.

My problem was outside the classroom. I was terrified of the playground. The children ran around screaming, laughing, and playing games I didn't know how to play. I had never been around children except for my cousins, who visited only occasionally. I didn't know how to relate to anyone my own age. During recesses I hid in the bushes at the edge of the playground and waited for the bell to ring. If a teacher found me and sent me back to the playground, I would get in the longest line for the swings. There I felt safe because I had a legitimate place to be for a period of time. When I got up to the front of the line I ran off to find another long line. I didn't know how to swing, and I feared looking like a dummy.

During my second week, as I was standing in line for the swing, one of the boys asked me, "Hey, skinny, what's your name?"

"Stormie," I mumbled.

"You're kidding!" he yelled. "Hey, guys, listen to this! Her name is Stormie!"

As everyone started to laugh, I felt my face turning a deep red. Then someone yelled, "Hey, Stormie, how'd you get such a stupid name?"

"That's easy," someone else added, "I'll bet she was born in a storm drain."

"Or maybe she's a storm trooper," said another.

I felt panic inside me as I struggled unsuccessfully to fight back tears. I breathed a shaky sigh of relief as the bell rang and everyone headed back to line up for class. An intense feeling of loneliness gripped me, and I wanted to disappear from the face of the earth. How I longed for a normal name like Mary Smith so I would never have to be teased again!

My dad had named me Stormie when I was born because not only had I been born in a storm, but he always said that when I cried I clouded up a long time before the tears of "rain" came. Mother had wanted to name me Marilyn, but Dad said the name reminded him of someone he never cared for. They agreed to name me Virginia, after my mother, but it was a name that existed only on my birth certificate, for no one ever called me that. Eventually the name was changed legally to Stormie. It never bothered me until I entered school, and then I never heard the end of it.

Another problem I had was my speech. From the reaction of the other children I became aware that I didn't speak well. I couldn't form words correctly and I tripped on them, stuttering a little. On rare occasions when I took the initiative to speak to someone, either I spoke so softly that they didn't hear me and I felt rejected by their lack of response or else I stumbled embarrassingly over the words.

"Stormie speaks funny," laughed the children.

I dreaded recess and lunch—times when I had to relate socially to other children. There were no teachers or other adults who noticed my plight or even attempted to help me or draw me out. It was the Dark Ages as far as knowledge of the needs and inner workings of young children was concerned.

Home life was no better than school. Most of the time Mother's behavior was erratic and volatile. She would become suddenly angry and violent, punishing me for unknown transgressions. Other times she could go for days acting as if I didn't exist; nothing I did distracted her. At those times she lived in a fantasy world talking to imaginary people. Mostly they were people who had done her an injustice, and she told them off. I learned never to bother her at those times because she would turn on me violently.

One day I took Mother's pearl necklace from the small jewelry box in her bedroom so I could wear it for our school pictures. I kept it in my pocket until I got to school and then put it on in the bathroom. All the other girls had pretty dresses, but every day I wore the same red-checked shirt and navy-blue long pants. The pearls actually looked silly with that tomboy outfit, but I didn't realize it at the time. I also wasn't clever enough to realize that I would be in trouble as soon as Mother saw the pictures—I was just desperate to be attractive in some way.

A few afternoons later, shortly after I arrived home from school, Mother asked, "Have you seen my pearls?"

"No," I said, trying to mask my panic as I wondered where I had put them. I knew I had taken them off in the bus on the way home from school and put them in my pocket, but I had completely forgotten to return them to her jewelry box.

Grabbing my arm, she pulled me to the kitchen sink. "I'll teach you to lie to me," she threatened as she pushed a slimy bar of soap into my mouth until I gagged. "I found my pearls in the pocket of your blue pants. You stay out of my things and don't you ever lie to me again." After she removed the soap, I had to stand for awhile with the horrible burning sensation in my mouth before I could rinse it out. Oddly enough, that punishment was never a bad memory for me. It was the only time I recall being punished for something I actually did wrong. It seemed normal, and I was almost happy about it. When the photo of me wearing the pearls arrived from school sometime later, she only laughed and I was relieved.

Somehow I survived first grade. However, two months after I started second grade, Mother took me on a trip to visit Aunt Delores, who lived in Omaha, Nebraska. I loved being there because Mother was nice to me around other people and my cousins were great company. The only problem, as we gradually realized, was that my mother didn't intend to return home. My dad later said that there had been no fight, not even a discussion that would lead him to suspect that she was leaving for good. I did overhear her confide to my aunt that she thought Dad didn't love her and that farm life was too hard.

I entered school in Omaha, and it was even more terrifying than in Wyoming. These were city kids, not farm kids. They were better dressed, more self-assured, and more knowledgeable. They had a set of mannerisms and expressions that were foreign to me. It became painfully obvious that I didn't fit in.

At lunch time we had to travel in pairs to the cafeteria, but I was always the odd person. Every day that I walked alone my embarrassment increased.

My loneliness became so intense that one day after lunch, as I was standing in the playground waiting for the bell to ring, I became desperate for someone to play with. I decided to approach a group of five children who were standing around a small tree piling snow on its branches. I joined in and tried to laugh like they were laughing. Suddenly the largest girl turned to me and said, "You don't belong here. Get out! Who asked you to play?" The other girls added, "Yeah, go away!"

The pain of their rejection penetrated like a knife. I turned and ran across the playground, blinded by the hot tears streaming from my eyes. I came to the edge of the field, but I couldn't stop. I crossed the street and ran the short distance home to Aunt Delores' house. Once inside, I tore up the stairs to my room, crawled into bed, pulled the covers over my head, and sobbed into my pillow. Mother and Aunt Delores had gone shopping and Uncle Mark was asleep with his hearing aid turned off, so no one knew I was there.

As I relived that experience over and over in my mind, I wanted to die. Was there no one on earth who would give me the time of day? I wasn't hurting anybody. I just wanted someone to speak to me and to accept me in some way.

When Mother and Aunt Delores returned and found me, I told

them I was sick to my stomach and had to come home from school. I got away with that excuse for a few days, but when I was forced to go back I felt so hurt, so unloved and lonely, that I stopped trying. Aunt Delores, with her wonderful sense of humor, was the only bright spot in my life.

After Christmas we suddenly left Aunt Delores' house. Everyone was under the impression that we were going home, but that was not my mother's plan. We went instead to my mother's Aunt Grace in Grand Island. There I was enrolled in yet another school, and Mother immediately found a job.

Aunt Grace's home was a large, pleasant old two-story building like Aunt Delores'. It had a big front porch surrounded by lilac trees that were in full bloom in the spring and smelled wonderful.

Inside, the house was comfortable and clean, and Aunt Grace was always cooking something tasty in the kitchen. In spite of these nice living conditions, I missed my dad terribly. "When are we going back home?" I asked once again.

"I don't know. Stop asking me," my mother responded abruptly.

At this new school I resigned myself to loneliness. My only solace was reading books and writing letters to my dad. I simply endured the inner pain until school ended in June.

When Dad finally came to visit, Delores prompted Aunt Grace to inform Mother that it was time to go home to her husband. Since there was nowhere else to run, she reluctantly packed our things and we returned to the farm. Mother was despondent and immediately became her ill-natured self. Still, I was glad to be home with Dad.

We weren't home for long. The following winter a severe blizzard killed much of my father's livestock. Then his crops were ruined by a series of violent hailstorms. The hardships of Wyoming farm life were too much. Mother and Dad had heard about the easy life in Southern California, so we packed our belongings and headed west for an unknown destination and hopefully a better life for us all.

# CHAPTER FIVE

# GROWING PAIN

The "better" life was a small gas station in Compton that Dad leased along with an old, run-down shack of a house for us to live in. The front door of the house was four steps from the back door of the gas station, so grease and dirt became a way of life. An empty field adjacent to us was a breeding ground for rats, which had no problem finding their way into my bedroom. Occasionally they got brave enough to climb up my bedspread and run across the bed. When that happened, I was paralyzed by fright and unable to sleep.

Dad worked 14 hours a day, from seven in the morning until nine at night, six days a week. When he was not working, he was always "dead tired." Considering how hard he worked, we barely survived.

Our poverty was obvious. No one lived in a worse house or drove a car that was older than ours. And even though I was able to get five new dresses for school—one for every day of the week—they were of such poor quality that they soon looked dowdy and ill-fitting. We ate so poorly that my hot lunch at school seemed like the finest gourmet meal. I went to bed hungry many nights when there was nothing in the kitchen but a nearly empty jar of mayonnaise and a bottle of ketchup. Usually I lived on peanut-butter-and-jelly sandwiches.

Between the hunger and the rats, life seemed hopeless. My escape was to dream about being a beautiful movie star. I would make millions of dollars, wear beautiful clothes, be chauffeured in a limousine, and live in a palatial home kept spotless by a full-time maid. Everywhere I went, adoring fans and handsome suitors would give me the love I had never known at home.

There was a glimmer of hope when my sister was born. For awhile she provided Mother a new lease on life. And I was ecstatic. Though Suzy was nearly 12 years younger than I was, I viewed her as a companion—someone to talk to, to relate to, to love and hold. I saw her as my ticket out of intense loneliness. Also, seeing my mother care for someone else gave me hope that maybe she would care for me too.

One afternoon when I arrived home from school, I could hear Suzy, now three months old, crying in Mother's bedroom. I went into my bedroom to attack a pile of homework. Suddenly Mother was standing over me. As I looked up, she dropped Suzy into my arms.

"Here! She's all yours."

"But I'm doing my homework," I protested.

"Don't argue with me. From now on Suzy is your responsibility. When you're not in school, you take care of her."

"What about drama? I was going to try out for the play."

"You come right home when school is out!" she yelled. "Do you understand?"

I felt overwhelmed. How was I going to keep up on my homework? I had finally started to make some friends, but now I wouldn't have a spare moment to develop those friendships. I couldn't bring anyone home. The house was too filthy to have someone see it, and Mother didn't want anyone in the house anyway. I tried to resent Suzy for being such a burden to me, but I couldn't. She was sweet, good-natured, and loveable, and I grew attached to her. She became my total source of affection.

One morning shortly after my twelfth birthday, I woke up with a throbbing headache. I could barely stand up straight because of the cramps and back pain. I stumbled into the bathroom to show my mother the blood on my nightgown.

"Well, now you have the curse of all women," Mother said in disgust, as if what happened was my fault. She had never, of course, warned me about the changes that would occur in my body. Her attitude communicated that I had done something irreparably wrong.

As my breasts began to grow, I noticed that the other girls in school were wearing pretty little bras. Tentatively I asked Mother to let me buy one too.

"We don't have money to waste on you!" she snapped. She went to her bedroom, came back a few minutes later, and threw her maternity nursing bra at me.

"There," she said. "You've got your bra. Now get out of my sight."

"I can't wear this!" I protested.

"And why not? It was good enough for me."

"But it's way too big. Can't I buy my own bra? Please, I'll earn the money myself."

"No you can't! I didn't have nice things when I was a kid. Why should you?"

There was no further discussion, so I had to wear what she gave me. I was mortified in gym class when I had to undress in front of the other girls. I tried to hide as much as I could, but was quickly discovered. "Where'd you get that thing?" said one girl with a loud voice. "Nobody wears that." I wanted to crawl into my locker and disappear as all the girls started laughing.

True to my mother's erratic nature, she shocked me one Sunday morning by saying, "Get dressed. We're going to church."

"Church?" I expressed my shock. We had never been in a church outside of a few weddings and funerals and the times Aunt Delores took us. "Where on earth did she get the idea to go to church?" I wondered. It seemed like such an uncharacteristically normal thing to do that I was eager to go.

I got Suzy ready and we drove to a pretty little church just a few miles away. Mother listened intently to the sermon and must have liked what she heard, for we came back the next Sunday. A few weeks later Mother started teaching a Sunday school class while I joined the young people's program. As she began acting like a normal person, I was hopeful that Mother might start treating me nice too.

One great thing about church was that the youth group had

terrific beach parties and picnics. I fell hopelessly in love with nearly every boy in the young people's fellowship and tried anything to attract their attention. Because I was the poorest and the youngest, I thought the only way I could win them was to be an "easy necker."

Unfortunately, someone caught me necking in the backseat of a car in the church parking lot while a youth party was going on inside the fellowship hall. Whoever reported it called the pastor and he called my mother. "You've been out whoring," she yelled as she grabbed my hair, slammed my head against a wall, and began slapping my face with her free hand. "The pastor wants to see you. We're going down there right now and maybe he will pound some sense into you."

As I was brought into the pastor's office I felt terribly ashamed. Mother had so frequently referred to me as a whore and a slut that now I felt like one as I stood before him. Surely he must be angry.

But the pastor looked at me with eyes of compassion and love. He invited me to sit down and gently said, "I don't want a nice girl like you getting into trouble. I'm going to pray with you that this does not happen again."

"That's it?" I marveled to myself. He said nothing more except a short prayer that I didn't hear because I was so shocked. No beating? No punishment? How could it be? He treated me with respect and love, and I felt like I was given a second chance. I vowed to never forget his mercy and never to do it again—at least not around the church.

While I was in junior high school, our family left the filthy shack and moved to a relatively nice house in a lower-middle-class neighborhood. Mother always improved during the first few months after a move. It was like a new beginning, and she tried really hard to take care of the house and keep an attractive appearance. Unfortunately, she couldn't keep it up for long, and then she sank even deeper. She became irritable and mean and never said anything encouraging or smiled with approval. She called me obscene names, and corporal punishment was her sole mode of dealing with me. The only physical contact I had with her was when she slapped me across the mouth or struck my head.

Soon she was sleeping most of the day and roaming the house at night carrying on imaginary conversations. One night in a fit of rage—I have no idea what prompted it—she took the big family Bible she had bought after joining the church and hurled it out the back door, across the patio. It landed in a plot of dirt. I gathered she was mad at God and the church. She apparently forgave God, because in a few days the Bible was back inside the house again. However, she did not forgive the church, and we never went back.

She made friends with a few of the neighbors on our street, and while she never became so normal as to have them over, she was at least cordial. But when they were not around she screamed and raged at me for no apparent reason. Her vocabulary became liberally sprinkled with the most disgusting profanity. She only referred to me in filthy names, the nicest of which were pig, whore, and slut. Suzy was learning to talk very well and began to pick up some of the filthy words that Mother used and to treat her dolls like my mother treated me. Mother was horrified. Fearing that the neighbors would notice, she carefully cleaned up her language and controlled her actions better in front of Suzy.

Her discipline was consistently inconsistent. She got furious if I tried to clean our filthy house, yelling, "This is my house, not yours! If I want it clean, I'll do it myself." Yet when I did something seriously wrong, like the time I took the car out for a drive before I had a driver's license, or set the bedroom curtains on fire while smoking, she said nothing. Her behavior made no sense, so I never knew what to expect. Her constant degrading words and abuse built such a deep hatred inside me that I began to wish she were dead.

Of course I couldn't bring anyone home from school. I never knew from moment to moment what condition Mother would be in. I was always aware of the fact that I lived in a crazy house—not like the homes of normal people. There was no laughter, no fun, no peace in our lives, and no hope for it ever being any different.

I seldom saw my father. He left for the gas station before I

got up and often returned home after I'd gone to bed. As far
as my sister, Mother had an obvious affection for her. In fact,
she went to the opposite extreme. While I was treated with
violence and hatred, Suzy received no discipline whatever. Sometimes I wondered if Mother was trying to make up for the way
she treated me. Despite the obvious discrepancy, I never felt
jealous. I was glad that Mother could actually be nice to someone
on a regular basis. Besides, Suzy was cute and affectionate, and
she loved me. She was a little pal, my companion.

During my last year of junior high, I spent a night away from
home with a girlfriend, Mary Hammil. It was the first time I had
ever spent a night with a friend. Mother was very angry about
my going, but I did it anyway. When Mary and her mother
brought me back the following night, Mrs. Hammil joyfully told
us the news that she was two months pregnant.

A week later as I walked in the door of our house after school,
Mother grabbed me by the hair. She slammed me against the
kitchen door and began slapping me as she screamed, "You
murderer! You murderer! You've killed an innocent child! I hope
you're happy with yourself, you selfish bitch!"

My mind raced. What could I have done? Maybe I had left
the front door open and my sister had gotten out and been hit
by a car? "I don't know what you're talking about," I yelled
back. "I didn't hurt anyone."

"You killed Mrs. Hammil's baby. It's your fault. You didn't
listen to me. I hope you're satisfied, you murderer!"

"What baby?" I spit in her face. "Mrs. Hammil doesn't have
a baby."

"She lost her baby!" Mother screamed at the top of her lungs.
"She had a miscarriage and it's your fault because you made her
pick you up and drive you home. That's why the baby's dead.
You murderer!"

I pulled away, dashed into my room, slammed the door, and
fell in a heap of sobs on my bed. "Oh no, God, no!" I cried.
"The baby's dead and it's all my fault. Everyone will hate me.
No one will have anything to do with me anymore."

After awhile I started to calm down and tried to think rationally. I had to call Mary. I had to know what she thought about this. I opened the door and tiptoed toward the phone. Mother saw me. "Don't touch that phone. It's my phone, not yours."

The next day at school I asked Mary what had happened. "Oh, nothing," she replied casually. "Mom just started feeling sick and she went to the hospital and the baby miscarried. She's all right."

"My mother says it was my fault," I said sheepishly. "She said when your mom drove over to pick me up that day it injured her badly."

Mary laughed. "How silly! My mother had been driving all along. Your mother's nuts."

I laughed with her, but inside something tightened and my heart hardened even more against my mother. *Never*, I determined, would I let her devastate me like that again. She might beat me and try to destroy me verbally, but she would never penetrate the hatred I had for her. From now on I would look upon her as a crazy animal, never to be trusted.

• • •

Mother attempted to make Christmas enjoyable that year, but it was an empty time for me. The season where all families were happily together only pointed up the loneliness I felt, and I ached for it all to end.

Mother surprised me on Christmas day by giving me a small green diary. She gave me other things too, but I felt that this was an unusually thoughtful gift, and I cherished it. I loved to read and write, and any free moments I had were spent writing stories, plays, poems, and song lyrics. I loved anything that had to do with writing, and the diary would be a wonderful way to express my pent-up feelings. I was so anxious to begin writing in it on January first that I wasn't even disturbed when I lost one of the two keys that came with it.

As I began keeping a daily record of my thoughts and activities, I particularly made note of who noticed me each day and who didn't. I was desperate for affirmation of my worth and nearly begged for it from everyone I knew. At the same time I was suspicious of people who paid attention to me, feeling that there must be something wrong with them if they did. Because there was never any closeness, communication, or emotional contact in my family, I tried to meet those needs through boyfriends. When that didn't work, I fantasized in my diary. Though I continued to do well in school, it was not enough to sustain the emptiness, loneliness, and desperation I felt. "Isn't there someone who can love me?" I used to cry at night to a distant and vague God somewhere out in the universe.

Mother seemed to know everything I did, as if she had hired detectives. What I *was* doing wrong seemed mild compared to her accusations, however. The degrading, filthy language she used to address me and the slaps on the mouth I received suddenly and for no apparent reason became more unbearable. I began having nightmares again about her coming after me with a knife.

Soon she had me thinking that maybe it was I who was going crazy.

"Where is your white skirt?" she asked me one day.

"In my closet. Where else would it be?" I retorted disrespectfully.

"It's not there. You've done something with it. You're giving your clothes away to your friends," she accused. Then she ranted on about my negligence.

I searched through Suzy's room, the laundry, and the pile of ironing but couldn't find it anywhere. I didn't consider looking in Mother's room, for she was very protective of her private property and I was never allowed to look in her closet or drawers.

Late that afternoon, as I went into my closet for something else, there was my white skirt hanging right in front.

"Here's my white skirt!" I yelled to my mother. "Did you put it here?"

"Me put it there? It was probably there all along. You're so blind. You must be going crazy. Your mind is very sick. I think you're mentally ill," she said with authority.

Although these incidents were common and I suspected that

she planned them, part of me began to believe her. "I am going crazy," I thought. "I can't cope with life. I'm a misfit. I don't belong anywhere. I can't think clearly. I feel lost." I began to question why I was even alive.

One evening I was across the street at a girlfriend's house watching her prepare for a date. She was a beautiful girl and very popular with the boys—everything I desired to be but wasn't. As I compared myself to her, my depression became unbearable. By the time I left her house to return home, I was filled with pain and self-loathing. When I opened my front door, I met two angry stares. Dad said, "Where have you been? What have you been doing?"

Before I had a chance to answer, Mother's venom began to spew out. "You've been whoring around the neighborhood like a slut. You've been with. . . ." and she began to list names of boys I liked.

I fled to my bedroom. How did she know all those names and details? Sure I'd been attracted to those boys, but I had certainly never mentioned them to her. How could she have known my thoughts?

Mother followed me into the bedroom to continue her accusations. She spit out her words between clenched teeth: "Your father and I have decided you can't go across the street anymore. You can't see your friends after school and you can no longer use the phone." She couldn't threaten me with taking away my allowance because I didn't get one, or saying I couldn't go someplace special because I never went anyplace special. But what few privileges I'd had were now gone.

When she finally left the room, I didn't cry. It was as if I'd been returned to the closet and I was a little child again. Fear, terror, hopelessness, and futility flooded over me, and I could not withstand the magnitude of this force. The voice in my head said, "It will never be any different." If that was true, I could no longer bear to face another day.

I waited until the house was quiet, then slipped into the bathroom, opened up the cabinet, and proceeded to empty every medicine bottle and swallow every pill. I swallowed 1½ bottles of Bufferin, plus pain-killers, sleeping pills, and a couple of prescription drugs. When I was done I went back to my room, put on a clean nightgown and robe, and laid down in my bed knowing I'd never wake up again. This wasn't a plan for getting attention or shocking people into caring. I just wanted to end the agony inside me.

When I opened my eyes again, I could not focus. The room was spinning and I felt weak, dizzy, and sick to my stomach. I rolled over, noted the sunlight, and tried to focus on my clock. It was one P.M.

What happened? What went wrong? Why was I still alive? Gradually I remembered. Sometime in the middle of the night, Mother had held me over the bathtub and forced me to drink some vile thing until I vomited.

I stumbled to the bathroom and locked the door. The empty bottles were in the trash. Most of what I had taken was aspirin. I looked at the other bottles. The sleeping pills and pain pills were old, from the time right after Suzy was born, when Mother had trouble resting. Maybe they had lost their power. Obviously they weren't enough to kill me, but just enough to make me very sick.

As I returned to bed, I reviewed all of Mother's accusations the night before. Where had she gotten that information? How did she know about those boys? Then it clicked. The diary! The lost key! Everything was in my diary, and she was using it to spy on me. Even my most private thoughts were subject to her scrutiny and dissection.

From behind my closed door I could hear the muffled sound of Mother running the vacuum cleaner. Whenever something horrible happened, she ran the vacuum. It was her way of denying the problem and appearing to be perfect. And what was the problem? That I was good for nothing, a disgrace to the human race.

Or could it be that *she* was the problem? I had seen enough families now to realize that my mother was not normal. Something was desperately wrong with her. Lately she had started talking about people watching her through the TV or following her when she left the house. When Dad or I had tried to dissuade her, she became hysterical, and the force of her hysteria overwhelmed us. The number of people trying to "kill" her was constantly increasing—communists, Catholics, blacks, whites, the rich, the poor, Baptists, Armenians, the Kennedys, and on and on until the list eventually included everyone we knew.

When I finally got up late that afternoon, Mother didn't say a word, not even to acknowledge my presence or find out how I was feeling. And I said nothing to her. It was as if we had silently agreed to never mention the incident to anyone.

Two days later I returned to school. "Flu" was the explanation on the note from home. I wasn't sure why I was alive, but the crisis was over and for some reason I didn't feel like dying anymore. Maybe it was because I knew Mother realized she had gone beyond the bounds of decency. However, I entertained no hope that she would ever change. Telling Dad was out of the question. I knew that if I ever mentioned anything to him, Mother would accuse me of lying and I would get punished. He always believed her.

Mother, of course, still didn't extend herself to me in any way, but she stopped going for the throat. We went back to doing what our whole family did best—pretending that nothing was wrong. The only solution for my life was to finish high school and then leave home as quickly as possible. All of my activities became geared toward that goal.

# CHAPTER SIX

# ABIDING HATRED

My strategy for escape had several elements. First, after we moved again before my junior year in high school, I revised my ways of gaining attention at my new school. I traded dirty language and loose actions for more respectable methods, such as running for school office and acting in school dramas. I found that if I practiced my lines long enough, I could speak in a way that no one would suspect I had a speech problem.

In spite of the improvement, I knew I needed professional speech therapy. So as soon as I turned 16, I began working in a department store in order to earn enough money to buy a car and pay for voice lessons. When I had earned 200 dollars I told Dad about my plan, and one evening he said he'd seen an ad for a little old Ford. "Let's go check it out," he said. I was thrilled with Dad's interest. He could relate to me well when it came to cars.

The car wasn't much to look at, but Dad said it had a good engine and that with a few minor adjustments in his gas station it would be in good running condition.

"What color do you want to paint it?" Dad asked.

"Blue. But I can't afford it."

"Isn't it your birthday next week?" I couldn't believe what he was saying. But sure enough, on my birthday, Dad drove the car into the driveway. It was purring, and it was painted my favorite shade of blue. Mother watched me through the window as I gave Dad a big hug and took the car for a spin.

Mother glared at me when I finally got home. "I didn't have

a car when I was a teenager," she sneered. "Why should you have one? Think you're something special, don't you?" I silently walked past her to my room and slammed the door. Through the closed door she shouted, "And what makes you think you're going to take voice lessons? I never had singing lessons. You're not going to have them either."

In spite of her opposition, I started studying with a voice teacher. Even with professional help I soon discovered that overcoming my speech problems was going to be hard work. The tension in my throat was so great that it took time just to get my jaw unlocked and the throat open. I spoke so rapidly that slowing my speech and making it more intelligible took hours of boring practice and then yielded only barely distinguishable results. Out of frustration, I ended up in tears after nearly every practice session.

I finally saw the fruit of my labor when I got the lead in the school play and became Senior Class Treasurer. Dad was happy for me. Mother was mad. She continued to remind me that I was still a whore and a slut no matter how many things I did. "You'll never amount to anything, you worthless _____," she would hiss as I left for my voice lesson.

The next part of my plan was to earn enough money to afford college. Following graduation, we moved to a small apartment near Knott's Berry Farm. I found work there, and so did my dad. The gas station was losing money, so he decided to try a regular nine-to-five job.

Early one morning on my day off, I decided to clean the tiny room that my six-year-old sister and I shared. I couldn't stand her mess any longer. Every drawer and her side of the closet and bedroom were filthy and cluttered with things that should have been trashed long ago. Suzy helped for awhile, then went outside to play. Mother entered as I was putting the finishing touches on the room. She had just awakened, and her eyes were puffy and burned with anger as she asked, "What do you think you're doing?"

"I've just finished cleaning up our room," I said with pride. With teeth gritted, her steel-blue eyes burned a hole through my heart as she said, "I told you if I wanted this house clean I would clean it myself. This is not your house, it's mine." Then she went to the closet and pulled out all the books and toys I had so neatly organized and threw them on the floor. As she shoved everything off the shelves, then began to empty the drawers on the floor something inside of me snapped. This was too much! I began to scream—open-mouthed, nonsyllabic, hysterical, depth-of-my-being screams.

Then I lunged at her to try and stop her. Quickly her right hand struck me hard across the ear and cheek and part of my eye. The blow stunned me, and before I had time to consider what I was doing, I struck her as hard as I could across the face, the same way she struck me.

She was shocked and so was I. I couldn't believe I had done that. Now my fear of getting stabbed in the middle of the night was far greater. I didn't wait for any further reaction. I ran immediately out of the room, grabbed my purse, and left the house.

I started to cry in the car, then stopped myself. "She's not worth crying over," I said out loud. "She's just a hateful old witch and not worth the tears. It won't be long before I'm out of there, and then I'll never have to see her again."

•   •   •

After a few semesters at several other colleges, I wound up at UCLA, majoring in music. It was a relief to be away from home and in a somewhat normal environment. But coping wasn't easy. My emotional needs were so intense that I frequently experienced fits of depression. That didn't stop me from trying to find fulfillment through relationships with men. I became involved easily, yet commitment frightened me, so I refused to get too close to anyone.

Married men were particularly attractive. I became romantically involved with a professor. I was miserable, yet I was drawn to a situation where I called the shots. Because he was married, all of our meetings were secret, and I could choose when we saw each other. It was flattering to think that someone so highly regarded and intelligent would find me attractive, yet the guilt and secrecy were overwhelming. I was glad when summer came and I went back to work at Knott's Berry Farm.

This time my job was acting and singing in a melodrama at the Birdcage Theater. I was the heroine, and the actor who played the hero was a handsome, talented comedian named Steve Martin. He was bright and sensitive, and what began as a relationship sharing poetry, philosophy, thoughts, and dreams turned into my first normal, head-over-heels-in-love romance. Steve made me feel beautiful, feminine, and desirable for the first time in my life. However, our destiny did not include marriage. So after our season together there was no sad parting, only an uncalculated drift. It would prove to be the only relationship in the first 30 years of my life for which I would have no regrets or bad feelings.

The following school year I started dating Scott Lansdale. When he invited me to go back East and spend Christmas with him and his family, I jumped at the opportunity. I would take any excuse to avoid being around my mother, especially during the holidays.

The Lansdales were wealthy and their home was everything my home was not. It was large, sprawling, beautiful, and clean. Even the windows that looked out over the beautifully manicured lawn were spotless. Scott's parents were normal, and I loved them. Scott teased me, saying that I liked his parents more than I liked him. That was fairly accurate. I would have given anything to have traded mothers with him.

Mrs. Lansdale was a gentle, sensitive woman who got up early every morning to fix breakfast. She treated me as if I was worth something, and it was hard not to contrast her to my own mother. We quickly became close friends, but not close enough for me to share the intimate details about my past. It was too embarrassing to tell anyone about being locked in a closet as a child, or having to listen as Mother wandered the house at night, answering voices that only she heard. Perhaps if I revealed this to Mrs. Lansdale she would reject me. After all, I reasoned, if a parent rejects you, you must be the rejectable type.

One evening after a big party at the Lansdale house, all the guests had left and Mr. and Mrs. Lansdale went upstairs to bed. Scott and I stayed in the luxurious party room in the basement and had a few drinks by the fire. In my desperation for love I was careless, and it proved to be a night I would later regret bitterly.

A few weeks after returning to L.A., I learned from my father that Mother's condition had worsened. He had consulted a doctor, who diagnosed her mental illness with a string of medical terms, of which "schizophrenic" and "paranoid" were the only ones I understood. So it was confirmed that more than just meanness and a hateful disposition were motivating my mother's behavior. There was something definitely wrong with her— something that had a name.

Mental illness was not openly discussed at this time and did not produce a sympathetic response. It was a reflection upon family members, as if their sanity was suspect too. Dad and I kept it quiet, and Aunt Delores agreed to fly in and help Dad have Mother committed.

"You need to be there too," Aunt Delores instructed me on the phone from Omaha. "She should know that we are united in our belief that this is best for her. The doctors say that if she can be convinced to go on her own to the hospital, half the battle will be won. The response of patients who turn themselves in is far better than those who have to be taken forcibly."

"But, Delores," I cautioned, "she will never go for it. She won't go peaceably and she will never let you take her."

Everyone but me seemed to think there was a good chance she would respond well. However, I knew Mother's dark nature far better than anyone else and was convinced the scene would be ugly.

The date was set for a week later, and I was to meet Delores at Mother and Dad's home. It was arranged for my little sister to be away that night. Dad, Delores, and I would lay the plan out for Mother. She would see the wisdom in it and would go calmly with us as we drove her to the mental hospital.

"They're dreaming," I thought. "They really don't know her at all. My mother is totally convinced that she's right and the rest of the world is wrong, that she's innocent and all others are guilty, that she's normal and everyone else is crazy. There is no way she'll admit there's something wrong with her."

In the meantime I tried to prepare for finals at college, but was so sick I couldn't eat or sleep, let alone study. I had grown increasingly ill since the holiday. At first I figured it was flu, but as it persisted, I finally went to a doctor and learned, to my horror, that I was pregnant. The news devastated me. I stumbled out of his office and made my way to a pretty little church just off campus. I sat in the empty sanctuary and tried to examine my options. None were good.

Marriage was out of the question. While I would have gone for that solution in an instant, I knew that Scott was repulsed with the idea and no longer wanted to have anything to do with me. He was a brilliant law student, an important man on campus, and the pride of his family. No way would he throw it all away just to right a little mistake.

Suicide was an option. But what would that do to my sister and father? Here we were on the brink of having my mother committed to a mental hospital. It would destroy them. But having the baby would be even worse. I was sure my family would rather that I be dead.

Where could I go? What could I do? I slipped off the pew to my knees and prayed. "God, please get me out of this mess," I cried.

I don't know how long I knelt and cried and prayed. But when I finally got up, I had heard no answer from God.

After that I became so nauseated that I couldn't eat or sleep. When the day came to confront Mother, Aunt Delores flew into Los Angeles. I was so sick I could barely drive, but somehow I made it to my parents' home. Delores greeted me at the door and I immediately began to shake. I went into the bathroom to try to pull myself together. I was grateful for the strength of Aunt Delores and was glad she was there. If only I could tell her the truth and go home with her to the pretty rainbow-colored room

I had once stayed in upstairs in her house. If only I could crawl between those clean colorful sheets and pull them over my head until this nightmare went away.

"Oh, God," I cried. "There is no way out. I'm trapped."

I came out of the bathroom and told my aunt, "I can't stay. I've got finals in the morning and I don't feel well. I can't bear to see the scene that's going to be here tonight. Please forgive me, Delores, but I have to go. Can you explain it to Dad for me?"

My aunt looked disappointed, but promised she would call and let me know the result.

I made my way back to my UCLA apartment in Westwood Village and threw myself onto the bed. I was too sick and distraught to study for finals. I would have to rely on the work I had done all semester to carry me. "Oh, God, give me a good memory," I cried. Why was I praying? Did God hear me? Was there even a God?

Early the next morning Aunt Delores called. "Are you feeling any better?" she asked.

"A little. I'm heading for my exam in a few minutes. How did it go last night?"

"Not good. When we approached your mother about going peacefully to the hospital she became hysterical." My aunt took a deep breath before describing it. "I've never seen her like that. She screamed at us and said we were just like all the other communists who were out to get her. She called us horrible names—you can't believe the things she said."

"Yes, I can. She says those things to me all the time."

"We tried to talk reasonably. She screamed, '*You're* all crazy, *I'm* not! There is nothing wrong with me.' Then she ran to her room, grabbed her purse and car keys, flew out the door and into the car, and was gone before we could stop her."

"Where is she now?"

"We don't know. She didn't come back last night. The doctor informed your father that he could sign some papers and the police would pick her up and have her committed."

There was silence.

"Well. . .what did he do?" I pushed her to tell me.

"He broke down and cried and said he just couldn't do it," she described painfully. "He feels that if he doesn't have her committed maybe she'll snap out of it."

I knew that he had visions of insane asylums out of the horror movies of the past and felt there would be no hope for her there. As cruel as she had been to him over the years, he still loved her enough to stick it out in hopes that someday she would "snap out of it."

"So it's up to you, Stormie," Aunt Delores' deeply exhausted voice continued on the phone. "The only one who can do anything for your mother is you."

"Me?" I choked. "You've got to be kidding. There's nothing I can do with her. We've always hated each other."

"Yes, I know," she sighed. "I'm afraid your mother was a terrible mother."

I couldn't believe my ears. Someone else knew that she was a horrible mother. I gathered strength in her remark because the recognition of that truth by someone else made me feel like I wasn't crazy after all. At the same time, I felt the responsibility of the world on my shoulders. I was pregnant and sick, and my dad and sister needed me more than ever now that Mother had left. I couldn't disappear for a year to have a baby. My suicide would destroy them. There was only one place left to turn.

# CHAPTER SEVEN

# CHOICES FOR DEATH

"Stormie! How are you!" Julie's voice chirped over the phone. "I'm not as good as I'd like to be," I answered. I'd met Julie the previous summer while working at Knott's Berry Farm. "I really need your help. Do you remember when you confided in me about the abortion you had? Well, I need to get in contact with the doctor who performed it."

I held my breath as I waited for her reply. If she refused to help me, I didn't know where I would go. Abortion was never mentioned in public. In fact, Julie was the only person I had ever heard speak the word to me.

"You know the police are cracking down," she said. "The doctor who did mine was jailed."

"Oh, no! What am I going to do? Please, Julie, I really need your help. I've got to find someone who can do this."

"I do have some contacts. Let me see what I can do. Hang on, Stormie. It will take me a few days to get back to you. But I'll call, I promise."

It was two weeks before I heard back from Julie. During that time Dad called to tell me that Mother had finally returned home. She had disappeared a few times before, but never for so long. As usual, no one asked where she had been or what she had done. We would proceed as always, pretending like nothing had happened.

Julie called the next day with news. "I've found a doctor just over the Mexican border in Tijuana."

"I don't care where it's done. I don't even care if he's a doctor.

I just want out of this misery. How much?''

"Six hundred dollars.''

"Six hundred dollars!'' I gasped. "I don't even have 50 dollars!'' I paused. "Never mind. I'll get it. Tell him yes and let me know when.''

I called Scott and asked him point-blank for the money. After some reluctance and questioning whether I was really pregnant or just needing some money, he gave in. I was extremely hurt by his remarks, but took the money.

With 600 dollars of cash in hand, I drove to a predetermined meeting place in a deserted area off the main highway to Mexico. There a man who was the liaison with the doctor met me and another woman with her husband who were going for the same reason. Apart from some attempts at light joking conversation, no one spoke as we drove the 60-minute drive to the border. I was afraid, but decided that no matter what happened it had to be better than being pregnant and sick. The nausea was unbearable.

We had no problem at the border; the guards obviously knew the driver. We drove to a small nondescript house in an old, dirty, residential section of Tijuana. A Mexican woman met us at the door. Once in the living room with the door shut, the doctor came out and greeted us.

Because I was so nervous, I volunteered to go first. I was guided to the back of the house via a long dark hall. I entered what I expected would be a bedroom, but the door opened to a hospital-like operating room. I put on a gown and lay down on the table as instructed. As the anesthetist put a needle in my vein, the doctor leaned over me and said, "Oh, by the way, if you die during this operation, I'll have to dump your body out in the desert. You understand that I can't risk danger for myself and the others by giving your body to the police. I just want you to know that going in.''

"Does that happen often?'' I questioned, my heart filled with fear.

"No, not often,'' he replied matter-of-factly. "But it does happen. I don't enjoy doing that, but I have no choice.''

So many times in my life I wanted to die. Now the thought of dying frightened me. "God, please," I prayed silently, "let me live and I'll be good."

"Ten, nine, eight, seven. . ." The next thing I remember I was lying in another room with the anesthetist preparing me to go home. Immediately I noticed that for the first time in weeks I didn't feel like vomiting. The nightmare was over! It didn't occur to me that I had just destroyed a life. All I could see was that I had escaped death. I had no remorse—only elation that I was still alive and had gained a second chance.

"Thank you, God," I prayed. "I'll be good. I'll do all the right things. I'll appreciate what I have instead of complaining about all I lack. I'll find out more about you, God, and I won't make the same mistake again."

The prayer was simplistic, but sincere. I meant every promise, but I soon discovered that I was too weak to fulfill any of them. After I returned to school, I fell right back into the same old habits and thought patterns.

That summer I was hired as a singer for a popular theater-in-the-round that did live musical comedy with different guest stars each week. The hours were long because we rehearsed one show during the day and performed another at night. To save money, I moved back home with my parents, but was there only to sleep.

Mother adopted a new policy after she returned home. She stepped up her aggressive hatred toward Dad and backed off on me. She now viewed my father and Aunt Delores as the enemy. Because I wasn't present during the night of the scene, I was not considered a traitor. Suzy was never in question. She was neutral ground for everyone.

Many times I found Suzy upset over Mother's bizarre behavior. Because I had basically raised her for the first six years of her life, I had managed to somewhat protect my sister from Mother's mental problems. But once I started college and was gone a great deal, she had to cope alone.

Late one night I came home and found Suzy crying. "Are you upset because of Mom?" I asked.

"Yes," she sobbed.

I hugged her and stroked her hair as I said, "There's something wrong with Mom. She's very sick, and she won't go to the hospital. So we have to take care of her as best we can. Try not to take anything she says or does personally because she can't help it."

I couldn't believe how well I had spoken those words. I despised my mother. I did not have one ounce of pity for her; the only pity I felt was for myself. Yet I was convincing enough that Suzy was encouraged and seemed to cope better after that.

Suzy's relationship with Mother was never scarred like mine. With me there was irreparable damage, and it seemed that because of our warped relationship, I found it increasingly difficult to cope with life. The emptiness and pain I felt deepened each year. My periods of depression got worse, the anxiety within me increased, and suicidal thoughts met me every morning when I awoke. On top of all that, I battled chronic fatigue as I drove myself with work in a futile attempt to bury my emotions.

My final show of the summer was "Call Me Madam" with Ethel Merman. I loved the show and I loved working with Ethel. The thought of it ending and my going back to UCLA was depressing. So when a fellow singer asked if I'd be interested in touring with the Norman Luboff Choir, I immediately said yes and kissed school goodbye.

For the next nine months I toured the United States with Norman Luboff, which presented me with some unanticipated problems. Living with 30 other people in the confines of a small bus, without even the luxury of a private room at night, meant that I had to hide my depressions and giant insecurities and put up a good front all the time. It was exhausting.

Once a week I would call home to check on my sister. One evening after a show I called from Georgia and Mother answered the phone. She was livid about my being with Norman Luboff: "Because of your high visibility, they're going to find me and kill me." Apparently the fact that "they" were already watching her through the TV and had her house bugged didn't matter. "Don't you forget that you are worthless," she snapped. "It doesn't matter that you sing with that fancy choir—you're still a nothing. A nobody.''

Mother was crazy, I knew that. So why was I shaking as I hung up the phone? I knew that what she was saying was not true, yet I was destroyed every time I heard those words. She still had the power to devastate me, like the little girl she had locked in the closet. When she caught me in a weak moment, she could plunge me into the pit of depression for weeks. Part of me knew she was nuts. The other part believed every word she said. Why did Mother have this hold over me?

I went downstairs to join some of the singers who were waiting for me in the hotel restaurant. I was so depressed I could barely speak or eat, so I excused myself early, went back to my room, and cried myself to sleep.

By the next morning I had pulled myself together enough to join the group for breakfast. I could even manufacture a smile and a few jokes. One of the young men noted, "Ah, I see you're manic today." I found the comment amusing but painful. Any reference to my mental instability fed an inherent fear that I might become like my mother.

I came off the tour distraught and emotionally exhausted. Trying to maintain a good front had taken its toll. Living in close quarters with people for that length of time only pointed out how odd I was compared to everyone else. I felt like a failure, and I went home and stayed in bed for several weeks.

I was shaken out of my lethargy one day when I was invited to audition for a new TV musical variety show that CBS was airing in the summer of 1966. I did everything I knew to make myself look and sound good, but when I saw the beauty and talent of the other girls, I was so depressed that I went home and climbed right back into bed.

When the contractor called a week later to tell me I was one of the four singers on the show, I was shocked. My joy was immediately mixed with fear. Obviously I had done a good audition, but how long could I keep up the front? My anxiety attacks were getting worse, and I never knew when they would happen. When they occurred, I had to hide in the nearest bathroom holding my stomach while I convulsed with stifled sobs, feeling as if a sword had been run through me. How long could I cover *that* up? Other times when I was afraid my throat tightened and I would lose my voice. What if that happened on this job?

In spite of all my fears, I took the job and made it somewhat successfully through the summer series. After that I retained an agent and got opportunities to sing, dance, and act on one TV show after another that were offered to me along with commercials and record sessions. I had opportunities to perform with stars like Danny Kaye, Jack Benny, Jimmy Durante, George Burns, Dean Martin, Jerry Lewis, Mac Davis, Stevie Wonder, Ray Charles, Linda Ronstadt, Sonny & Cher, and many more. Usually the auditions went great, but when it came time to perform, depression would overtake me or an anxiety attack would render me mute so that I was unable to deliver what I'd promised.

One evening my agent, Jerry, called. "Why did you turn down the part in that movie today, Stormie?" he demanded. "After all your auditioning and my hard work you just walked out on the offer. I can't understand what is the matter with you."

"I'm sorry, Jerry," I searched desperately for an answer that would explain it. "At the last minute I just couldn't go through with it."

"Go through with what? You had the part. All you had to do was show up for work."

"I know. I'm sorry, Jerry. I'm really sorry."

After a long silence in which I could almost hear his mind turning, trying to make sense of the things that I did to jeopardize my own career, he said goodbye and hung up.

It was impossible to understand my struggle. For years I had dreamed of doing the things I was now doing. But all the modeling, commercials, television shows, and acting could not convince me I was attractive or talented. No matter what glamorous and wonderful things happened to me, l still saw myself as ugly and unacceptable. Just a few hours after the ecstasy of attaining a new goal, I felt worse than ever because I thought, "If this doesn't make me feel better, what will?"

Despite past failures, I kept looking for the perfect relationship. Appearances meant a lot to me, so I picked men who seemed sophisticated, educated, and cultured. I wanted to be part of any lifestyle that was opposite to the way I grew up. Tommy fit the bill perfectly.

We were a total mismatch. I was out to have all my needs met—to be loved unconditionally, to be close, to be touched emotionally. Tommy, however, only wanted a good time, and any suggestion of commitment or marriage drove him away. I knew he wasn't good for me, yet his attractive appearance and flamboyant lifestyle made me want to believe that eventually he could fulfill my need for love and security.

All my grasping for love caused me to end up in the same situation that two years earlier I had promised God would never happen again. I got pregnant. As before, I had nowhere to go and no one who wanted me in that condition. But this time my main concern was for my career. Getting pregnant was definitely a bad career move, and without my career I would cease to exist. To make things even more complicated, I was scheduled to tour Europe, Africa, and South America for the next three months with a well-known singing group. I was leaving within the week so I had to act quickly.

This pregnancy made me even sicker than before. The abortionist in Mexico was nowhere to be found, so on recommendation of a knowledgeable source I flew to Las Vegas to try and make connection with a certain doctor there. I went to his office and begged him to do the operation. He was suspicious of me because I didn't work in Las Vegas and wanted to run a test to determine for sure that I was pregnant.

"How long will it take to get the results back?" I protested.

"Two to three days," he answered.

"I can't wait that long. I'm leaving on a three-month singing tour in two days. I need the operation right away."

"This is a setup, isn't it?"

"What do you mean?" I asked, knowing that he thought I might be a setup for the police.

He remained thoughtful and silent for a moment, then said, "No, I can't do it."

"Please," I begged him. "If you won't do it, send me to someone who will. I'm desperate. I have the cash."

The doctor remained firm in his decision and left the room.

Later that afternoon I got a phone call at my hotel. The voice on the other end of the line said, "Do you need a doctor?"

"Yes. Please, can you help me?"

"I have a doctor who will do it. Twelve hundred cash."

"I've got it. How soon can it be done?"

"I'll pick you up at three o'clock."

Suddenly I felt scared. "This is a real doctor, right?" I questioned. "And he'll put me to sleep and I won't feel any pain?"

"Of course," the voice mumbled and hung up.

At three o'clock a short, stocky, balding man came to my door. He was nervous and constantly mopped his sweaty forehead with a dirty white handkerchief. I got in his car and we drove a short distance to an obscure, low-class motel near the center of town. We entered through the back door and took the elevator to the second floor. He had a room key and we quickly entered one of the rooms. Until now I had thought this operation would be a breeze like last time, but as we entered the sleazy motel room I knew I was wrong.

"Where's the doctor?" I panicked. "Where's the anesthesiologist? Where's the equipment?"

"Shh! You gotta be quiet. People will hear you." He snapped. "The doctor will be in as soon as you're ready. Let me see the cash."

I gave him the money.

"Take off all your clothes from the waist down and lay face up on that chest of drawers."

"You've got to be kidding!" I said. "Where is the doctor? I want to see him first."

"Look, do you want the operation or not!" he spoke gruffly.

Seeing no alternative, I did as he said. The man then put a blindfold tightly around my eyes and tied a gag over my mouth. "You must not see the doctor or make any noise," he explained. "These operations are extremely dangerous now. The police are cracking down. We can't give you anesthetic because we must move fast if there's any problem. Believe me, this is the best way."

I was numb with fright as he tied me to the top of the chest of drawers. No anesthetic? My heart pounded wildly. I didn't know this man. He could take my money and leave me there. Then I heard the door open quietly and someone else enter the room. The two of them whispered briefly and I could tell the other person was a man. Soon I heard the clanking of surgical tools.

Then the real nightmare began. The first man placed himself across the top half of my body while the "doctor" began the work of the abortion. As he scraped and cut, I began to cry. I gagged and retched and experienced the most excruciating pain of my entire life. It seemed endless. I groaned so loudly that the man placed the full force of his chest over my face to stifle the sounds. I was afraid I might smother. Finally there was one excruciating cut on the inside of me that felt like it must have severed the baby from the uterine wall. It was beyond any pain I could possibly have imagined. A few seconds later it was over, and the doctor left the room immediately.

The man untied me, took off the blindfold and gag, and the phone rang. He answered it, but I was in such pain and shock that I didn't notice what he said. I slid off the chest and stumbled toward the bed for my clothes. Nausea, sobs, and pain racked my whole body.

The man hung up the phone, turned to me, and said angrily, "Clean up this mess. The police are downstairs and the place is swarming with FBI agents."

Just as he said that, I threw up all over the bed and my clothes. Vomit and blood covered my legs. The man, full of disgust, ran to clean up the mess around the chest of drawers. What had been cut out of my body lay in bloody paper towels on the floor, and he wanted that evidence against him destroyed. "Finish cleaning up and flush everything down the toilet," he instructed as he fled from the room.

I did not want to be found in this condition either, so as sick as I was, I picked up all the blood-soiled paper towels and followed his instructions. With terry towels from the bathroom I wiped the blood and vomit from my legs, the bed, the chest of drawers, and the floor. I cleaned off my clothes as best I could and hurriedly put them back on. Tears mixed with sweat, mascara, and vomit ran down my face. I was still convulsing with sobs.

The man came back relieved. "There was a kidnapping downstairs. It has nothing to do with us. I'll finish cleaning this place; you go fix your face and hair." A few minutes later he drove me back to where I was staying.

In contrast to the last abortion, when I felt relieved to be alive, this time I felt depression, failure, and disgust. It had been so ugly.

Two days later I flew to the East Coast to begin the singing tour. My bleeding continued for weeks, and eventually I had to enter a hospital for an operation to stop it. But the pain of the memory never stopped. Every time I saw a baby I felt it all over again. I mourned and felt an emptiness unlike any I had ever known. I wasn't the same after that. Mentally I began to spiral downward.

Would there ever be any end to the hopelessness I felt, or was I doomed to this kind of painful existence for as long as I lived? Where could I find the answers? Who could help me?

# CHAPTER EIGHT

*Stormie*

# MOTHER AND MENTAL ILLNESS

"And so you see, Dr. Foreman, that's when I began to drown myself in my work. It's the only thing I can count on even though I can't always depend on myself to do a good job. I thought marrying Rick would bring me some security, but I'm suffering more than ever."

I looked at the kindly gentleman who had listened to my story unfold over the last few months. He helped me understand much of what had happened, and now I could see where my fears came from and how they controlled me. Talking with him was a wonderful relief, for no matter what I told him he never made me feel like I was crazy.

Neither of us, however, could understand the origin of my mother's hatred and why she treated me the way she did. Yes, she was mentally ill, but that doesn't necessarily result in cruelty and violence. Now that I had told my story I had an unshakable desire to find out more about her.

"Dr. Foreman, I want to go back to Nebraska and talk with my mother's family. I've got to know how she came to be this way." He thought it was an excellent idea. Rick didn't care what I did, since there was nothing left between us but indifference on his part and resentment on mine. My absence was a relief for both of us.

I flew to Nebraska and talked with my mother's father, her two sisters, Jean and Delores, plus other aunts and cousins. It was difficult putting all the pieces together because everyone remembered the past a little differently. I had been told that seven members of a family will give seven different accounts of the same event. It certainly proved true in this case. One thing that *was* consistent was that everyone cried as they spoke of my mother and the past. The tragedy of her life could not be overlooked.

I didn't tell anyone my purpose for being there. How could I add to their hurt by saying that Mother had abused me and now I was trying to rise above the scars? How could I say that my life was falling apart and I was seeing a psychiatrist to help pull it together? The words "psychiatrist" and "insane" were closely linked in some people's minds. I knew I wasn't crazy, but I did have serious doubts that I would ever be normal. My only hope was that I would learn to cope. Revealing my problems to the family could only be a hindrance to that end. I was determined not to let anyone learn the truth.

After a week of questioning I was able to somewhat piece together Mother's life. Although it was apparent that she was not abused as a child, her life was definitely scarred by trauma. She was born Virginia Faith Campbell, the middle child of three girls. Her place in the family was typical of many middle children—lost in between. She was beautiful and well-liked but also stubborn, lazy, and obstinate. Her bright and lively personality made a good impression at social gatherings, but on a one-to-one basis with certain members of the family she was cruel and cold. During the Depression people were concerned with survival and not the emotional balance of a family member, so her undesirable character traits and strong will usually went unchallenged.

When she was 11, Virginia had an unpleasant encounter with her mother, who was nine months pregnant at the time. Apparently her mother verbally rebuked her for something she had done. Virginia insisted that she was being unjustly accused, stomped her feet, and talked back saying, "You're wrong! I didn't do it!" She was sent to her room, where she silently wished her mother dead. A few hours later her mother went into labor, and at the hospital she died in childbirth along with the baby. As children frequently do, Virginia felt responsible for what happened and believed her mother's death was both a punishment and a rejection of her. Uncensored guilt and unbearable grief led to deep emotional scarring from which she never recovered.

The shock of the death overwhelmed Virginia's father, and the burden of caring for his three daughters was more than he could handle. The girls were separated and passed around among different relatives and friends. Because of that, Virginia felt isolated and alone. This was during the Depression, and having an extra child to feed and clothe was not always considered a blessing. Virginia believed that the various foster parents she stayed with favored their natural children over her in affection and material goods. Whether true or not, she believed it, and the perceived injustice instilled her with anger and bitterness.

She became attached to one certain family in which the other young girls were attractive and possessed qualities that she greatly desired. Virginia tried to emulate them and did her best to make the whole family like her. But just as she was allowing herself to have strong feelings for each member, the father of that family killed himself. No one knew the reason for the suicide, but Virginia once again assumed that it was because of her. "I'm responsible for all the deaths in my family," Mother had once told me gravely. I now understood why she thought that way.

Gradually it became too hard for Virginia to cope with the real world. She believed she was responsible for the deaths of two of the most important people in her life, and because she was at an age where she was unable to understand or verbalize her feelings, rejection took root. With everyone around her forced to deal with serious problems of their own, there was no one to help her. So she invented a world she could deal with and understand, where she was the center. In her creation she did no wrong, but was persecuted unjustly. Unable to cope with the mountain of guilt she faced daily, in the world of her own making she was blameless.

During her late teenage years, Virginia contracted a severe case of scarlet fever and came close to death. When she recovered, certain family members observed that she was never quite the same. Her emotional instability became more apparent and her already changeable personality exhibited hot and cold mood swings that defied logic. She tried desperately to get out of the small town where she lived and attend college or study music, but there was no money for that, and in addition her father strongly opposed it. This frustration added to her growing bitterness and insecurity.

As a child my mother had been put in the closet a few times by her father as punishment for minor infractions. Even though those incidents were infrequent and of short duration, she was severely indignant and vocal about her dislike of it. She was jealous of both her sisters and had mentioned to me many times how she felt they had consistently received better treatment. Because of that she was especially cruel to her younger sister, Jean, and put her in a closet a few brief times for punishment.

After hearing these stories, I began to feel sorry for my mother. She was someone to be pitied instead of hated. She had been trapped by her environment and the circumstances surrounding her life. A stronger person might have worked through the problems, but she survived the only way she knew how to, and her mistreatment of me was part of that survival.

This didn't excuse her actions, but it made them understandable. She locked me in a closet so she could better cope with life, and simply forgot how long I was left there. She was angry at her mother for dying, angry at her dad for not helping her when she needed it most, angry at the suicide, angry at her sisters (whom she thought were favored over her), and angry at God for the circumstances of her life. She was filled with repressed rage, which she vented on the most likely recipients—her younger sister Jean, me, and later my dad.

Many people realized that Mother was mentally unstable, but few knew how bad she was because of her ability to appear so normal at times. Even the ones who were aware of her bizarre behavior did not recognize the seriousness of her illness. Out of curiosity, I asked certain people when they first realized that my mother was different. I received a variety of answers.

"When she was in her late teens," said her younger sister Jean, "right after she had scarlet fever."

"She was always emotionally fragile," said older sister Delores.

"After she had been married a short while," said many.

"She was physically frail from the beginning," said her father, "and her personality was always difficult. It's hard to believe that her mind has deteriorated this badly . . ." His sad voice trailed away.

The night before I was to leave, I lay in bed and thought about all I had heard. I recalled a rare conversation I'd had alone with my dad early one morning before Mother was awake. "When did you first realize there was something wrong with Mother?" I had boldly questioned him.

"I noticed it first on our honeymoon," he said. "She thought someone was following us and refused to stop at the hotel where we had reservations. We traveled to four different places before she finally felt safe enough to stay in one. I could see that there was no one following us and couldn't understand why she was so afraid."

I was completely shocked that he had known about this from the day they were married. I silently questioned his sanity while marveling that he had put up with this for so long. He must have really loved her to overlook all that.

As I turned out the light and pulled the covers up to my chin, I felt deep unrest. There were no clear-cut answers about Mother. Was she born with a chemical imbalance? Did the trauma of childhood losses cripple her? Was she never called to account for her actions, and so she became unaccountable? Was her brain damaged by the high fever during her bout with scarlet fever? Did she have signs of mental illness way back in her teens which no one recognized? Was it all of these things? I couldn't answer these questions, nor could anyone else.

After hearing everyone's stories, I felt I knew Mother better. Yet all that information only stirred up my own pain even more. I thought that knowing the truth would make a difference, but it didn't.

"What do I do with all this information?" I thought as I tried vainly to sleep. "I can see why Mother is the way she is, and I feel sorry for her, but it doesn't change the way I feel inside. I still hurt. I still ache. I still feel like a prisoner of my past. I understand everything, yet I understand nothing.''

I cried into my pillow as despair overtook what little hope had been raised over the last few months. "What am I supposed to do now?'' I sobbed to no one.

# IT'S WHO YOU KNOW THAT COUNTS

I flew home from Nebraska more miserable than I was before I left. Rick had not lifted a finger to keep the house clean while I was gone so it was a mess when I arrived. I looked at my house and I looked at my life and I couldn't cope with either of them anymore.

I stared into the bathroom mirror as I undressed for bed. I looked old. My skin was sallow, wrinkled, and broken out. The pores were large. My hair was dry and thinning. The gray hairs had steadily increased over the years with every new trauma. My mind was also gray. There were no bright colors in my life. My eyes were dull and lifeless, with dark circles under them that I could no longer hide with makeup. I was 28 years old but I looked over 40. My health was not responding to good nutrition and exercise as it had in the past. I had a sinus infection and constant low-grade nausea that had gone on for months. I felt unloved, undesirable, unattractive, and more locked up than ever. My emptiness knew no bounds. I saw only the hopelessness of my life. All my methods for survival had failed. The new season of the Glen Campbell Show was due to start in a few weeks, but this time I knew I could not pull it together again.

"God," I said silently, "I don't want to live anymore. Things will never get better and life makes no sense. Please let me die."

Suicide was the answer. Only this time I wasn't going to slip up. I knew the difference between a sleeping pill and an aspirin, and I would make no mistakes. It would be clean. I would arrange for all my money to go to Dad and Suzy and the death would look like an accidental overdose of drugs and booze. I would be out of my misery without inflicting pain on anyone else. I made plans to secure enough pills to do the job. I was dying everyday anyway, so why not end this torture.

The next night my Christian friend, Terry, called me to do a record session as a background singer. During a break she abruptly said, "I can see you're not doing well, Stormie. Why don't you come with me and meet my pastor? He's a wonderful man and I know he can help you."

I hesitated.

"What have you got to lose? I'll pick you up and take you...okay?"

"Okay," I said, acknowledging that I really didn't have anything to lose.

Two days later Terry picked me up and drove me to a restaurant, where we met Pastor Jack Hayford from the Church On The Way in Van Nuys. He was a warm, effervescent man with a direct gaze and exuded a confidence that might have been intimidating had it not been tempered by an obvious loving and compassionate heart. He spoke with a remarkable balance of eloquence and down-to-earth vernacular. Although he was possibly ten years older than I was, everything about him was youthful. I kept looking for phoniness, shady motives, discrepancies, or manipulation, but I never found any of them. He was unlike anyone I'd ever met in my life.

Pastor Jack, as Terry called him, listened intently as I shared briefly about my depression and fear. I was still trying to keep up a good front even at this late hour in my life. I didn't want either of them to know I was nauseated and fighting an infection that wasn't responding to any method of treatment. I saw any admission of weakness as a sign of failure. I definitely didn't want them to know the details of my mother and childhood.

He worked his way into a conversation about God with such ease that it was like he was talking about his best friend. He made God sound like a touchable person who cared about me.

"How much do you know about Jesus?" he inquired.

"Just a few details," I said, recalling my past experience with church. "I know about His birth in a stable and that He was put to a cruel death on a cross for no reason. He was supposed to have been a good man. Other than that I really know nothing."

"Have you ever heard of the term 'born again'?"

I looked at him with a vague expression.

"Jesus said that He was the Son of God and that unless we are born again, we cannot see the kingdom of God. He said, 'My Father's will is that everyone who looks to the Son and believes in Him shall have eternal life.' Looking to the Son means accepting Him as Savior and thereby being born again into God's kingdom. It's a spiritual birth, not a physical birth. It's the opportunity to not only secure your eternal future, but your future in this life as well. You can begin life anew, and your past will be forgiven and buried."

I was fascinated as he spoke about how the Holy Spirit would come into my life and transform my circumstances. Something inside of me thrilled over such a possibility.

"It happens in the spirit realm," he explained, "but it also affects your physical life in practical ways."

Pastor Jack never asked me if I wanted to identify with Jesus, but rather talked of Him as one would tell stories about a beloved father. This was different from the many times when people had walked up to me on the street, pushing a piece of paper in my face and talking harshly about repentance, sin, and salvation. They seemed to think of themselves as superior over those who weren't like them, and because of that I wanted no part of their lifestyle. But this was different.

Two hours flew by, and near the end of our time together, Pastor Jack asked me, "Do you like to read?"

"I love to read!" I responded eagerly.

"If I give you some books, would you read them this week?"

"Sure," I promised.

Terry and I followed him to his office at the church, where he carefully selected three books from his well-stocked shelves. Handing them to me, he said, "Let's meet back at the restaurant in exactly one week. I want to hear what you think of these."

"Great," I said with enthusiasm. My new reading assignment

gave me something to look forward to.

Talking with Pastor Jack and Terry had been a great reprieve from the immovable oppression in my life, but it ended when I returned home. As Terry drove off, the nausea returned and I couldn't wait to climb into bed.

I began reading the books the next day, soaking in their contents like a sponge. It was as if I was transported out of my dreary life into another world.

The first book was *The Screwtape Letters*, by C.S. Lewis. It is a characterization about a devil who wrote letters of instruction to his nephew Wormwood. The letters spoke of how to destroy people and how to lay traps and wait for victims to fall into them. Of course, I was educated and sophisticated enough to not believe in a devil. All my Science of Mind teaching and other occult religions had taught that there was no evil force except what existed in your own mind. If you could control your mind, there would be no evil in your life. So the idea of a devil was amusing, yet fascinating. As certain real-life situations were presented in the story, C.S. Lewis seemed to have a logical, almost believable explanation for them.

The second book was about the work of the Holy Spirit. Again, even though I had heard about the "Father, Son, and Holy Spirit," I never thought of the Holy Spirit as a person with power to change lives, or that He could manifest Himself through someone by different spiritual gifts. This too was fascinating and seemed logical.

The third book was the Gospel of John, the fourth book of the New Testament in the Bible. Pastor Jack had given it to me in the form of a separate book, and I read it in one sitting. The words on each page came alive with meaning, and I felt the vitality of those words somehow entering me, bringing life to my life.

By the end of the week I was feeling a little better physically, and when I met Terry and Pastor Jack at the restaurant, I was eager to talk.

After we ordered lunch, Pastor Jack looked at me in his direct manner and said, "Well, what did you think of the books?"

"I believe they are the truth," I replied.

He smiled and let me continue.

"I don't know why, though. I don't believe in the devil."

He smiled again, unflinching at anything I said and calmly explained that the way I believed was exactly one of the traps that C.S. Lewis had written about.

"The devil wants you to believe he doesn't exist, that Jesus isn't the Son of God, and that there is no Holy Spirit with power working in lives today, for then he's rendered you totally impotent," he explained.

I began to see the wisdom in what he was saying. I was indeed caught in the trap. Pastor Jack talked about life and God in a way that made me hunger for more.

After we finished our lunch, Pastor Jack invited us back to his office to pray. Seated across from Terry and me, he looked directly at me and said, "Stormie, you said you believe the books I gave you were the truth. Does this mean that you want to receive Jesus today and be born again?"

"Yes, I do," I said softly and without any hesitation.

He led me in a prayer and I repeated after him: "Jesus, I acknowledge You this day. I believe You are the Son of God as You say You are. Although it's hard to comprehend love so great, I believe You laid down Your life for me so that I might have eternal life and abundant life now. I confess my failure and that I am a sinner. I confess that I can't live life without You. Come into my life and fill me with Your Holy Spirit. Let all the death in my life be crowded out by the power of Your presence, and this day turn my life into a new beginning."

It was simple and easy. I was born again and filled with the Holy Spirit. I left the office feeling light and hopeful, though I still didn't fully understand what it all meant. Terry invited me to come to church with her and her husband on Sunday, and I accepted. As I was not strong enough emotionally or physically to make it there on my own, they came by the house and picked me up. It had been 15 years since I'd been inside a church, and when I entered this one I noticed immediately that it was unlike any I'd ever seen before. The structure and decor were plain compared to the fancy churches I'd been in, although very neat and clean.

"So glad that you're here!" bubbled one of the hostesses as I entered the front door. Though I was wearing jeans and a T-shirt and the hostess was in her Sunday best, she wrapped her arms around me and gave me a big hug. I appraised her cautiously and decided that her smile was genuine and her motive pure. I soon discovered that her friendliness and caring quality were typical of nearly everyone there. It was hard to ignore the exuberance, the laughter, and the absolute joy of life that came from the 300 or so people in the overcrowded sanctuary. I felt like I was attending a party, compared with the somber churches I had been in years earlier.

As I settled into one of the comfortable seats near the front, I sensed a spirit of peace settle over my mind. I felt strength coming into me just being there. Spiritual things were not new to me, since I knew there was a spirit realm from all my occult practices, but this was totally different. Instead of experiencing the fear that I had previously associated with anything spiritual, I now sensed a supernatural presence of love so powerful that it permeated the air and even bathed the floors, walls, and seats.

"There's life here," I thought to myself. "And the life is real."

Pastor Jack came onto the platform and immediately began to lead us in songs of worship to God. The congregation sang hymns and choruses of praise that were so powerful they nearly elevated me out of my shoes. As their voices rose, so did my spirit, and I couldn't help but compare them with the painfully timid congregations I had heard in the past that barely mumbled the words into their hymnals while an overzealous soprano dominated our attention. Again the word "life" came to my mind as I tried to label the comparison.

"All hail the power of Jesus' name, let angels prostrate fall!" the full voices soared in almost a shout. "Bring forth the royal diadem and crown Him Lord of all!"

"His name is Jesus, Jesus. Sad hearts, weep no more! He has healed the brokenhearted, opened wide the prison door. He is able to deliver evermore," came the words during a more tender moment. Sometimes it affected me so profoundly that I couldn't sing at all but only stand, listen, and cry as the worshiping voices penetrated every fiber of my being. I gained strength from each new song and felt a release of tension from down deep inside as stress oozed out of my body.

"The Bible says to lift up holy hands to the Lord," directed Pastor Jack, and I, along with everyone else, responded with upraised hands of worship. When I did that, I felt as if I had just let go of myself and the load I was carrying. I was offering it up to Him, and I felt Him taking it from me. Again I cried.

When the worship time ended, Pastor Jack began to speak, and it seemed as if he was speaking only to me. The Bible, or Scriptures, as he called them, came alive as he taught on a story that happened thousands of years ago but had a direct bearing on my life right now. He told of the Israelites being set free from Egyptian captivity and then wandering around in the desert for 40 years because they wouldn't listen to God and do things His way.

"That's me," I thought. "I've been doing things my own way and wandering around in the wilderness. Oh, God," I cried quietly, "I want to do things *Your* way now."

As we were in the car heading home, Terry asked me, "Well, what did you think?"

I thought for one brief moment, then replied, "I think I'd better not go to Church On The Way anymore without waterproof mascara and a box of Kleenex."

Terry laughed, since she was well aware of how much I was moved by the worship, the teaching, and the powerful presence of the Spirit of God in the service.

I was eager to return the following Sunday and every Sunday after that. I was still too weak to make it on my own, so each Sunday morning Terry got me out of bed with a phone call and picked me up at my house. Every time I entered the church, peace would overtake me. Healing and strength came in waves, and I got glimpses of hope for my life. Never had I heard as great a teacher as Pastor Jack, and I hung on his every word. He always brought the teaching around to where I was living, as if he had prepared his sermon to speak directly to my need. Later I realized that was the Holy Spirit working in my life, and that everyone felt the same way I did. At the end of each sermon, as the point was driven home, I had to fight back convulsive sobs. This time it was crying that cleansed and healed me, and I sensed a refreshing and renewal in my being when it was over.

Whenever Pastor Jack invited the congregation to receive Jesus, I silently made that commitment again. Just hearing that because of Jesus I could be forgiven of everything I had ever done wrong, and that now I could make a fresh start, brought life to my bones.

Every time I entered the church I cried. It was the cry of a lost little girl who had been wandering for a long time, and though she had tried to keep herself strong throughout her wandering, the minute she saw that her daddy had found her, she sobbed. Every Sunday I realized all over again that my Daddy God had found me. My Daddy God loved and cared about me when I couldn't love and care about myself.

Unfortunately, the jolt back to "real life" started as soon as Terry drove me home from church. The moment I entered my house I began my descent slowly back into depression, until by the following Sunday morning I could barely get out of bed. Gradually, however, the peace carried over a little longer, until eventually it lasted all of Sunday. Even Rick couldn't destroy it. However, the more joyful I became, the more Rick retreated in the opposite direction. His negative attitude fully blossomed and he became more difficult and critical, finding nothing good to say about me or to me.

One morning I came home from church bubbling over with the joy I felt inside. Rick was watching television and made no attempt at communication.

"Rick, this church is so great! I feel wonderful when I come out of there! I wish you'd come with me just one time."

"I've told you before, I don't want to talk about it," he snapped. "If you want to waste time with your creepy Christian friends that's your business, but leave me out of it."

"Rick, please let me tell you about Jesus," I persisted in hopes of penetrating the wall of his emotions with the truth I'd found. "Jesus has changed my life..."

I stopped as Rick stood up and growled with anger in his eyes, "Don't you *ever* mention that name in this house again!" Then he walked out of the room, leaving me feeling like I'd been slapped in the face and the door shut on what little communication possibilities were left to us. His anger was so intense that I knew I must never mention Jesus to him again. All that remained between us now was resentment and we seldom spoke to one another.

As my insides became more solid, the externals of my life began to change. Little by little some of my bad habits disappeared without my even trying.

"Want a cigarette?" a girlfriend offered one day at lunch.

"No thanks," I replied.

"Let me buy you a drink. How about a brandy, or a scotch?"

"No, I really don't want anything."

"Want to get high on some grass tonight? My boyfriend has got some great marijuana from South America, and we could drive over to his apartment and pick it up."

"No, honest, I'm fine. I just don't have the desire or need for those things. No offense," I foolishly apologized.

"You're getting weird, Stormie," she said, her voice turning serious.

"Please don't worry about me. I may be weird, but I'm very happy." I was met with a quizzical stare.

"Look, I'm not chemically addicted to these things; I only used them for emotional solace. Now that my emotional needs are being met by Jesus, I simply don't have the need for them anymore."

"You *are* getting weird, Stormie," she repeated, then changed the subject.

Within a few weeks I did something brave. I had my long, trademark-blonde hair dyed back to its natural color of chestnut brown. I was beginning to suspect that being the woman God made me to be might not be all that bad, and I wanted to find out who that was. I knew it would mean losing work, and sure enough, no one wanted a dumb blonde comedienne who was brunette. But the loss of work didn't bother me. I was beginning to feel better about myself, and it had nothing to do with work.

About that time the Glen Campbell Show was canceled. The two main recording and TV contractors I had worked for in Hollywood developed cancer and died. A singing duo that I had performed in for several years in some of the nightclubs around town suddenly dissolved when my other half decided to go off on her own. To add to all that, early one morning I received a phone call from my commercial agent.

"I have an interview for you this morning," she chirped on the other end of the line.

"What's it for?" my voice wary of her answer.

"A cigarette commercial. They want a pretty blonde about your size."

"I can't do it," I said with a combination of determination and fear.

"You can't do it! Why not?" she controlled her impatience.

"First of all, I'm not a blonde anymore. And second, I don't think smoking cigarettes is good for you. I can't be part of something I don't believe in, and I don't believe in convincing people to buy a product that's bad for them."

"Stormie, this is the sixth commercial interview you've refused to go on because it involves liquor, cigars, cigarettes, or costumes that you think are too revealing." She was obviously disgusted with me. "If you can't accept these commercials, then there is absolutely nothing we can do for you."

"I guess you're right," I said slowly. "I'm really sorry."

"We'll send you a release from your contract in the mail," she snapped, and hung up.

I replaced the receiver, stunned by what had just transpired. Part of me felt great relief, but the other part was afraid because my last avenue of revenue was shut off. Suddenly there was no money coming in, and I knew I could no longer support Rick in that big house. The pressure to come up with all that money each month was more than I could bear. That, coupled with the fact that he was becoming even more critical and cruel, pushed me to the edge. Life seemed hopeless when I was around him, for he was a constant reminder of all my failures and what a rejected person I had been.

That afternoon I found an apartment and that night I informed Rick I was moving out. We hadn't even been married the two years I'd planned, but I couldn't take any more of it. I told him he could have the house and everything in it that was his. I would take only what I had brought into the house when we were married or purchased since then.

He agreed, and appeared to take the news very calmly. But I knew he was concerned about having to find a job and pay his own bills. I was so wrapped up in my own feelings that I couldn't see that he battled with self-doubt too. I still couldn't discern anyone's problems but my own.

I moved immediately. Since I had only a few possessions, within one day I had hung every picture and put away every book and dish. Because the TV and recording industry was very slow, all of my close friends were out of town on tour. I had no one to talk to, so my relief over not having to support Rick and that house was mixed with loneliness. I felt that my life had been turned upside down and that everything that didn't belong was being shaken out. The only problem was that there was nothing much left—just the church. The church was a refuge, my only place of security and peace.

During one Sunday morning service while the congregation was praying in small groups, Pastor Jack walked to the back of the church where I was and whispered that he wanted to see me in his office as soon as possible. I was excited to go because I loved Pastor Jack, and any chance to talk to him was welcome. Besides, I had written my first two Christian songs and could hardly wait to show him.

Once in the office his mood was very serious. Pastor Jack was not interested in my songs, but only in the fact that I had filed for divorce. "God's ways don't allow for divorce," he told me. Then he showed me all the Scriptures to back it up and spent an hour explaining them.

I didn't attempt to blame Rick, nor did I try to explain

anything. I took full responsibility for the marriage and its failure. Whatever penalty there was for deceiving Rick into marrying me, I was willing to pay it even though that thought was
terrifying. My choices, as I saw them, were to go back and live
with Rick or else give up my salvation and the church and get
a divorce. I knew there was only one choice: I would never go
back and live in hell with Rick.

As if he'd read my mind, Pastor Jack's face softened as he
leaned forward across his desk and said, "I know you would
rather die than go back to a situation where you've been so
miserable."

"I can never go back," I said, suppressing the tears. It was
still important for me to keep up a good front, so I struggled
to keep from crying. I was grateful that he understood my
feelings, and if I had to leave the church, he knew the reason.

Then he did something totally unexpected. He came over beside
my chair, got down on his knees, put his arms around me, gave
me a firm hug, and said, "I want you to know that whatever
you decide, I still love you and this church is still your home."

Now I could no longer control the tears that poured down my
cheeks. Never had I faced such unconditional love. I tried with
all my might to choke back the immense swell of uncontrollable
sobs that lay just below the surface. "If I let them loose, Pastor
Jack might see what an emotional mess I am and change his mind
about letting me stay in this church," I reasoned.

I left with a promise to return for more counseling, and
considered it a great victory that I had not completely fallen apart.
I was grateful to God that I didn't have to leave the church and
that I could be loved even when I failed. It was my first experience with this kind of love, the depth of which I had never before
imagined. I expected judgment. This was what I lived with before
I met Jesus. Instead I found God's love. And I was soon to discover that it went far deeper than I even dreamed possible.

# CHAPTER TEN

# THE DELIVERER

I ripped open the large white envelope from a motion picture company that I had worked for well over five years earlier.

"Another residual check!" I exclaimed gleefully to no one. It was only 276 dollars, but it would cover the rent, buy the groceries, and pay off the two bills sitting on my desk.

"God, you are so good to me!" I prayed thankfully. "Every time I need to pay a bill, You send money from the most unexpected places."

I had lost track of how many times the Lord had done this over the last few months of no steady work. He had sustained me in many other ways too. Because of the extra time I had, I was able to spend many hours at the church, especially in the counseling offices. With no regular work, I was having to learn what it meant to put my identity in Jesus rather than my last job. It was a slow and painful process.

I was also learning about "fellowship." What a strange, "churchy" word that was to me when I first heard it! It reminded me of tea and cookies after a women's meeting, or a potluck dinner in the basement of a church. I soon discovered that it was much more than coffee hour, however. It involved getting to know other believers and entering into a caring and sharing type of relationship with them. I entered these new relationships with caution. The difference between my believing friends and *non*believing friends was like two different worlds. But I found a strong bond between people who love the Lord that made other relationships seem shallow by comparison. That common bond was compelling and irresistible.

"Growth is a relational experience," Pastor Jack would say. "You do not grow except within relationship to a body of believers."

I understood this to mean that there needed to be ongoing circulation with other believers in order for me to experience real growth. I learned that fellowship expands the heart, bridges gaps, and breaks down walls in us, leading us to realize who God made us to be. I wasn't sure exactly how it worked, but I knew that it did work.

•  •  •

I woke up with a start Sunday morning and realized immediately by the brightness of the sun shining through my bedroom curtains that I had overslept. In spite of all the Lord's blessings, the counseling at the church, the times of joy and peace, and the support of other believers, I still struggled with periodic depression. I was constantly exhausted from the struggle to rise above it. I suffered from insomnia, and after tossing and turning for hours I would finally fall into a deep sleep toward the morning. When I woke up I felt as if I hadn't slept at all.

"Church starts in 20 minutes," I groaned to myself. "There's no time to wash my hair or put on makeup. I'll just have to sneak in and hope no one I know sees me."

I quickly dressed, ran a comb through my hair, grabbed my Bible, and rushed to the car. Sunday morning church was my lifeline. Missing it was absolutely out of the question, no matter what my condition.

I pulled into the church parking lot, jumped out of my car, and ran to the church entrance, where I bumped unavoidably into Paul Johnson and Terry. As we greeted each other, they turned and waved excitedly to someone driving into the parking lot.

"That's Michael Omartian. He's coming to this church for the first time," Paul explained.

"Great!" I said, to cover my alarm and kicking myself for

not at least putting blusher on my cheeks. I wanted to escape before he saw me looking so awful, but it was too late. Michael was out of his car and over to us in an instant.

"Michael, look who's here—it's Stormie!" said Paul.

"Hi, Michael." I tried to sound joyful. "How have you been?"

"Good," he nodded. He looked wonderful. Even though his hair was too long and in need of a good shaping, he was still the best-looking man I'd ever seen. I excused myself and rushed into the church alone. I couldn't bear to sit next to them in my disheveled state.

As soon as the service began, I started to cry and didn't stop until it ended. I don't know what the people sitting around me thought and Pastor Jack must have wondered what effect his message was having on me that morning. All I could think of was how I had blown everything. I could see now that when Michael first came into my life, God had provided him as an opportunity for me to make the right decision. I had heard the truth. I had been attracted to God's light in him, but had resisted it. I had my chance and typically I made the wrong choice. Now it was too late.

"Oh, God," I cried, "I've messed up everything. These past 29 years have been a total waste. My life is shattered in a million pieces that can never be put back together again. Oh, Lord, I'm grateful that You've given me hope and peace and eternal life, but as far as my life ever amounting to anything, how can it happen? It's too late." I muffled my sobs into an already-soaked tissue.

In the midst of my utter distress I heard God speak to my heart words of comfort: "I am a Redeemer. I redeem all things. I make all things new. Whatever you've lost I will restore. It doesn't matter what you've done. It doesn't matter what's happened to you. I can take all the hurt, the pain, and the scars. Not only can I heal them, but I can make them count for something."

My tears flowed without end. How could God ever accomplish all that? Yet I sincerely believed that all things were possible with God, and His words gave me hope. "God, I surrender my life to You. Don't let me ever be in the wrong place again," I prayed.

Until this moment I had only received His life. Now I *gave* Him mine. As I viewed the failure and rubble of my past, I knew I couldn't navigate on my own anymore. I wanted God to take my life and do with it what He wanted. He would certainly do a better job than I had ever done.

After church there was no way I could slip out unnoticed. Michael stopped me at the door and mentioned that he had just bought a new car the day before. "Would you like to go for a ride?" he asked.

"Great," I said, again beating myself for not at least putting on some lipstick or eye makeup before I left home.

During our short drive we caught up on the past two years. "You've done well, Michael," I smiled. "I hear you're the hot new piano player in town. Remember, I told you so."

Michael laughed. Then his countenance became solemn. "I hear you're divorced."

I looked down and nodded my head yes. "It's okay if you want to say 'I told you so.' Everyone was correct in their predictions."

"I feel like I failed you by not pressing the reality of Jesus into your life," said Michael. "Had I tried harder I possibly could have made you understand. You might have received Him and none of this would ever have happened."

"I can't tell you how many times I wished you had forced me to listen. But it's too late now. That's all in the past, and the important thing is that I know Him today. Please don't blame yourself. It was what I saw in your life that attracted me to Jesus in the first place. I saw Him in you and Terry and later Pastor Jack—I just didn't know it at the time."

I was shocked when Michael suggested that we meet and talk again the following weekend. "Surely You have blinded this man, God, or else he feels sorry for me. I couldn't look worse than I do today," I said out loud on the way home in my car. "God, don't let me make another mistake," I prayed. "If I shouldn't be with Michael, I'm willing to not see him anymore." I was serious about that, and it was further evidence that my prayer earlier that morning in church was sincere.

I felt no uneasiness about seeing Michael the following weekend, so when Saturday night came I washed my hair, carefully styled it, and put on my makeup with the hand of an artist. When he met me at my front door he must have wondered if I was the same woman he had seen the previous Sunday. We went out to dinner that night and saw each other every weekend after that over the next many months. When we made arrangements to go out for dinner *during* the week, I knew it was serious.

I especially loved going to church with Michael on Sunday mornings. After the service, we would go out for lunch and talk about the teachings from the Bible and what the Lord was doing in our lives each week. Praying together drew us closer to each other as we continued to grow and learn about God's ways.

We both began to see the importance of obedience and the rewards when we were obedient to the Lord's commands. We learned that God's ways are good and that we could trust them. All that learning was an exciting adventure, and we were never bored with it or with each other.

After nearly a year of dating, Michael asked me to marry him. I didn't have to ask him for time to think it over, for I'd already thought through the possibility in depth. As much as I wanted to spend the rest of my life with Michael, I feared making another mistake. "God, let Your perfect will be done concerning our relationship," I prayed day after day.

"Michael, there's something I need to tell you," I said bravely. "There are things I've done that I have never told anyone."

I proceeded to confess everything of my past to him, for I wanted this to be a relationship of total honesty, no matter what the risk. His look of concern turned to a grin when I finished and he said, "That's it?"

"Isn't that enough?" I replied.

"The way you were talking I thought perhaps you were wanted by the FBI for armed robbery."

I laughed and sighed with relief, "You mean you still want to be friends?"

"I want to be more than friends," he answered, and I knew at that moment I had found the right man.

• • •

Once we were married there were many problems to work through. Fortunately, the problems were not between *us*, but each of us individually was dealing with scars of the past, and being married surfaced those things.

Michael was never, in any way, abused as a child. He had a wonderful family. But his mother, whom I loved dearly, had been a domineering woman with extremely high expectations to which Michael felt he never lived up. She told me soon after we met that she had made mistakes as a mother.

"I was way too hard on him as a child," she tenderly confessed to me one afternoon. Her big, expressive brown eyes were filled with hurt and remorse. They conveyed the guilt that torments any parent upon realizing that he or she has made a mistake with a child and that there is no going back. "He feels he can never live up to the family's expectations, and it's my fault," she sighed heavily.

"Michael is a good man and a great husband," I encouraged her. "The problems of the past are definitely a reality, but he's getting over them and God is using them to show Himself strong in Michael's life. Please don't feel bad. It's all being healed. Really."

She was somewhat comforted, but still concerned.

The difference between Michael and me was that Michael suffered from feelings of never living up to what was expected of him while I suffered from the belief that no one ever expected anything of me. Part of me always felt like a misfit that should never have been born. Fortunately, the great love and trust that Michael and I had for each other provided a strong bond that laid the groundwork for the healing that was to come.

I gradually discovered that while receiving Jesus as my personal Savior and being born into the kingdom of God was instant, allowing Him to become *Lord* over my life was a process. I let

Him have more and more of me as I went along, but each time I thought I had given Him my *all*, I discovered I had only given all I could. If I wanted to live in peace, enjoying God's full measure of blessing, I had to obey God's Word—not in the strict, legalistic sense, but with an attitude that says, "Show me what to do, Lord, and help me to do it."

In order to live in obedience to God's Word, I needed to find out what His Word said. So I bought a large, heavy Bible that had four different translations in it. I read the Bible from beginning to end in one translation, then began all over in another. People who saw me lugging that huge Bible to church must have thought me exceedingly spiritual. I wasn't—just exceptionally hungry.

As my hunger for God's Word grew, so did my desire for more teaching. Attending church once a week was not enough, so I added Wednesday and Sunday evenings to my schedule. This also opened up possibilities for making more new friends, and I found associating with them a significant source of strength and encouragement.

I had always written songs, but now I began to take my writing seriously as more and more song lyrics about Jesus came to my heart and mind. I could barely write them down fast enough as they came stream-of-consciousness style. I rewrote and pared and honed until I had the right word with the right note and each song said exactly what I wanted it to say. The thrill of hearing these songs recorded by Christian artists, and knowing that God was using them to bring happiness to people, was a privilege I valued highly. I believed this was part of my reward for obedience.

Michael and I soon realized that we had neglected to take one very important step of obedience—that of being baptized in water. Jesus Himself was baptized in order to do what was right, and He commanded us all to do the same.

Still cautious about doing something that was merely a religious ritual as opposed to taking a step of obedience with understanding, I studied further. I found out that baptism in water was an act of obedience by which the lordship of Jesus in your life is declared. The past is washed away in the water and you come up cleansed while it remains buried. There was nothing magical about the water itself. The power is not in the water, but in being obedient to the Word of God whether you understand it fully or not. All steps of obedience, and this one especially, carried with it the opportunity for deliverance, freedom, and wholeness, and I desired everything that God had for me. After discussing it with Michael one afternoon, we were baptized together that same night. I didn't feel any different afterward, except that I had the joy and confidence that comes from knowing you've obeyed God.

Still, through all the growth, I continued to struggle with depression. Oddly enough, my depression seemed to be growing in intensity. Every morning when I awoke I was plagued with thoughts of suicide. It was like a bad habit I couldn't break. However, I wasn't shy about asking for help at church. I was so convinced that Jesus was the answer to every need that I regularly visited the counseling office. The counsel I received always helped, but the problem of depression was never completely eliminated.

I could not understand why. I had the gift of eternal life and total forgiveness from Jesus. I had a loving pastor who taught me much about God and the Bible. I had a wonderful husband and financial security, so I no longer had to work to survive. Yet I still felt like I had nothing to live for. What was the matter with me? Was a part of me missing, just like with my mother? I was still afraid that I would end up crazy like her. If I had all I wanted and still felt lacking, if I had much to be happy about and yet remained depressed, if I had everything to live for and still wanted to die, then what hope was there for me? I was certain that Jesus was the answer to my every need, and if He couldn't help me, then nothing could.

As the suicidal feelings increased, Michael urged me to call the counseling office again. I was embarrassed at the frequency with which I made appointments there, but the staff didn't seem discouraged by this. They ushered me into the assistant pastor's office and I told him about the length and severity of this depression, plus the suicidal feelings that weren't letting up.

He thought a moment, then said, "I think you'd better see Sara Anne."

Sara Anne turned out to be a pastor's wife and a member of the regular counseling staff at the church. She was steeped in the Word of God and had great faith to pray for and see people set free from emotional pain. She was highly knowledgeable about people with my kind of problem and was one of the most powerful ministers of God I've ever met.

I entered her office and sat in the chair across the desk from her. She looked up from her papers and gave me a big smile. She had a beautiful face of intelligence, understanding, and warmth, and I felt comfortable in confessing my problems and past to her. She listened for a long time, nodding thoughtfully and seeming not the least bit shocked by anything I said.

"You need deliverance," she stated matter-of-factly when I had finished talking. "Do you know what deliverance is?"

I shook my head. I had heard the term but didn't understand it. It sounded like a strange activity involving red-eyed demons and whirlwinds, but I could tell by her calm demeanor that this was not what she meant.

"Don't let the word 'deliverance' frighten you," Sara Anne explained. "It's a process of becoming everything God made you to be. Deliverance removes all the past brokenness and bondage from a person's life so that the real *you* can come forth. A lot of people are afraid of deliverance because they think it will change them. But deliverance doesn't *change* you; it *releases* you.

"I'm talking about oppression and not possession," she continued. "There are spirits that attach themselves to you. They can come into anyone's life through the work of the devil, who has been allowed to influence our lives through our own sin. Our responsibility is to pray for deliverance from whatever oppression is tormenting you, whether fear or suicidal thoughts or whatever. Second Corinthians 1:10 says that Jesus will *continue* to deliver you. Deliverance is like salvation in that we don't earn it. It is God's gift to us."

She continued, "I think we should fast and pray and meet again next week to see what God wants to do for you. Certain deliverance will not happen in your life except by prayer and fasting."

"Fasting?" I gulped.

I had heard about fasting because Pastor Jack taught about it. In fact, the whole church was supposed to fast every Wednesday. I guess I thought Pastor Jack was speaking to the church staff, the elders, and the superspiritual. Surely he wasn't talking to me.

"Yes, there is a certain kind of release that will not happen in your life without prayer and fasting. It is an act of denying yourself and positioning God as everything in your life. Fasting is designed to loose the bonds of wickedness, undo heavy burdens; set the oppressed free, and break every yoke."

"Fasting...of course," I said hesitantly, unwilling to reveal my true feelings of concern that I might die in the night if I went to bed without dinner. "How long?" I held my breath.

"You should stop eating Sunday at sundown and I will see you Wednesday morning at ten A.M.," she said confidently.

"Do I just drink water during this time?" I questioned.

"Yes, water. You don't have any physical problem that would prohibit you from doing that, do you?"

"Oh, no," I answered, trying to think of something.

"Now during that time you must be much in prayer. Ask God to bring to your mind every wrong sexual relationship or encounter you've ever had, every sin you've committed, every occult practice you've been involved with, and list them all on paper. Bring it with you next week."

"I'll be writing day and night," I thought to myself in horror. "What are you going to do with the paper?" I asked, trying to mask my concern.

"When you've confessed it all and we've prayed, you will tear it up and throw it away."

"Good," I said with great relief, and she laughed heartily at my response.

I left Sara Anne's office feeling hopeful that God was going to do something for me. The fast actually seemed like an adventure, and I was glad I was being forced to do it.

The first two days of the fast brought no problems. I worked on my list of failures and drank water every time I felt a hunger pang. On the morning of the third day, as I was getting ready for my appointment with Sara Anne, she telephoned to say she was sick and needed to postpone our meeting for one week.

Instantly my hopes were dashed to the ground. I could hear the congestion in her lungs, and she could barely talk. She was apologetic, and of course I understood. But instead of seeing this as the devil's attack upon her body, I believed the devil's lie that there would never be deliverance for me.

"See, it's never going to happen," I heard the voice in my head say. "You've had these depressions for 20 years. It's never going to be any different. You were a fool to hope otherwise."

During the week that followed, the depression became so bad that when Michael wasn't home I lay in bed for hours from sheer exhaustion. Sara Anne instructed me to fast again, just as we had the previous week. I had lost all hope of anything being accomplished through it, but I fasted anyway. Out of obedience I would do what Sara Anne said and let her discover for herself that nothing was going to change.

On the morning of the third day I wearily got out of bed and dressed, half-expecting the phone to ring and the appointment to be canceled. But no one called. Just before I left, Michael and I prayed that God would work a miracle.

Once in Sara Anne's office, we got down to the issues immediately. She had me renounce all my occult involvement, specifically naming each type of practice and asking God for forgiveness. "Let your astrologers come forward," she read from the Bible, "those stargazers who make predictions month by month, let them save you from what is coming upon you. Surely they are like stubble; the fire will burn them up. They cannot even save themselves from the power of the flame."[1] "Let no one be found among you who...practices divination or sorcery, interprets omens, engages in witchcraft, or casts spells, or who is a medium or spiritist or who consults the dead. Anyone who does these things is detestable to the Lord."[2]

What the Bible said about the occult was pretty clear. If you are aligned with it, you cannot be aligned with God. I remembered Pastor Jack saying, "The occult is real in its power, but wrong in its source. It derives its power from the realm of darkness."

At first I didn't want to believe that these things were wrong. I had always thought of them as a method for getting closer to God. But I believed what Jesus said and that the Bible was God's Word. So if God said these things were wrong, I was willing to give up my involvement with them. Yet somehow, in my lack of complete spiritual awakening, I had never thought to *verbally* break the ties I had established with the realm of darkness. I thought that to just stop practicing these things was enough. But I was wrong. I had been aligned with evil and had never sought to identify and break its powerful hold over my life. When Sara Anne read those Scriptures, I knew that this was exactly what I had to do. She instructed me to renounce each practice specifically, and so I did.

"Heavenly Father," I began my confession, "I bring before you my involvement with spirits other than Your Spirit. In the name of Jesus I renounce astrology, I renounce fortune-telling, I renounce Ouija boards, I renounce reincarnation, I renounce seances, I renounce numerology, I renounce tea-leaf reading, I renounce horoscopes, I renounce automatic writing, I renounce sorcery, I renounce hypnotism, I renounce Yoga, I renounce astral projection, I renounce spiritism, I renounce ESP, I renounce tarot cards, I renounce palm-reading, I renounce mind control, I renounce transcendental meditation, I renounce levitation, I renounce false religions. I recognize these practices as satanic and I confess my involvement as sin. I bind these powers of darkness and in Jesus' name I break any hold they have had on me."

When I was finished and Sara Anne had prayed over me, I felt like a huge weight had been lifted off my chest.

Next I took my list of sexual failures, the drugs, the abortions, and any other wrongdoing I had recalled and presented them before the Lord. I confessed each one as sin and asked for God's forgiveness for them.

Then we addressed the problem of my mother. Sara Anne

instructed that I say, "God, I confess hatred for my mother and I ask Your forgiveness. I forgive her for everything she did to me, I forgive her for not loving me, and I release her into Your hands."

About this time I began to cry, partly because of the relief of being free from the heavy load of failure and guilt and partly because I felt the gentle, healing presence of the Holy Spirit in the room.

With that preliminary foundation laid, we moved on. Sara Anne called Andrea, another counselor, into the room to pray alongside her. While I sat in a chair, they put their hands on my head and worshiped God for many minutes. I kept my eyes closed and felt as if the roof on the small room was being raised with the joy of their praises.

One by one they addressed spirits that had tormented me or had an oppressive hold on my life. Spirits of futility, despair, fear, and rejection were mentioned as were spirits of suicide and torment. I was not demon-possessed, but these spirits had oppressed me at points where I had given them place through my sins of unforgiveness and disobedience to God.

When Sara Anne felt that the oppression was finally broken, she relaxed her grip on my head and rested her hands on my shoulders. She began to speak, not in the powerful voice of authority that she used to address the oppressive spirits, but in a soft, almost-angelic tone. I recognized that she was giving a prophetic message, one that would change my life forever.

"My daughter, you have been locked in a closet all your life— first physically and then emotionally. But *I* have the keys. *I* have the keys."

Tears rolled down my cheeks and into my hands that I had held open on my lap. It was a gesture of openness to His words as Jesus unlocked the place where I had been held prisoner for all my life.

"I'm giving the keys to you," the word continued. "Whenever you feel the devil trying to lock you up again, use the keys I have given you. Use the *keys* I have given you."

"God has also given me a Scripture in Isaiah for you," Sara

Anne said as she turned to her Bible lying open on the desk. " 'Speak tenderly to Jerusalem, and proclaim to her that her hard service has been completed, that her sin has been paid for, that she has received from the Lord's hand double for all her sins.'"

Looking up at me she said, "I know the Lord told me to give you that, but I'm not sure what the words 'double for all her sins' means for you."

"I know what it means," I assured her. "I have always felt that I paid double for everything. Life has been twice as painful and twice as difficult for me than for anyone else. God is saying no more of that. The hard times are finished and the consequence of my sin has been paid."

It was all over. I was drained. With a big, loving smile, Sara Anne gave me a warm hug and said, "God moved in your behalf today. You're going to feel like a new person."

"I already do!" I said in return. I wasn't sure of all that had happened, but I felt like a thousand pounds of dead weight had been lifted off of me. I really *did* feel new.

"I know this may seem like a strange question," I continued, "but do you think I should change my name? I mean is 'Stormie' a legitimate Christian name? As a child I used to hate being teased about it, and even though now it has proven to be a name that people remember, I've always desired to have a normal name like Marilyn. Maybe I should change it to that. I thought as long as I'm a new person, I should have a new name. What do you think?"

Both women listened thoughtfully, and after a moment of silence Andrea replied, "No, I believe you are supposed to keep your name and let it be a testimony to the work that God has done in your life. You've come out of a stormy childhood, but God calms the storms of our lives. I know He is going to do that completely in you. Whenever someone questions you about your name, let that be your opportunity to share about God's goodness."

I felt her advice was a word from God, so I laid the issue to rest once and for all. I thanked them and hugged them both goodbye.

"Now go and walk in all the freedom God has given you," Sara Anne instructed. She directed me to read my Bible and pray every day and to attend church three times a week. "This gives you a good armor of protection from the devil, who will attempt to steal back the territory in your life that has been taken away from him," she explained. "It's not that what has been accomplished by God can easily be undone, but the devil could certainly undermine it by causing you to doubt and fear again."

I left her office dazed and almost numb. As I drove home I tried to remember all that happened. I had gone there without much hope. I believed that God *could* do something, but I didn't know whether He *would* do it for me.

I had sensed the presence of God in the whole process. What it would all mean in my life, I didn't know. And what were the keys that God was talking about?

Michael was gone when I arrived home. I ate some fruit—my first food in nearly three days—and went to bed. A few hours later Michael came home and woke me up from a sound sleep.

"Tell me what happened with Sara Anne." His voice reflected the concern on his face. This had been a draining time for him too, but my own emotional paralysis had blinded me to it until now.

Halfway through the story he interrupted me: "Your eyes look totally different, Stormie. They're peaceful, not fearful or worried. But it's even more than that...I can't explain it...tell me more."

The next morning I awoke without any feelings of depression whatever—no thought of suicide, no heaviness in my chest, no fearful anticipation of the future. I waited all day for it to return, but it didn't.

Day after day it was the same. I never again experienced those feelings, nor the paralysis that accompanied them. I had gone into that counseling office knowing Jesus as Savior, but I came out knowing Him also as my Deliverer.

# CHAPTER ELEVEN

# THE KEYS

After my time of deliverance, I spent the rest of the year learning what the keys were that God had given me. I knew that Jesus held the keys to life, and by receiving Him and being born again, the doorway to life after death had been opened for me. Then He unlocked the door of my emotional closet that day in the counseling office with Sara Anne. Now I found that the significance of the keys extended far beyond that. If I were to experience more life in *this* life, there were keys I needed in order to unlock doors on a daily basis—the doors to peace, wholeness, fulfillment, love, abundance, growth, ongoing deliverance, fruitfulness, and restoration.

One such key was spending time daily in *God's Word* and letting it be written indelibly on my heart and in my mind so that it shaped my actions and thoughts. I had no trouble believing that the Bible was God's Word because after I received Jesus the words practically leaped off the page teeming with life. Because of this I developed a hunger for more of the Word to feed and fortify the places in my spirit and personality that were starved or severely undernourished. I carefully memorized certain verses and spoke them out loud in order to cut through the dark times of my life with power. I read even when I didn't understand what I was reading or was too tired to assimilate much. Pastor Jack taught that it was like eating a meal. "Do you know what you had for lunch last Tuesday?" he asked.

"No," I shook my head.

"But it still fed your body, didn't it?"

"Yes," I nodded.

"Well, even though you may not remember a word you read from the Bible last night, it still fed your spirit."

I discovered right away that for me to get through a day successfully, I needed to read the Bible first thing every morning. It set my mind on the right path from the beginning and gave me a solid foundation on which to build my day. Anytime I was tempted to fall back into the old habit of thinking of myself as a failure or feeling fearful and depressed, I took out the Bible again and read. As I did, I could feel my attitude reverse and my mind fill with peace.

The key of God's Word was also spiritual ammunition to stand against whatever was opposing me. Now I could understand the authority and power given to me through Jesus. When I became fearful and heard a voice in my head saying, "You're going to end up mentally ill just like your mother," I would speak out loud the Scripture from the Bible that says, "God has not given us a spirit of fear, but of power and of love and of a *sound mind*."[4] I'd repeat that over and over until the fear was gone.

Another key was *prayer*. King David's words "Early will I seek thee" resounded in my mind, and I knew that I needed to be up early every morning, not only reading the Bible but also spending time talking with God and listening for His reply. I took my every concern to Him.

Prayer, like the Word of God, helped to change my thought habits. For 30 years I thought, "I'm no good. I'm ugly. I'm worthless. I have no talent. No gifts. I'm undesirable. There's something wrong with me. I don't deserve to be alive." But now I recognized these thoughts as lies and not in line with God's truth. They responded quickly to prayer, whereas before they had responded to nothing. The lying thoughts had no power now that the Father of Lies had no hold on me. The key of God's Word helped me to see the truth and stand in it, and the key of prayer secured God's help in the matter. Reversing bad thought habits had to be worked out on a daily basis, and taking my needs to God in prayer was the key to a peaceful and fruitful day filled with victory.

Every morning I would come before God in prayer and say, "Jesus, I proclaim You Lord over my life and I commit myself to You this day. Help me to bring every thought that I have under Your rulership." Then I would list all the specific needs that I wanted Him to take care of at that time. As a result I saw the frayed ends of my life begin to be smoothed out. Because I was praying, my life was no longer left to chance.

Along with prayer came the key of *confession*. I learned that I must daily confess everything in my heart that was sin. I used to think that sin meant smoking, drinking, drugs, and sexual immorality, and since I was no longer involved with any of these, and I hadn't murdered anyone or robbed a liquor store, I was exempt from sinner status. How wrong I was! I discovered that "sin" was an old archery term meaning to miss the bull's-eye. Anything other than direct center was sin. That realization opened up a whole new world for me. Anything less than God's perfect will for my life was sin. In that light, I had plenty to confess. From my critical attitude to self-hatred, white lies, and selfishness, there were many things I was doing that I never even realized were wrong. Again I prayed as David did, "God, create in me a clean heart. Show me my secret sin and cleanse me from all unrighteousness."

I learned that the rage I held inside from childhood was sin even though it began when I was too young to understand it and even though there was a good reason for it. Sin is never justified no matter who commits it or what age they are. God never approves of sin, but He does make provision for it through Jesus, and the key to experiencing that provision is confession. When I didn't use my confession key, I got tied up in guilt and was miserable. As difficult as it was, I had to confess on a daily basis.

Through confession I became aware of my own jealousy. When I would see beautiful women with talent, I would immediately compare myself with them and fall short. I came to see this as the seed from which jealousy grows. Secretly I wanted what they had. As I confessed this before God every time it happened, gradually I began to be free of those feelings. In fact, I grew in that area so much that I began to appreciate the beauty and talent of other women, as one can admire anything of God's creation. What a relief to no longer be threatened by another person's gifts! With that barrier down, close relationships developed quickly and easily.

Another important key was *forgiveness*. Forgiving others, especially my mother, became something I had to deal with daily. I confessed forgiveness for her in the counseling office and thought I had taken care of it until the very next time I saw her. Then all the old feelings of hatred, frustration, bitterness, and anger came forth like a flood, and along with them came their partners, defeat and low self-esteem.

"God, I forgive my mother," I confessed daily whether I felt like it or not. "Help me to forgive her completely." I knew without a doubt that harboring unforgiveness would keep me from the wholeness and blessing God had for me, and that it would make me sick physically. I knew I could never be completely whole as long as I had any unforgiveness. I had to keep working on it. It was during this time I learned that forgiveness doesn't make the other person right, it makes *you free*.

God was faithful to answer my prayer, and forgiveness for my mother developed in me to such a point that I was eventually able to see her as God made her to be and not the way she was. I saw how the traumas of her life had misshaped her, and how she, like I had been, was a victim of her past. Only she never found the way out. Every time I pictured the 11-year-old girl who lost her mother and felt responsible for it, believing that life and God had deserted her, I felt deep sadness inside. I cried over her life and wished that somehow things could have been different. I saw her like I had never seen her before, and instead of hating her I felt sorry and began praying for her healing.

I read up on the subject of mental illness and began to understand that Mother's brain did not function like the brain of a normal person. I had known that long before, but always blamed her for it. Now I saw that she really couldn't help herself. She was at the mercy of disassociated, unorganized thinking patterns that made no sense. Her illogical and inappropriate behavior, like laughing when I was hurt or becoming enraged when I cleaned my room, were normal for someone in her condition. There was a short circuit somewhere. Everything she imagined was completely real to her, and common to those with the same illness. Her mind simply could not sort things through clearly. I felt pity for her and regretted all the times I had been mocking and cruel in my attitude toward her. I now had respect for how well she navigated life considering all she had going against her.

My ability to absorb this knowledge about my mother was directly related to my forgiveness of her. But forgiveness not only made me a more compassionate person, it also allowed me to recall good memories of my mother. Previously, because my hatred and unforgiveness had been so overpowering, no good thoughts of her were ever allowed to stay with me. But now, one by one, things I had long forgotten, or never even acknowledged, popped up in my memory.

I flashed back to Mother making pancakes for me when I was three, and how she smiled and exclaimed with pride that I had eaten five of them. When I was in third grade, Mother and Aunt Jean came to town one hot afternoon and surprised my class at school with cups of ice cream for each child. How proud I was that she had done that! When I was nine, Mother gave me a birthday party and invited all the girls in my class. She served a full dinner, with slices of watermelon, ice cream, and cake for dessert, and then she and Dad took us miniature golfing. We were very poor, and that must have cost them greatly.

On the day of my twelfth birthday I came home from school feeling sorry for myself because no one had remembered. I went to my room and saw that it had been cleaned and straightened. On the bed was a box containing a beautiful turquoise wool suit that I had dreamed about owning. Mother had bought it for me. At Christmas she always cooked a big dinner, made popcorn balls, and bought gifts for the family. I could see now that she had tried hard to make the season something special even though it must have been terribly difficult for her. Every part of life must have put tremendous pressure on her, but I never before saw her misery—only my own.

I had forgotten these events because immediately after each

one she always did something hideous to cancel out any good that had been accomplished. But now, because I had forgiven all the cruel acts, I could just focus on the kind ones. What a relief this brought, as well as a sense of fulfillment! The bad memories began to diminish and the good memories increased, paralleling exactly my level of forgiveness toward her.

I did have a major setback every time I saw Mother in person, however, because even though I became more forgiving of her, her hatred toward me increased along with the progression of her mental illness. However, with practice I was able to work through the problem more quickly each time. Forgiveness became an art: The more I practiced, the better I got at it and the freer I became.

Another key was *saying yes to God*. Every time I thought I had all my problems solved, I found myself at another crossroad. I knew that God was asking me to give myself to Him in ever-deeper commitment. The more I understood what was accomplished in Jesus' death on the cross, the more I realized He was asking me to nail parts of myself to the cross and let them die too. Just as I had given up my dyed-blonde hair, drinking, smoking, and drugs, I now had to give Him my dreams about becoming an actress or someone important. These were all things in which I had placed my identity. But God wanted my identity to be in Him.

I had desired as a child to be an actress or a singer—someone that people would love. It was the only way I thought I could be worth anything to anyone. God was telling me, "You must know that you are worth much to me whether you accomplish anything or not. Even if you are rejected in the world's eyes, you are valuable to me."

Everything I desired of God to be implanted in me couldn't happen until I let my own life go. So now, with these major deliverances taken care of, God began His cleanup program. Excess baggage had to be eliminated, the most major of which was self. All my desires to be noticed, to be somebody, to do something great had to be given up to Him. My dreams had to be *His* dreams, the ones *He* placed in my heart. They couldn't be the ones I thought I should have, or needed for the purpose of making other people like me.

"Okay, Lord," I finally said with much reluctance. "I give up my desire to be anyone important or to do anything significant. I will no longer regard not being a success in the world's eyes as a failure, because You love me the way I am." I stopped doing all TV shows and studio singing. I did nothing but go to church, take care of my home and husband, and watch all my dreams come crashing down as a part of me died a little every day. The death process was long and painful.

Nearly three years later I was in a large Bible study at church. Just before the start of the final class, the assistant pastor, who was also the teacher, came up to me and said, "I have been praying for you and I feel that God has shown me you are to begin singing again."

"He did? I am?" I exclaimed with surprise.

"Yes. There is deliverance and healing for others that He wants to work through you. You are to tell what the Lord has done for you and sing the songs He has put on your heart."

"That's wonderful!" I responded with mixed emotions. I was eager to serve God, but still miserably aware of my inabilities.

"I want you to begin tonight and sing for the group."

"What!" I jolted as I felt my mixed emotions turn to one single emotion—terror. "I can't do it tonight."

"Do you feel in your heart that God has called you to minister His life to others?" he asked firmly.

"Well, yes, but I thought I would have more time to prepare."

"This has been a class in ministry development, and this is the last night of this class. These are people who love you. You need to take a step of faith, and tonight is the time to do it. This will be your beginning point."

"But you don't understand," I continued to plead. "I can't sing. I have serious speech problems, and when I'm afraid, my throat closes off and I lose my voice. That's why I never sing alone, and I haven't even sung in a group for a long time."

"God is asking you to be willing to fail in front of all these people. Are you willing to sacrifice your pride to be obedient to God?''

"Pride! Me?'' I protested. "I'm the one who has been humiliated all my life. I've always struggled with a low opinion of myself. How could I have pride?''

"You do have pride. You're too proud to fail in front of others. You're overly concerned about their opinions. You've been comparing yourself to others for years. That's pride, Stormie. If you don't sing now, you're giving in to it.''

As difficult as this was to hear, I could see the truth in all he was saying.

"What'll I sing?''

"Sing one of the many songs you've written,'' came the obvious answer.

My heart was pounding and my legs were shaking as I got up in front of the people.

Slowly I swallowed my pride, closed my eyes, and cautiously sang "All the Time in the World.'' My throat was so tight and pained that I could barely croak it out. My face was hot and perspiring. It was truly terrible and totally humiliating. I sang as badly as anyone could possibly sing, but when I was done, everyone in the room clapped and cheered. I opened my eyes and was surprised to see expressions of love, support, and caring, and even some people with tears. As awful as the experience was, I felt like something had been broken in the spirit realm.

A few weeks later I began receiving invitations to speak and sing, and it was apparent that God was calling me out into public ministry. "I don't really sing,'' I told the people who called because I wanted them to know my problem right away.

"That's okay—we want *you*,'' they replied.

After a few months of explaining to people that I wasn't really a singer, so don't expect too much, God spoke to my heart and said, "Don't say those words anymore.''

"But God, they'll think I don't realize that I have vocal problems. They'll judge me. How mortifying not to be able to explain this to anyone.''

"*I'll* decide who is the singer,'' I heard God say. "The singer is the one in whose heart I put my song. Take your eyes off of what others think and put them on me. You will not sing to win prizes and favor. You will sing to bring deliverance to those who have been locked up and hurt just as you have.''

I couldn't see how this was all possible, but I soon realized that it could only be accomplished through the aid of the keys and my willingness to say yes to God and step out in obedience. So the death I went through became a door that led to life. It was opened by the key of saying yes to God.

Shortly after that, God showed me another very important key—*the key of praise and worship*. It was to be a key that would unlock many doors, but especially that of fear.

Anytime I felt the walls of life closing in and my emotional closet door slamming shut, I would clap my hands, sing worship songs, and praise the Lord out loud. I didn't stop until I felt the walls come down and the door unlock. Whenever I saw the cloud of depression trying to settle on me again, I would do the same until it lifted. When I heard the lies of my past shouting, "You're worthless, you'll never amount to anything, you're no different, you'll never change," I would say, "Thank You, God, that You are all-powerful, that You reign in my life and in the midst of this situation. Thank You, Lord, that You love me and have made me to live in health and power and victory and joy and peace. Thank You that in my weakness You are strong.'' On and on I went until the black cloud over my head evaporated and the fear was gone.

My husband and I had been recording albums together since we were married. On the first two, "White Horse" and "Adam Again," he was the soloist while I sang background and wrote all the lyrics. However, on the next three albums, "Seasons of the Soul," "The Builder," and "Mainstream," he insisted that I sing a solo or duet with him on some of the songs.

Those albums, plus the concerts we did together and my speaking engagements, were all very frightening. The only way I got through them was with praise. Every time fear came over me, I began to thank God for all He had done in my life and for the voice He *had* given me. There were many times of failure, when I forgot to praise altogether and allowed the fear to control me. But more and more I had success in that area and saw myself and my circumstances being transformed. Praise was the key that got me through impossible situations in my life.

One more key was *fasting,* which I began to do on a regular basis. Because of this there was ongoing deliverance and freedom. Every time I fasted, it was like getting a holy oiling so I could slip through the clutches of the devil. I positioned God as everything and nothing else could hold me. With every denial of myself I gained more of Jesus, and more of Jesus meant more peace, love, and wholeness. Along with the entire church I fasted and prayed every Wednesday. But several times a year, when I felt the need for a deep spiritual as well as physical cleansing, I went on a three-day fast. The benefits far outweighed the discomfort and inconvenience, so I looked forward to each time of fasting.

By using all the keys that God had given me, I began to function more like a normal person. I could see I was on the road to wholeness. The keys were so effective that I was eager to learn more about God's ways. Apparently God was eager too, for I embarked upon a time of major spiritual housecleaning that had unexpected practical application in my life.

CHAPTER TWELVE

*Stormie*

# PLAYING BY THE RULES

"Why do you call Me 'Lord, Lord,' and do not do the things which I say?"[5] Jesus' words from the Bible struck my heart with the distinct impression that I needed to do more in the area of obeying God. "If anyone loves me, he will obey my teaching. My Father will love him, and we will come to him and make our home with him."[6] Obviously there was a link between the presence of God and obedience. I didn't want anything in my life that separated me from the presence of God, so I set about to study further into God's Word to find out more about His directives. This was not done out of guilt but rather out of deep conviction and a desire to be all that God made me to be.

As I studied the Bible, my conviction grew. How many times in my past had I begged God to do what I wanted Him to do, yet I never even bothered to find out what He wanted *me* to do? How often had I been mad at God for not giving me what I wanted, yet it never entered my mind to find out what *He* wanted? I came across the Scripture "If anyone competes as an athlete, he does not receive the victor's crown unless he competes according to the rules."[7] How foolish I was to demand that God let me win at the game of life while I refused to play by the rules! The more committed I became to living God's way, the more I saw that the way I had been living wasn't pleasing to Him. There were certain steps of obedience I needed to take. God had accepted me the way I was, but He wasn't about to leave me that way. One-by-one He began to surface things in me that needed to be done away with, and He usually didn't have to search too far.

For some time I had been feeling uneasy about certain possessions in our home. Early one morning I came across the Scripture
"Do not bring a detestable thing into your house or you...will
be set apart for destruction,"[8] and I knew that my housecleaning
ing day had arrived. I set about to search and destroy any
"detestable thing" I had brought into our home. I went through
every inch of our house and threw out whatever was not of God
or was even questionable in nature. Sixty or seventy expensive
hardcover books on the occult went into the trash, along with
all paintings, sculptures, wall hangings, hand-painted trays, and
miscellaneous artifacts that exalted other gods. I even got rid of
things that in themselves had no meaning but were a reminder
of my first marriage, an old boyfriend, or an unhappy time in
my life. These things I *gave* away because they could be put to
good use by other people who had no negative ties to them.

Out went the tapes and records that had ungodly lyrics on them.
Out went the magazines and novels that exalted lifestyles and
thinking patterns that were opposed to God's ways. This all might
have sounded like a witch-hunt to anyone who didn't understand,
but it wasn't. It was a sound-minded decision to separate myself
from anything that separated me from God. I had experienced
enough of God's blessings to know that I wanted *all* of what He
had for me. When I finished housecleaning I felt so light, clean,
and joyful that I could hardly contain myself.

I decided that since I and my house had been born again, it
was time that my wardrobe was too. I threw out tight pants,
revealing sweaters, low-cut dresses, and sexy outfits that were
not befitting the daughter of a king or glorifying to the God of
the universe. I marveled that I had worn these things to church
and didn't once receive stares of condemnation from Pastor Jack
or Anna, his wife. They never made me feel like I was less than
anyone else, although I certainly gave them reason to. When I
showed up late for church in my tight jeans and skimpy T-shirt,
with no makeup and uncombed hair, they always welcomed me
as if I were the guest speaker. They accepted me like God accepted
me—the way I was. And their love was a major part of my self-
acceptance and healing. But they, like God, were committed to

seeing me move on in the Lord. And they, like God, did it with love and not condemnation.

As I threw the clothes, books, magazines, records, and art in the trash, I knew I had to do the same with certain habits and relationships. I stopped watching offensive TV shows and became very selective about what movies I went to see. Filling my mind with violence, foul language, disrespectful use of God's name, and other people's sex acts did not make me feel good in my spirit, and I knew it didn't feel good in God's Spirit either. The Bible said I was the temple of the Holy Spirit of God, so how could I enjoy the fullness of His presence if He was being crowded out by all that was opposed to His ways? As I separated myself from these things, I felt more and more fulfilled and happy.

I gradually realized that certain of my unbelieving friends were a bad influence on me. They had a drawing power in them that attempted to pull me away from all the things of the Lord and back into my old life. Even though I still cared for these people, I knew the relationships had to go. My method for handling those particular friendships was quite simple. All I had to do was tell them about my new life in Jesus and invite them to share it. The ones who responded remained as friends and those who didn't were gone within a short time.

Some spiritual housecleaning happened without my doing anything. One day I woke up and realized that my fear of knives was gone. I don't know how it happened, but I assumed it was because of God's promise in the Bible that says, "Perfect love drives out fear."[9] It also says that "if anyone obeys his word, God's love is truly made complete in him."[10]

I could see that there was a definite connection between obedience and receiving God's love. Through my obedience I was able to receive more of God's love. God's love in turn crowded out my fears. The greatest illustration of that was the complete disappearance of the fear of knives without my even realizing it. This was a prime example of receiving deliverance just by being in the presence of God.

Through my steps of obedience I began to see things more clearly. I identified the occult spirits that I had aligned myself with as being the same spirits that inspired the Sharon Tate murders. I had *felt* aligned with that evil because I *was* aligned in the spirit realm.

For the first time I saw abortion for what it was—the taking of a human life. What had never entered my mind before now came in with full conviction. I recalled my feeble bargain with God before the first abortion: "Get me through this and I'll be good." What a joke! I didn't know what good was, and even if I had, there was no way, without Jesus and the power of the Holy Spirit that I would have ever been able to accomplish it.

When I had my abortions I firmly believed that the baby's soul and spirit entered his body only at the time of birth. It was a theory I had been told back then, and I had believed it. It never occurred to me that I was taking the life of another person. "It's not a human being," I reasoned, "but just a mass of cells." Because I believed that, I had little conscious guilt about what I had done. That, however, didn't make it any less wrong or the consequences any less shattering. Even though I had confessed my wrongdoing earlier and been released from the guilt of it, I still lacked a full understanding of how deeply I had violated God's ways. As I read the Scriptures, it became clear that God's purposes and plans for that individual were established from the moment of conception. Whether it was legal or not, whether I felt guilt or not, the facts were the same: I had destroyed a life in which God had placed gifts, talents, and purposes. That death manifested itself in my own life as I felt myself dying inside a little more each day. I thought I was saving my life by having the abortions when actually I was taking away from it. This slow death continued until I broke the bonds of it in confession and deliverance.

As I became more knowledgeable of God's ways and more obedient to His rules, I could see that every rule and every commandment was established by God for our own benefit. It wasn't to make us miserable and keep us from having fun, but to bring us to the greatest level of fulfillment. God laid the ground rules because He knew that this is how the game could be won.

Every new step of obedience that I took also brought increased physical health. I began to gain a little weight, which was more attractive on my painfully thin frame. It became easier for me to eat and exercise the way I knew I was supposed to, and as a result my skin became clearer and my hair stopped falling out. Overall, my health improved greatly. God cared about the total person, and His healing and restoration extended to every level of the human personality.

The most astounding result of my obedience to God's ways was that the more I walked in obedience, the more emotional wholeness I enjoyed. There was a link there, too. Of course no one can be perfect, but it wasn't a matter of being perfect; it was a matter of the heart and the will—a heart that says "I love You, Lord, and I love Your laws" and a will that says "I *choose* to walk Your way." That attitude of heart and decision of will allowed the Holy Spirit to accomplish obedience in me. He *enabled* me to do what was right.

How good God is! He freely gives His love, His presence, His healing, His deliverance, and His emotional restoration to all who are willing to play by the rules He has established.

# THE FACE OF THE ABUSER

I was shocked when I didn't get pregnant immediately after Michael and I made the decision to have our first child. Judging from my past, I thought that conceiving a child would be no problem for me. But when month after month went by, I feared I was paying retribution for the abortions I'd had. Still not fully understanding God's mercy and grace, I could not comprehend a love so great that it reached beyond the confines of my failure and recovered everything that had been lost. Nor could I fathom a God who did not punish as I deserved.

Michael had been in counseling for some time regarding his fear of traveling. It wasn't a fear of airplane crashes, but rather an intense anxiety about being away from the security and familiarity of home. It was something he knew he had to get free of, and he was concentrating on that particular problem. So the fact that I wasn't pregnant didn't concern him as much as it did me.

One morning as I was again praying to conceive a child, God spoke clearly to my heart. He said, "You are going to have a son and he is going to be conceived in Jerusalem."

I shook my head, pounded my ears a couple of times, and said, "Would you mind repeating that please?"

There was no repeating, but the original words resounded in my head.

"Surely I'm making this up," I thought. "But then again, why would I make up something as ridiculous as that?" I pondered it off and on for a few weeks and then dismissed it from my mind.

A few months later I came home from a church meeting with a brochure that Pastor Jack had given our Bible study group about a tour that he and Anna were taking to the Holy Land. They were asking 30 people to go with them so anyone who wanted to go should sign up immediately. I casually remarked to Michael about what fun that would be, and he abruptly said, "Let's do it."

"Do what?" I asked, not expecting his next remark.

"Let's go with Pastor Jack and Anna to visit the Holy Land."

"What?" I exclaimed. "You've got to be kidding! You don't like driving to San Diego overnight, let alone taking a plane clear across the world for three weeks. Are you joking?"

He wasn't joking, and over the next few months we readied ourselves for the trip. During the two weeks before our departure I became quite ill with a lung infection. For awhile it appeared as though we wouldn't be able to go, but I recovered just in time and off we went.

At the beginning of the tour, Michael did fairly well with his travel anxiety, but by the fourth day he was suffering severely. Late one evening he broke down and said, "I just can't make it. Do you mind if we forget the trip and go home?"

"No," I said, concerned. "Do whatever you need to do, but we must call Pastor Jack. We shouldn't leave without his counsel."

We hesitated to call Pastor Jack because it was near midnight and the tour had an exhausting schedule, but Michael was determined to take the first flight out. Pastor Jack came to our room immediately, talked with Michael for a long time, then prayed for him to be free of the fear and insecurity that was tormenting him. He took Michael in his arms and held him as a father would a son while Michael sobbed. I witnessed the love of God working through a compassionate pastor and an obedient son and I saw deliverance and healing happen in my husband because of it.

As a result of that night, we stayed on the tour and there was a total turnabout in Michael. Five days later we finally had a free day in Jerusalem, and because of the intensity of the tour it was the first chance Michael and I had to spend time alone with each other. After that day the hectic schedule resumed. We rose before dawn, went full speed, and fell exhausted into bed at night.

When we arrived at the Sea of Galilee I became extremely ill. I was dizzy and nauseated every day and could not keep any food down. It got progressively worse, and we tried unsuccessfully to get an earlier flight out of Israel back to California. The only solution was to send me on to Tel Aviv to stay in our hotel there and wait for the rest of the group to catch up.

When we finally left Tel Aviv, our plane made an emergency stop in Paris for mechanical reasons. I was taken to the hospital there and given a shot to control the nausea and vomiting and to ward off dehydration long enough for me to get back to California. Even so, the ride home was miserable. I was so violently sick that everyone, including me, thought I must have food poisoning.

Being pregnant didn't occur to me because I associated the violent sickness of my first two pregnancies with my own psychological rejection of them. But once in California, I soon found out that I was indeed pregnant and that my extreme illness during pregnancy was a condition I had inherited.

All the talk I'd heard for years about my grandmother dying in childbirth flooded my mind with fear. My mother's frequently spoken words of "Once you have children your life is over" played repeatedly in my brain. I was afraid—afraid of the violent nausea and pain I felt in my body day and night, afraid that I might die in childbirth like my grandmother, afraid that my life really was over, just as my mother said.

Mother's reaction to my pregnancy was hard to read. She was more concerned with all the people who were following her. She said the President of the United States was having her watched and that the communists were going to kill her because she knew too much. There were times when she seemed so normal and her story sounded so convincing that I wondered, "Wouldn't we feel terrible if what she's been saying is true and all this time none of us believed her?" But then she would give herself away by saying that Frank Sinatra and the Pope were conspiring to have her shot. I guess if I were convinced that they were trying to have me shot, I might be more concerned with that than the birth of my first grandchild. It's hard to say. Anyway, I was disappointed that she didn't seem to care.

Dad, on the other hand, was very excited, yet also worried. I was so sick that by the end of four months I had lost 13 pounds. On a body still too thin, this did not look attractive. Dad was well aware of our family history of serious pregnancy complications and his concern was evident.

I called Sara Anne about the problem. I knew my fear had to go, and I thought the nausea and pain might be caused by it. She assured me that I was not the same as my grandmother and that this was also a different time, so I would not be dying in childbirth. She also pointed out that what my mother taught me on the subject was a reflection of her own feelings and totally opposite from the Word of God, which says that children are a gift and a blessing from the Lord. Then she prayed for me to be free from the fear. As she did, I felt a heaviness lift immediately. Unfortunately, the nausea and the pain remained.

When nothing helped my condition, I became increasingly concerned that I might lose this baby. One evening while crying out to God about it, the words He had spoken to me nearly six months earlier flooded my memory.

"You are going to have a son and he is going to be conceived in Jerusalem."

I thought back. Michael and I had been together on that one free day in Jerusalem. First because of my lung infection, and then because of the hectic traveling schedule, it was the only possible time I could have conceived. I was amazed as I put all the facts together. "God," I said, revealing the magnitude of my faith, "if this turns out to be a boy then I'll know I really heard from You."

When I told Michael all that God had spoken to my heart he was relieved. Over the next difficult months of the pregnancy I hung onto God's words, repeating over and over to myself, "God has ordained this pregnancy and He will bring forth this child."

Four weeks earlier than planned I suddenly went into heavy labor. The baby was positioned sideways and unable to be born naturally, so I had to have an emergency cesarean. We were frightened, but I still kept hearing God's words to me over and over. Just as predicted, a healthy baby boy was born on June 25, 1976—right on Pastor Jack's birthday! Christopher Scott Omartian was immediately our most memorable souvenir of the Holy Lands.

Very soon after bringing the baby home from the hospital, old feelings that I thought were dead began to rise up in me. All the rage and hatred I had ever had for my mother returned in full force. I looked at my beautiful boy and thought, "How could anyone treat a precious child the way my mother treated me?"

"God, why am I feeling all this?" I questioned. "Haven't I forgiven her?" I didn't yet realize that when God begins a work, He keeps perfecting it. All of these negative feelings were surfacing because God wanted to take me to a new level of deliverance. I felt like I was going backward and that I had lost the deliverance I had already received. But God's truth was that as long as I was following Him, I would go from "glory to glory"[11] and "strength to strength."[12] It was God's desire to give me more freedom in this area than ever before, and now was the time for me to receive it. What surfaced was something I had no idea resided in me. Only having my own child would fully expose it.

I was determined to be a good mother—in fact the best mother possible. After all, I was well aware of the pitfalls of bad mothering. "I will never be like my mother," I pridefully told myself. "My child will have the best care I can give him."

One night when Christopher was just a few months old, I couldn't get him to stop crying. Michael was working late and I was alone in the house. I tried feeding him, but that didn't help. I changed his diaper. I put warmer clothes on him, then cooler clothes. I held him and rocked him. I tried everything a mother can do, but it made no difference. He screamed all the more. In the middle of his crying I was close to crying myself.

The frustration built until I finally snapped and lost control.

I slapped my baby on the back, the shoulder, and the head. My heart pounded wildly, my face burned, my eyes were blinded by hot tears, and my breathing became shallow and labored. I was out of control.

The baby's screaming suddenly became a rejection of me. "My son doesn't want me because I'm not a good mother" was the lie I heard in my head. Because rejection was so foundational for me, it pushed me over the edge.

"Stop crying!" I screamed at him. "Stop crying!"

I realized I was one step away from throwing him across the room. The energy inside me was limitless, and I knew if I yielded to it I could injure him badly—maybe even kill him.

The only alternative was to get away from the baby. I laid him in his crib, ran to my bedroom, and fell on my knees beside the bed. "Lord, help me!" I cried. "There's something horrible in me. You've got to take it away, God. I don't know what it is. I don't understand it. I love my baby more than anything in the world. What's the matter with a mother who hurts a child she loves? Please, God, whatever is wrong with me, take it away." I sobbed into the bedspread.

I was on my knees before God for nearly an hour. Finally the baby's screaming subsided. He had cried himself to sleep.

Michael came home before the baby woke up again, but I didn't tell him anything. I couldn't. I didn't know what to say. It was too mortifying to even think about it, let alone confess it to my husband. When the baby woke up he seemed to be fine. He acted as if nothing had happened, and so did I.

Four or five days later it happened again—the baby crying, the feelings of rejection, something snapping inside me, my emotions going out of control, the desire to beat and beat, catching myself just in time, putting the baby in the crib, going into my bedroom, falling on my knees before God, and crying to Him for forgiveness and help.

I was flooded with guilt. What kind of mother was I? All my good intentions were melted by the fire of rage that burned within me. Again I stayed on my knees until I felt the intensity of what gripped me lift and the forgiveness of God flood in to wash away my guilt. God's love sustained me in the terrible loneliness I experienced because of the secret I couldn't bear to share.

Over the next few weeks I began to understand some of what was happening and why. The face of the abuser became clearer. All my life I had looked at my situation from the standpoint of one who has been abused. It was shocking to discover that I had all the potential in me to be an *abuser*. It was built in me from childhood. I had seen that violent, out-of-control behavior before—in my mother. I knew it wasn't my child that I hated. It was me. And now I also saw that it wasn't *me* that my mother hated; it was herself. My compassion for her grew.

I eventually confessed all this to my husband, and to my relief he was not horrified. Surprised yes, but not fearful, repulsed, or rejecting of me in any way. He offered to pray with me anytime I needed it, and added, "You know, I get irritated too when the baby doesn't stop crying."

"It's more than that," I tried to make him understand. "In between the times I lose control, I experience what I believe to be normal irritation and frustration. What I'm talking about is different. It's way out of proportion to the offense. It has an energy that derives some kind of pleasure in hurting, and it isn't satisfied until it's been fed. Taken to its extreme, it is the same energy that causes someone to be a mass murderer or rapist or to commit other acts of violence. I can see that the more abusive and violent the childhood, the more serious the offense that may be committed."

With Michael's support I called Sara Anne and told her the situation. She prayed with me, and we both believed that as long as the baby was safe, I was mature enough to work this problem out alone with God. She told me this wasn't going to be solved through instant deliverance. This was a step-by-step process, a little at a time.

Sara Anne was absolutely right. The healing process from my child-abusing tendencies was long and slow. I prayed about it nearly every day over the next few years and what the Lord showed me through it all was how much He loved me.

In the beginning I found it shocking to find child abuse hidden in my personality. What I was facing was a little-understood problem at that time. I had always thought of child abusers as scum-of-the-earth, insensitive, uneducated, despicable, low-life types. As I looked at that image of them and then examined myself, I didn't feel that I fit into any of those categories. My husband and I had a music ministry, we had positions of leadership in our church, and we led a prayer group that met in our home. No one would ever have imagined I was struggling with this problem. Was it possible that the common denominator between all abusive parents is that somewhere in their past they were abused too? If so, what about my mother? She wasn't abused as a child. As I checked into this, I saw that there were other factors to consider.

People who abuse their children have emotions that have never been fed. A child needs love and affection, and without these the child fails to develop emotionally and becomes crippled in that area. Whether caused by trauma, having love withheld, verbal abuse, physical abuse, or sexual molestation, the emotions have shut off and stopped growing. The body grew because it was fed food and the mind grew because it was stimulated, but the emotions never grew. Down inside every abuser is a child that needs to be loved into wholeness. My mother had not been abused, but through great trauma and tragedy she felt rejected and unloved. Whether it was real or imagined, she still suffered the same consequences.

This gave me increased compassion for abusive parents. Like me, they were caught in a trap. Once started, child abuse was something that would be passed on from generation to generation unless it was stopped. I knew that the power of God was the only thing to stop it. Fortunately, in spite of my intense feelings of rage, I stopped just short of child abuse because of the healing I'd had. Without that I, too, would have been an abusing parent.

When Christopher was 3½ years old I wrote a song called "Half Past Three." It was the prayer I prayed time and again during his early years. I cried desperately to God daily to help me raise him because I knew I couldn't do it on my own. That little boy was the most wonderful gift God had ever given me, and the thought of harming him was too painful a prospect to bear. I prayed, "God, don't let Christopher suffer the way I suffered. Don't let him feel unloved or rejected like I did. Don't let me damage him in any way."

After the song was finished, it was months before I could sing it through without crying. When I was finally able to talk about what happened and sing the song in public, I knew I had been healed. Performing it for the first time in concert, a hush came over the crowd as I sang:

> Only half-past-three,
> And yet you've got a way of taking self-control from me.
> Only half-past-three—
> Who knows at four-and-twenty where you'll be?
> Sitting on a mountaintop
> Or at a poor man's table,
> Leading sheep from anywhere
> As far as you are able?
> I want you to know love the way that I never knew it.
> I don't want you to travel life the way that I've been
>     through it.
>
> Oh, Lord, don't let me ruin things with faults and weak
>     displays.
> Don't let me make a monster from a perfect piece of clay.
> It would be so easy to do,
> Unless You take what's inside of me
> And replace it all with You.
>
> Only half-past-three,
> A curly-headed shadow who is never out of mind.
> Only half-past-three,
> With eyes that want to trust that you are kind.
> What else do I ever see
> Preparing him for solo flight,
> But all the possibilities
> For good, for bad, for love, for fright?

I don't want him to ache inside the way I did for years.
I don't want him to have to shed more than his share
    of tears.

Oh, Lord, help me to teach him all that You have taught
    to me.
Show me how to guide his footsteps and when to set him
    free.
Give him a time to know You
And a place inside Your kingdom
For when his time is through.

Sometimes I think, Oh, Lord, It's getting very late for me.
But the sun is just about to rise on half-past-three.[13]

I was unprepared for the response. A flood of people who had
been through similar experiences came up to me afterward. I had
no idea how great was the need of emotional healing for those
who had been damaged in childhood, and also for people who
were carrying on the tradition with their own children. Everywhere I went the response was overwhelming. I received hundreds
of letters from people crying out for help who had been victims
of the past and were now trapped in their present circumstances,
with no vision of hope for their future.

"If there was deliverance and healing for me, then there is for
you too," I told them. "You *can* get free of the past and the
paralyzing hold it has on you. Things *can* be different. But it
can only happen through Jesus. In the Bible it says, 'From *the
Lord* comes deliverance!'[14] He is the deliverer. He is the healer.
Without Him I would not be whole.

"The way it happened for me was by simply spending time
in God's presence," I continued. "God asks us to make Him
the center of our lives and to continually seek His presence. When
we do that, His presence answers our every need. In His presence there is deliverance, for the Bible says, 'Where the Spirit
of the Lord is, there is freedom.'[15] The Bible also says, 'He will
deliver the needy who cry out, the afflicted who have no one to

help.'[16] Just by my repeatedly crying out to God, He met me in my need each time. He is there for those without a counselor, without anyone to talk to, without someone to understand.''

"Why did it take 3½ years?" people often asked me.

"Deliverance from child-abusing tendencies took time because I needed to learn a new way of thinking," I explained. "I needed to learn to seek God's presence *before* I looked for any other solution. When I didn't understand, I turned to Him for understanding. When I didn't have the answer, I turned to Him to find it. When I was confused, I turned to Him for clarity. It was a *walk* of life that had to become a *way* of life. It's good to seek counseling, but no one can live in a counselor's office. We have to become better acquainted with *The* Counselor. So when you don't know what to do, seek God's presence in prayer and worship," I advised. "Stay there long enough to let Him love you into wholeness."

I laughed at myself for the calm manner in which I gave advice. My healing process was "gradual" but it seemed "endless" at the time I was going through it. My first deliverance from suicidal depression and destructive feelings of worthlessness was instant. The deliverance from the fear of speaking and singing came as I obeyed God and entered into praise and worship of Him. It still goes on. The deliverance from child-abusing tendencies was a process of 3½ years. As long as it seemed, it did have a beginning and an end. During that 3½-year period I felt God walk with me step-by-step. I felt His love reach down and heal me little-by-little. Up until that time I thought He only loved other people, or that He loved me sometimes, depending on whether I was good or said and did the right things. In the end I fully believed that God loves me all the time. After that I was sure God had taken care of every area in which I could possibly have problems. What was left for Him to do except restore the relationship between me and my mother?

# CHAPTER FOURTEEN

*Stormie*

# THE REWARDS OF OBEDIENCE

Growth, growth, and more growth came over the next year. Michael and I had a new house built, and the building process took much longer than we expected and cost more than we anticipated. I related the whole experience to the Lord building us: The process takes longer than we think it will and the cost is greater than we expect. But, just like with the house, the rewards are far beyond our dreams and well worth the wait.

Lately, as I spent time with God, I had one consistent request: I asked Him repeatedly to heal my mother and restore the relationship between us. However, it seemed that every time I prayed for her, expecting God to do something, she got worse.

Dad retired from working at Knott's Berry Farm, and he and Mother moved to a five-acre farm in central California. It was perfect for him, being the farmer at heart. He loved to raise cows and horses and plant gardens. With no more city stress and pollution, but rather leisurely working outside in the clean air and eating fresh fruits and vegetables from his garden, I could see his life being extended by this way of living.

At first the move appeared to be good for Mother too, but as always before, her surge of normality was only temporary. This time she sank into her fantasy world even quicker and deeper than before. Her bitterness and hatred was now all directed toward Dad. In her hysterical moments, Dad's method of coping was to calmly walk out of the house and leave her to fight by herself. This incensed her so much that one day she picked up a dead tree branch, crept up behind him as he was stooped over pulling weeds in the garden, and sent it crashing across his back. Another time, on a freezing winter day, she turned on the garden hose and drenched him with water.

As her actions became more openly hostile and violent, I became more concerned about Dad. I asked the church to pray about her condition at one of the services. Thousands of people prayed, and I thought God would answer and Mother would be healed. However, instead of getting better, she got worse, this time with a new twist.

It was now normal for Mother to sleep all day and prowl the house at night, fighting imaginary enemies. One morning she woke Dad at three A.M. She had been cooking since midnight, and had a full meal prepared and the table set for eight people. She told Dad that her voices had informed her I was coming for dinner. Now they told her I was lost. She wanted Dad to drive her into town to search for me.

He accommodated her, as he always did. Anyone else would have hit her in the head or had her committed, but not Dad. He put up with her for reasons that only he can understand.

At 4:30 in the morning, I received a call.

"Stormie?" the voice of my dad questioned.

"Yes, what's wrong?" I quickly wakened.

"Your mother said you were coming for dinner tonight and that you were lost in town. We've been looking for you since three A.M. this morning. Are you coming?"

"Of course not, Dad. I'm still here in bed."

"I want you to tell your mother so she knows." He handed the phone to her.

"Where are you?" she said gruffly.

"I'm home in bed. Where am I supposed to be?"

"You told me you were coming for dinner." Her anger gained momentum.

We hadn't spoken in weeks and had not seen each other in months. The farm was a four-hour car ride away, so it was not the kind of trip anyone would make just for dinner.

"I never told you that. I haven't even talked with you. Where are you hearing these things?" I said, knowing full well where she heard them. I had long suspected that she heard the voices of demons and that they controlled her personality. I kept trying to point her toward the realization that she was listening to lies, but she refused to see it. She was actually blinded and *couldn't* see it. Her own personality was suffocated beneath thick bondage and she was unable to entertain rational thoughts. She hung up on me in total disgust.

In all my life I never saw my mother forgive anything or anyone. She was an injustice-collector of the highest order. She had on the tip of her tongue the name of anyone who had ever wronged her and could tell you the complete incident in full detail. She could relive it with all the intensity of feeling as when it first happened. And so, just as she never forgave Dad for suggesting that she go to a mental hospital, she never forgave me for not coming to dinner at three A.M. that morning.

About three months later Michael and I took Christopher to visit my parents. Immediately when I walked in their house I noticed the dining table.

"Why is the table so dirty?" I whispered to Dad. "The dishes are filthy. There is a quarter-inch of dust on everything and cobwebs on the glasses."

"Your mother set that table the night she called you and she refuses to put anything away," Dad explained. "She won't let me touch it either."

When I met Mother's cold stare, that familiar look of venom, it was clear that I was back on top of her hate list. She barely spoke to me, although she tried to be civil when others were in the room with us.

Michael, like many people, had thought of my mother as "such a nice woman" when he first met her. However, when we stayed with my parents for a few days one Christmas early in our marriage, Mother couldn't keep up the front. She had to communicate with her voices. She prowled all night speaking hateful things to those who were trying to kill her. She complained of people shooting her with laser guns and electronic rays and watching her through windows and mirrors and the TV. The FBI tortured her sexually, she said. I couldn't believe my ears. I had never heard her say the word "sexually" in my entire life, and here she was being tortured sexually by the FBI! "Imagine how surprised they would be to hear that," I thought to myself.

Michael was initiated early to Mother's insanity, but he never saw her in a fit of rage. Only a select few people had ever witnessed that, and it was definitely something they never forgot. I had seen it repeatedly as a child, far more than anyone else. Michael was spared.

Mother's hatred of me persisted throughout the day we were there. I tried to ignore it, but it was impossible. When it came time for dinner I said, "I'll set the table."

"The table's already set!" She spit out the words at me. "It's been set for four months, and you're going to eat off of it just the way it is."

"But it's dirty," I protested like a little girl trying to hide bitterness behind innocence. What was the matter with me that after all these years and all my healing and deliverance she was still able to reduce me to the most base emotions? I was supposed to be a Christian adult and a leader in the church, yet I felt like slugging this mean old lady. It appeared that the only time I could have pity on this poor, emotionally deformed person was when we were not in the same room. I was not able and would never be able to cope with her hatred of me in person. Michael and I cleared the table, washed all the dishes, and set the table again. Then we all sat down to a very solemn and tension-filled meal. When we left the next morning I said to Michael, "I can never go back there."

I called Sara Anne as soon as I arrived home and told her what had happened—how Mother devastated me every time I saw her and how upsetting the visits were for my whole family. I wanted to obey God and honor my father and my mother, but I was having a horribly difficult time.

"You don't have to go there to be destroyed by her," she counseled. "Honor her from your home. Call her, write her, send her gifts, pray for her, and love her from a distance. When God heals her, you will be able to visit. Of course go if the Spirit leads you to, but don't feel guilty if you are released to stay away for awhile. Give yourself time to be healed.''

Michael and I agreed this was sound counsel, and I tried to explain it to Dad.

''Why don't you just walk out and ignore her the way I do?'' he responded.

''I wish I could, Dad, but it just doesn't work that way for me. Here I am grown-up with a family of my own, and yet I feel the same way around her as when I was a child.''

He understood why I found her too upsetting to be around, and he agreed to come to *our* house for visits.

Now my prayers intensified.

''You're a Redeemer,'' I reminded God. ''You redeem all things. God, I pray, redeem this relationship with my mother. The most basic relationship anyone can have has been denied me. I've never had a mother-daughter relationship. Lord, heal her, I pray. Make her whole so that this part of my life can be restored.''

Then, as clearly as anytime in my life, I heard God speak. He said, ''I *am* going to redeem that relationship. I'm going to redeem it through your own daughter.''

I blinked. I shook my head. I swallowed hard and said meekly, ''But, Lord, I don't have a daughter.''

The silence was deafening. As I waited for God's reply I thought, ''I'm almost 40. My first pregnancy was horrendous. I don't think I can live through another one. I've always been defensive with anyone who suggested that we have another child. God does not require of me beyond what I'm able.''

I continued to fight the idea for a long time, until I realized I was fighting the will of God. I knew that God would love me whether I had another child or not. But if I wanted all the healing, wholeness, and blessing that God had planned for me, I had to lay down my life and again surrender my will to His. Once Michael and I made the decision to obey God, I felt immediate relief.

My relief turned to joy as I asked God not to let this pregnancy be like the first one, and He responded by comforting me with the words ''I will see you through it.''

I was shocked, devastated, and overwhelmed when this second pregnancy turned out to be physically even more severe than the first. Again violent nausea took over my body and I began losing weight immediately. The pain was as if someone had poured boiling water through my veins. Unable to stand or sit up, I stayed flat on my back.

"God, why?" I cried out. "Why this again? Have You deserted me?" But His words came back to me clearly: "I will see you through it." I realized that He never said this time would be different; He never said that in this world we would have no problems; He said that in this world we would have trouble, but *"I will see you through it."*

My condition worsened and I was admitted to the hospital and fed intravenously. My doctor, one of the best obstetricians in the city, tried everything possible. He refused to give me any medication for pain or nausea for fear that it might endanger the baby. I was grateful for his decision because I was sick enough that I might have taken anything for relief. Finally my veins gave out, and as soon as they removed the I.V.'s my condition got worse. I knew I needed a miracle, but I was too sick to pray anymore. All I could say was, "Help me, Jesus."

Every hour seemed like a week because of the pain and extreme nausea. I couldn't sit up. I couldn't read or watch television. I couldn't sleep. There was nothing I could do but lie in my hospital bed and cry. There was no relief.

Sara Anne visited often and read Scriptures to me hour-upon-hour. She massaged my legs, the only part of my body I could stand to have touched, and her eyes overflowed with compassion as she watched me getting worse.

One day I cried to Sara Anne, "I was a fool to go ahead and get pregnant after what happened the last time. Why did I do this?"

She reminded me of the truth the pain had blinded me to. "You did it as a step of obedience to God, remember? There is great reward for obedience, you know."

"I'm sorry, Sara Anna," I sobbed. "I just can't see it right now."

Then I heard God's words again. "I will see you through it." I didn't know if this meant that I was going to die and be with the Lord or that the doctors were going to have to take the baby to spare my life. Those appeared to be the only two alternatives, and neither was my choice. I couldn't bear the thought of leaving my little boy, and I knew if I lost this child I would probably never be pregnant again.

That night I dreamed about holding a beautiful baby girl, with dark hair, sparkling chestnut-brown eyes, and long, dark eyelashes. The picture of her was so vivid and lifelike that it gave me happiness just to think of it.

When my doctor determined that there was nothing more he could do for me in the hospital, arrangements were made for me to go home. Pastor Jack called me that night before I was to be discharged. He was very upset that I had regressed and even more upset about the possibility that they might have to take the baby.

I said, "Pastor Jack, I don't understand. I know God can heal me. I know I was supposed to have this baby. But the pain and nausea never let up, and I feel too weak to pray anymore."

There was love, compassion, and concern in his voice as he labored in prayer for me yet another time.

Sunday morning I was discharged from the hospital. The pain and nausea were worse than ever, and I was discouraged, to say the least. It was decided that if there was no change by the following Tuesday, taking the baby was the next step. There was nothing more that could be done, and time was running out.

At home in my own bed, little Christopher came into my room. He didn't run in happy to see me like he had always done before. He came in cautiously and kept his distance. I had not been a mother to him for four months, and now we were strangers. I couldn't hold him, read to him, or play games with him. Emotionally he was leaving me behind. He politely said hello, then ran out of the room to continue his life. It broke my heart.

Bob and Sally, two very close friends, came to our house with their children to temporarily relieve Michael from the burden of this whole ordeal. They made the meals for the day and kept

Michael and Christopher company. There was nothing they could do for me, so they left me alone. I was grateful.

At six that evening I almost jolted in bed. I sat up and said to myself, "What just happened?" It took a moment to realize that I suddenly felt no pain or nausea.

I sat in bed for a few minutes to see when it would return. When nothing changed, I got up slowly and walked into the bathroom adjacent to our bedroom. I looked in the mirror at my thin face and hollow eyes, then carefully walked back and sat on the bed for a moment. Still feeling no nausea or pain, I got up and walked into the den, where my husband was alone, watching TV. He nearly fell off the couch as he sat up quickly and said, "What's the matter? What are you doing up?"

"I don't know," I said in disbelief. "I suddenly feel different. The pain is gone, and the nausea too. It may come back any minute," I added, exhibiting great faith. After months of agony, I was afraid to hope that this feeling could last.

Michael looked at me in amazement and whispered quietly, "Praise God!"

I walked slowly out of the den and down the long hall into the kitchen, where Sally was cleaning up the dinner dishes. I hadn't eaten much of anything for months, and even with intravenous feeding I felt very weak.

She turned and said in a startled voice, "What are you doing out here?"

"I don't know what's happened, Sally. I suddenly feel better."

"Well, Hallelujah!" she lifted her voice. "Do you want something to eat just to prove that what you're saying is true?"

"Yes, quick, before it comes back again," I replied.

She gave me a bowl of sliced pears and some plain dry toast without butter. It tasted like the most wonderful gourmet meal. I ate it down, loving every morsel and thanking God for my reprieve. Even if it all came back up, to be able to chew something and swallow it was heaven.

We waited and waited, but the nausea and pain didn't come back. I went to bed and slept through the night. The next morning I received many phone calls telling me how fervently the church had prayed for my healing the night before in the Sunday evening service. Pastor Jack had not mentioned to me that he was going to have the congregation pray.

"Yes, I *am* feeling better." I told each person who called. I didn't tell anyone how *much* better, since I was still afraid it would all come back and I didn't want them to stop praying.

I waited until six o'clock Tuesday night—a full 48 hours—to call Pastor Jack at home and tell him what had happened.

I described to him in detail the events surrounding Sunday evening.

"Praise God, you've been healed!" he said exuberantly.

"I have?" I replied. "Do you really think so?"

"Stormie," he sighed patiently, "I *know* so."

"You mean it won't come back?"

"No, you've been healed. Did you know we were praying for you on Sunday?"

"No, I didn't know anything about it until Monday."

Obviously it was not my faith or prayers, but the faith and prayers of thousands of other people around the country, and specifically those in The Church On The Way, that healed me and saved my baby. I was filled with gratitude for the love and concern of my brothers and sisters in Jesus. God had given me a caring family like I had never dreamed possible. He had promised to see me through, and He did.

Two weeks away from my due date, I flew to New York to be with my husband at the Grammy Awards ceremony, where he won three Grammys for producing an album called "Christopher Cross." Christopher was the first artist to win the four top awards—Album of the Year, Record of the Year, Song of the Year, and Best New Artist—all in one evening. It was an exciting time, and I thanked God that He made it possible for me to be a part of a big night for my husband.

Soon after I returned home, the pretty little dark-haired girl with the chestnut-brown eyes and long, dark eyelashes that I saw in my dream was born. We named her Amanda Katherine. Right away I could see that this time everything was different. I had no more urges to batter or beat. No times of losing control. No rage, no anger, no inkling of the former problem.

I had known since the first incident with Christopher that I did not have in myself what I needed to be a good parent. I would always have to depend totally on God to help me raise my children. Because I couldn't do it without Him, I was forced down on my knees all the more to seek God's guidance and pray to be more like Him in nature.

As soon as I was recovered enough, I concentrated on making up for lost time with little Christopher. Every afternoon when Amanda was sleeping I took him someplace special—just the two of us. Although extremely proud of his little sister, it made him feel important and grown-up to kiss her goodbye and inform her that she was too little to go where we were going. In our three hours together, Christopher and I got acquainted again. We walked and we talked. We went to the park, to a children's movie, miniature golfing, to the toy store. This was *our* time, and within two weeks all that was damaged during those months of my infirmity was repaired. "Thank You, God, for giving me Christopher and Amanda," I said at least ten times every day, and I meant it with every fiber of my being.

With the cost of obedience taken care of, the rewards of that obedience were great. From the moment of Amanda's birth, the healing began. Just like an open wound heals slowly day by day, I felt a wound in my emotions, in my heart somewhere, begin to heal. Every day with Amanda brought more wholeness and more fulfillment.

At 42 years of age I went to my very first mother-daughter tea, presented at Amanda's preschool for Mother's Day. It was thrilling beyond description. I found myself feeling sorry for the two little children whose mothers didn't come. Always before that had been me; I never had a mother who came. Now I was getting to go as the mommy.

Amanda's pretty brown eyes sparkled and danced as she got up with her friends to sing the songs and recite the poem they had rehearsed for their mothers. Every few seconds she would steal a glance in my direction to see if I was watching her. I was.

God had kept His promise to restore my lost mother-daughter relationship, and He chose the perfect way to do it. The cost of obedience is great, but the rewards, I discovered, are far greater.

# CHAPTER FIFTEEN

# FINAL FORGIVENESS

"Do you ever get rid of the pain?" a young woman asked me after one of my speaking engagements.

It was a question I heard frequently from people who had been abused as children. I knew immediately the pain she was referring to.

"I don't know," I replied honestly. "You get healing. You receive freedom beyond what you thought possible, but I don't know if you ever get rid of the pain."

The pain of an abused child stems from a foundation of rejection. A constant "pain in the gut" becomes a way of life, and many people, like me, accept it as part of daily living. It's with you everywhere you go. Before I met Jesus, I silenced my pain with drugs, alcohol, work, or "love" relationships—methods which, in the long run, only served to make the pain worse.

Even in the happiest moments, the pain was always there waiting for the mere suggestion of rejection to bring it rushing in, reaffirming all the negative feelings I had ever had about myself. In times of weakness, suicide seemed to be the only solution. When I was 14, I wanted to die just to stop the pain. I used to beg God for a frontal lobotomy so I wouldn't have to feel anymore. After establishing my relationship with God through Jesus, I was able to take my pain to God in prayer on a continuing basis. It certainly had gotten better and more controllable, but it was still there.

Yes, I understood the young woman's question completely. After Amanda was born, I was flooded with requests to speak

about the restorative power of God. Amanda's birth had nothing
to do with their asking me, but I believe this sudden opening up
of ministry was because of my obedience. Again, it was one of
the rewards. It was also an example of God using the rubble of
my past to help others. Whenever I spoke, there were countless
people suffering from the same wounds and emotional scars I
once had. They felt like they were dying inside and needed to
know there could be life before death for them.

Another part of my ministry that sprang forth was in the area
of physical fitness. I had seriously studied exercise and nutrition
for 15 years and had been teaching exercise and nutrition classes
for some time. The classes became so popular that people were
calling from all over the country asking me to sell my exercise
tapes and class notes. This led to two "Exercise for Life" albums
and a book called "Greater Health God's Way" for Sparrow
Press.

I was thoroughly enjoying my ministry, my family, my church,
my God, and my life in general, but there was still a subtle unrest
in me. I've frequently been described as high-strung and fast-
moving, the type of personality that will always be active. That
part of me is God-ordained, but this was something more; it was
an unrest deep in my soul. And I might well have lived out the
rest of my life thinking, "Well, that's just me," had it not been
for Sara Anne noticing this in me.

"There is an unrest in your spirit, Stormie," she said. "I see
it surface occasionally. Let's both ask God to reveal what's
causing it. I know He wants you to be free from yet another
thing."

I was amazed. I thought I *was* free! At least that's what I had
been telling everyone in my concerts. Here I was, 42 years old.
I'd had deliverance and teaching for 13 years, and now I was
teaching others about the freedom they could enjoy. Was I yet
to need more?

"God, reveal to me what I need to be free from. What causes
this unrest?" I prayed.

I got no answer.

Nearly a week later, Sara Anne called early one morning to

tell me of a dream she had in which she believed God revealed to her my problem. "You have unconfessed hatred and unforgiveness toward your father," she explained.

"What?" I exclaimed with indignation. "No way, Sara Anne. This time you're wrong."

"Honestly, Stormie, I would not have thought of that myself. I believe the dream I had was definitely from God."

I was silent.

"Think about it," she continued. "See what God says to you."

"You don't understand, Sara Anne. My dad is sweet and nice. He has never done anything bad to me. He's never even laid a hand on me except for a couple of spankings which I deserved. He's a kind person. How could I hate him? Why do I need to forgive him?"

"See what God has to say about it," she gently repeated.

I hung up the phone, sat for a moment, and prayed, "God, what is she talking about? This is the most ridiculous thing I have ever heard."

Then suddenly, like a flash of steel penetrating my heart, I nearly doubled over with pain. I saw myself in the closet again crying silently, "Why doesn't Dad ever open the door and let me out?" The thought of it was so painful that I couldn't allow myself to see it anymore.

At church that night I told Sara Anne, "You were right. I can't talk about it right now, but I feel I'm supposed to fast for three days starting the Wednesday before Good Friday. Could you pray with me for deliverance from this after the Good Friday services?"

She and her husband agreed that this was the correct thing to do and that they and Michael should fast along with me.

"Ask God to reveal more and more to you over the next few weeks," she counseled.

In the car driving home I prayed, "God, show me everything I need to be free of concerning my dad."

I wasn't on the freeway more than three minutes when the pain penetrated to the center of my being. This time I began to sob hysterically. The sobbing hurt my whole insides. I was blinded by tears and could hardly see to drive, so I slowed down. As cars whizzed around me, I knew I needed to pull myself together immediately or there was danger of an accident. The force of whatever thing was in me was so powerful that I was afraid a full look into the face of it would be unbearable.

"God help me!" I swallowed and struggled to blink back further tears.

Over the next few weeks I began to see clearly that I did indeed harbor unforgiveness toward my dad for never once coming to my rescue when I was a child. He never let me out of the closet. He never pulled my mother off my back. He never once protected me from her insanity. I had been let down by the one person who was my protector, my covering. The unforgiveness I harbored was unconfessed because I had never allowed myself to consciously think angry thoughts toward him.

I had learned a couple of years prior to this that, much to my surprise, Dad didn't know about the times Mother had locked me in the closet. This knowledge relieved my mind, but it apparently didn't heal the wound. And it didn't release me from the bondage of a lifetime of unforgiveness. I learned the truth of the situation, but now I needed to apply *God's* truth to it in order to be truly set free.

The more this problem was exposed, the more it became apparent that we weren't talking about simply unforgiveness and anger. We were talking about rage—rage toward my dad. Because of this rage and unforgiveness, I had grown up to distrust all male authority—not all men, but only those in authority over my life, such as my pastor and my husband. I had never openly rebelled against them, and it never consciously occurred to me that I didn't have the utmost respect for them. So the symptoms of the problem were way down deep inside. The bottom line was that I felt if I was hanging on a cliff by my fingertips, any male authority in my life would walk on by and let me drop.

This bondage was manifested in my life by my extreme independence. I always felt that I had to keep everything together all by myself because I couldn't depend on anyone else to come through for me. It took a lot of constant energy to keep myself together like that. I could never rest.

Oddly enough, along with all this I started to feel like I was going crazy. I had heard there is a fine line between sanity and insanity, and I suddenly felt like I was walking on it. After a few years of *not* feeling that way, I couldn't understand what was happening, but the feeling was unmistakable. There is a definite sensation of losing your mind, and I had it. I'd often been concerned about ending up like my mother, but never felt I was that close to it until now.

Good Friday arrived, and we all met as planned in the counseling office. I confessed my unforgiveness for Dad, and as I did, the ray of steel penetrated my stomach again, only this time it unleashed a torrent of emotion unlike any I'd experienced in adult life. I recognized it as the pain I had felt as a small child locked in a closet with no one to help me. It was the same pain that would periodically well up in me with such force that I had to withdraw from my friends at school or double over against a bathroom stall at CBS.

The pain came to the surface in full force. I sobbed grieving sobs from deep in my being. They were sobs I had held back rigidly in my throat for years because Mother threatened to beat me if I cried. The pain felt as if I was giving birth to something bigger than my body could deliver—something tangible, something measurable.

Sara Anne and her husband anointed me with oil, laid their hands on my head, and commanded in the name of Jesus that any oppressive spirit that had a hold on my life be broken. One final surge of pain wracked my body, and then it was over. A new inner peace settled over me.

With the expulsion of that deeply buried unforgiveness and rage, the devil's final stronghold in my life was destroyed. I could see clearly now that the deeply repressed unforgiveness had led to a type of mental imbalance. Could that be what had happened to Mother—all her unforgiveness internalized to the point that her view of life became warped by it? I was sure it wasn't the only thing that leads to mental imbalance, but I knew for certain that a sound mind cannot exist with deep unforgiveness and rage. There is a direct tie between forgiveness and wholeness.

I also saw that deliverance was a process that happened in different ways at different times. Sometimes it happened by spending time in God's presence and walking in obedience to Him, such as the way I was delivered from my fear of knives. Sometimes it happened by crying out to God in prayer and exalting Him in praise, the way I did when I discovered my potential for child abuse. Sometimes it happened in the counseling office with the guidance of trained and qualified counselors, as it did when I was set free of paralyzing depressions. But no matter how it happened, it was always Jesus—the Deliverer—who set me free. He had come to strip away that which separated me from Him.

The next morning I noticed distinctly that I did not feel like I was going crazy. I felt completely normal, and the sensation of pending insanity never came back. It reminded me of when I was delivered from suicidal thoughts and I woke up the following morning without a trace of them. In the years since, they never returned. These were miracles I couldn't deny, nor could I have conjured them up in my mind. I only knew that once again I had a new level of freedom inside me. Another set of chains had been broken, another closet door unlocked.

Trust for my husband and my pastor came slowly and steadily after that. Michael was still human and made mistakes, but I no longer saw it as a lack of caring or concern for me. My relationship with him improved immediately because I began to worry less and let him handle things. Always before I felt I had to be in on every financial decision, and I'm certain my attitude made Michael feel as if I didn't trust him. Now I didn't care if I was even consulted, for I trusted that God would guide my husband in all things. What relief to not have to struggle to be in control of everything.

For the first time in my life I realized how little I knew about my father. No one ever volunteered information about him, and I never thought to ask. I had always subconsciously viewed him as a one-dimensional stick figure, but now that I was set free from all my unforgiveness, I discovered features of his personality and the quality of his character unfolded. The next time he visited, I learned that he was the oldest of eight children—

three boys and five girls—and because of this he carried a great deal of responsibility in the home. He was raised on a farm in Pennsylvania by devout Christian parents. His father was the superintendent at the church and his mother was the organist. I was surprised by this because I had never heard Dad say the words "church" or "God" in my whole life.

"Why didn't you ever go to church once you left home, Dad?" I questioned after he surprised me with this new information.

"In order to get to church we had to walk a mile-and-a-half through the fields," he answered. "We went two times on Sunday and every Thursday night no matter if there was hail, rain, or snow. When we got there we sat nearly four hours at a time on uncomfortable wood benches while the preacher ranted and raved about hellfire and brimstone. It was boring as could be, and children weren't allowed to move or make a sound. I've always believed in God, but I decided that once I left home I was *never* going to go through that kind of torture again."

I heard from other relatives that Dad was a very handsome man and that many women were after him. But he was shy and paid no attention to any of them until he met Mother when he was in his early thirties. She was only 24 and he was dazzled by her beauty and charming party personality. He fell in love with her and always remained in love with his first impression of her even after no trace of it remained in reality. Apparently the hope of her "someday snapping out of it" and returning to normal kept him going.

After I forgave Dad, I could see how much he really did love me. He never showed it openly because he was not comfortable doing that, but his love was there just the same. I discovered that even though a parent may love a child deeply, unless the child *perceives* that love he won't *feel* loved. Realizing this made me become more openly affectionate with my own children. Many times each day I kissed and hugged each one of them, and looked them in the eyes, and said, "I love you." Then, just to make sure there were no misunderstandings, every week I quizzed them.

"Does your mommy love you?" I'd ask.

"Yes, you do," they chortled and laughed.

"How much do I love you?" I questioned.

"A lot!" they replied without hesitation.

"Why do I love you so much?"

"Because I'm me!" they replied in perfect unison.

"That's right!" I cheered. "I love you because you're you."

In time I noticed that the pain in my gut was gone. The memories didn't bother me the way they used to. I came to a new level of rest like I had never before imagined.

Six months after that Good Friday counseling session, I spoke before a large group of people and told my story of God's total restoration. When I finished, there was a question-and-answer time in which a lady stood up and asked, "Do you ever get rid of the pain?"

With joy I smiled and answered, "Yes! For the first time in my life I can say that you really do get rid of the pain. It doesn't happen overnight, but it does happen."

# TOTAL RESTORATION

Mother had not left the house in five years, so spending another Christmas without her was not unusual. Dad came to our home, along with my sister and her family, and we celebrated together. Part of the gift that Michael and I gave Dad was a trip east to visit his relatives. We presented it to him early so he could leave and be back in time for Christmas Day with us. The day after Christmas, he returned to his own home.

During this time no one worried about Mother because she always loved being alone. It was her opportunity to talk to her voices and carry on unrestricted. A giant freezer in the garage was stocked full of food, so she was not wanting for anything to eat. When Dad returned after Christmas he found that she had not done any dishes for the two weeks he was gone and had not eaten much of anything during the last few days. Our first thought was that her characteristic refusal to do housework had caused her to stop eating when she ran out of dishes. When it appeared that she wanted to eat but couldn't, Dad concluded she must have the flu. Her mental condition had gone down at an accelerated rate during the past two years, so communicating was difficult. It was impossible to get an answer from her that made any sense. As she progressively lost touch with reality, she barely seemed like a human being anymore.

Just a few months earlier, Mother and Dad's little dog became sick and died. Mother refused to believe the dog was dead. She placed the body in the middle of her own bed and every day put food in its mouth, poured water down its throat, and talked to the dead body as if it were a living dog. Whenever Dad came near the dog, or mentioned burying it, Mother got hysterical. This finally convinced Dad that it was time to see about having Mother committed. He went for help but found that new laws made commitment much more difficult. He had to prove that she might physically harm herself or someone else. Since he could not prove that, his hands were tied.

After the dog had been dead on her bed for over a week, the smell of death was pungent enough to keep Dad awake at night in his bedroom down the hall. He knew he had to take action. Since Mother slept all day and prowled the house talking to voices all night, Dad waited until she was sound asleep about midmorning. He crept in, took the little corpse off the bed, and buried it in the field in back of the house. Anticipating what would happen when she awoke, he dug the hole very deep.

When Mother woke up and found the dog missing she was angry and hysterical.

"Where's the dog?" she demanded of my father.

"I've buried her. She's dead," he said with finality.

"She's not dead. You've buried her alive!" she screamed repeatedly as she ran for the shovel. She dug everywhere searching for the dog. She even dug right in the place where Dad had buried her, but the grave was deep enough that Mother never found her. She finally gave up looking.

After that, Mother's complaints about people shooting her increased. "They're shooting me with laser beams in my stomach and my breast. They're beaming rays into my brain. They want information, but I won't give it to them."

I pitied her, but not enough to visit. I no longer hated her and I did feel sorry for her, but her verbal attacks on me were unceasing. She acted as if she despised me, and even though I understood that it was self-hatred turned outward, I couldn't bear to be with her.

My sister always got along decently with Mother and visited her periodically. After Christmas she reported that Mother looked very bad; she had lost a lot of weight, her face was puffy, and her skin was yellow. My dad remained firm in his belief that she had the flu.

Just before Michael and I were to take the children on a family vacation in Hawaii, I called Dad to ask about Mother.

"She's better," he said. "She's staying in bed and I'm bringing meals to her. She's eating well now—not throwing up."

"Do you want me to come and help you with her?" I asked. "I'd be glad to do it."

"No, no. She's doing fine now," he assured me.

Our second morning in Hawaii, I got up before everyone else, as I always did, and went for a run on the beach. This was my time to talk to God. It seemed I could always hear Him more clearly away from telephones, obligations, and deadlines, and close to the beauty of His creation. The question of writing my life story about how God restored me to wholeness had been gnawing at me for months, and I needed to hear an answer from Him.

"What about it, God?" I asked. "I know I'm supposed to write this book, and I feel You're saying to begin now. Am I hearing You right? I need to know I'm hearing *You*."

I had been hesitant to begin the book because there was always the possibility that Mother could be healed from her mental illness and a published story of her past would be a painful reminder. Yet I felt a leading to begin right away. I prayed and worshiped as I walked on the rocks and sand, and then, as clearly as I have ever heard anything from God, He spoke to my heart, "The time is now to begin the book."

"It's okay to write it even though she's still alive?" I questioned.

"The time is now to begin the book," I heard again. I felt that familiar warm rush through my body and the immediate peace and joy that comes from hearing God's voice. I was certain I had His go-ahead.

When I returned to our room at the hotel, everyone was just getting up. We dressed and went out for breakfast, and I shared with Michael about God's release to start the book. He fully supported the idea.

As we returned to our room, I saw the red light blinking on the wall, signaling that someone had telephoned and left a message. Immediately I sensed that it was something serious. I called the front desk and received a message to contact my sister at my parent's home. I quickly dialed, anticipating bad news, for neither my sister or Dad had ever called me on vacation before. My dad answered.

"Dad, I got the message that you called."

"Your mother's very ill. We're trying to get her to a doctor, but she won't go. There's an ambulance here now, but she's locked herself in the bathroom and won't come out for anybody." His voice was distressed.

"Where's Suzy?"

"She's talking to her through the bathroom door."

"How sick can she be," I wondered, "if she's strong enough to lock herself in the bathroom?"

I heard Dad yell, "Suzy, Stormie's on the phone!"

Suzy's voice betrayed the seriousness of the situation as she spoke, "Stormie, Mom's really sick. You wouldn't recognize her. She must have lost 60 pounds. She's skin and bones and she looks awful. I think she's dying." Her voice sounded suddenly mature and I recognized that the weight of Mother's illness had been on her shoulders.

"Are you sure?" I asked in disbelief. How could it be that just a few days ago Dad said she was getting better and now she was dying?

"You should see her. It's frightening. She won't go to the doctor. She refuses to come out of the bathroom and go with the ambulance attendants who are here waiting. What should I do? She's in pain. She needs help." Her voice broke.

"Suzy, she's probably afraid of the men. Maybe she thinks they're going to kill her. If you can't get her to go with them, then let them go. After they're gone and she comes out of the bathroom and rests for a while, ask her if she will let you and Dad take her to the hospital. You're the only one she'll listen to. Ask her to do it for *you*, Suzy. Tell her you can't stand to see her in pain and that they'll give her something to help her.

Tell her you won't leave her, that you'll stay with her."

"Okay," she said with conviction and direction in her voice.

"We'll take the first flight out. I'll call and tell you what time we're coming in," I said, and hung up the phone.

There was a sudden urgency inside of me. I had to get home. "God, please help me to get there before she dies," I prayed as I dialed the airline ticket office.

There were no flights with seating for four people until midnight, and I wasn't going without my family. I was afraid to see Mother alone without Michael and my children.

We called the church and asked for prayer. "Pray that I get there before she dies," I asked.

It took us the rest of the day to pack, return the rental car, check out of the hotel, and make call after call to see if we could take an earlier flight.

Before leaving for the airport I spoke again with Suzy. She had followed my suggestion and Mother had agreed to go to the hospital. Suzy and Dad carried her into the car and drove her to the emergency entrance. Suzy stayed with her until she was admitted, given something for pain, and fell asleep.

"What did the doctor say?" I asked.

"Cancer. She's not going to make it. They're just going to keep giving her something for pain."

"Oh, no!" I said, filled with guilt over not being there, as well as sadness over Mother's intense suffering.

"Stormie," Suzy said after a brief pause, "don't feel guilty if you don't make it before she dies. . . . She's so bad that you don't want to see her like this."

There was silence as I choked back tears and tried to swallow and speak. "Thanks, Suzy. I can't tell you how much I appreciate your saying that." As much as I wanted to see my mother before she died, I also feared eternal anger from my sister and Dad for not being there.

We boarded the plane at midnight and arrived in Los Angeles at eight A.M. California time. We were in our house by nine A.M. and decided we had to sleep at least two hours in order to make the four-hour drive to the hospital safely. The alarm went off at eleven A.M. I hurriedly dumped the contents of the suitcases on the floor and repacked them with warm clothing while Michael fixed something quick to eat and made beds in the back of the car for the children to sleep.

I called my parent's home and there was no answer. I then called the hospital and insisted that they put me through to my mother's room.

"She's in critical condition," they protested.

"I'm her daughter!" I insisted.

Suzy's husband, Louis, answered the phone.

"Louis, we're leaving right now from our house. How is she doing?"

"I don't know if you'll make it," he said, his voice noticeably shaken.

"Louis, you can't be serious. You mean she won't last four more hours?" I asked in horror. I couldn't believe it. This was all happening so fast.

"You don't know what she's like." His voice quivered. "She doesn't look like your mother anymore. She's not the same person."

"We'll be there as fast as we can, Louis. We're coming straight to the hospital." He gave me directions and I could hear my dad and my sister talking as Mother moaned in the background.

We piled in the car and nearly flew there, hitting every green light and no traffic. In the car I broke down and began to sob. "Please, God, let me get there before she dies. Please, God, don't let her die before I see her."

Michael put his hand on my shoulder and steered with the other. I looked in the backseat and met two pairs of very concerned little brown eyes staring back at me. Amanda and Christopher were worried, too.

"I'm okay," I reassured them. "Mommy's just afraid that Grandma will die before we get there."

"That will be sad," said Christopher.

"I'll be sad, too," said almost three-year-old Amanda, not fully understanding but wanting to be like her big brother.

I had always been honest with my children and had shared with them truthfully as much as I thought they could understand. Christopher knew that my mother had mistreated me as a child, but he understood that it was because she was sick. "Grandma has always loved *you*," I reassured the two of them.

I prayed silently all the way there. Something inside of me hoped that Mother and I would see each other and that things would be different. Maybe she would be in her right mind and we could talk like normal people. Perhaps she would let go of her hatred of me for a few minutes and communicate as a mother to a daughter. I even had wild dreams of us telling each other we were sorry for the ways we hurt each other, and maybe I could even say, "I love you."

I thought back to all the times Mother complained about people shooting her in the breast, the head, and the stomach. It never occurred to us that she was talking about real pain.

I recalled my periodical calls to talk to Dad, and how he always gave the phone to Mother. She consistently answered in the same unfriendly tone.

"Hi, Mom, how are you doing?" I would chirp in my most phony happy voice.

"How do you think I'm doing?" she would begin, and then proceed to vomit all the garbage that surrounded her days.

"The FBI is shooting my head with laser beams so bad I can't think. They know I have communist secrets. The President of the United States is trying to get information out of me, and so are the Catholics and the Armenians and the Mafia and Frank Sinatra." From then on I couldn't get a word in. I would lay the phone down on the bed and check in about every five minutes. She would still be talking, not fazed in the least that I had contributed nothing to the conversation. Thirty or forty minutes later I would pick up the phone and say very loudly, "I have to go now, Mother. Goodbye." My dad mentioned that after talking with me Mother was always a little better and didn't have to complain as much to him. I looked upon those telephone times with my mother as saving Dad's life.

I thought about the last time I visited Mother and Dad. Out of the blue, she had popped into the den where I was sitting alone and said, "All those times I locked you in a closet. . .that never bothered you, did it?" The pitch of her voice came down at the end, implying that of course it never bothered me as opposed to asking a true question and looking for an honest answer.

Still, I was so shocked I could hardly speak. Was this the same woman who never admitted doing anything wrong in her life? Granted, she made it clear that she knew this closet thing was no big deal and that she was just curious, but she *did* at least admit to doing it.

I pitied her enough to not tell her the truth, but I still had sufficient fleshly qualities in me to caustically remark, "Oh, no, Mother, I loved every minute of it."

My snideness went totally unobserved. Mother heard what she wanted to hear, and with a slight smile she replied, "I didn't think it bothered you." Then she returned to what she was doing in the kitchen. Part of me rejoiced because Mother finally admitted she had locked me in the closet. What provoked her to mention it after all these years I really couldn't imagine. Maybe unconfessed sin never lets a person rest no matter what the circumstances.

While on the way to the hospital to see Mother for the last time, I thought over all these things and observed that God had left no loose ends.

Our trip took only 2½ hours, miraculously short of the four hours we had anticipated. Michael dropped me off in front of the hospital and I quickly ran up the long walkway to the main lobby while he parked the car. I asked for my mother's room number, and when the receptionist could not locate it my heart pounded. I feared that it was too late and that she had been taken out of her room.

"No, here it is. Virginia is in Room 3A, right down the hall."

The hospital was very small and it took only seconds to run to her room and open the door. There was no one else in the double-occupancy room but two old, very sick-looking ladies, neither of whom I recognized as my mother. The one farthest away was unconscious and hooked up to many wires, tubes, and a respirator. She had no teeth. My mother had teeth. She had never allowed a dentist to lay a hand on her.

The other woman was thin and frail, her pale blue eyes staring off to the side in a very pained and hopeless expression. "I must have the wrong room," I thought, and started to leave. But as I took a second look just to make sure, I saw that the pale blue eyes belonged to Mother. I hardly recognized her tiny frame.

"Mom," I said softly. "Mom, it's me, Stormie."

I cautiously approached her bedside. I was still afraid of her.

"Mom," I said louder. I shook her arm. "Mom, it's me, Stormie."

There was no response.

I positioned myself so that her blue eyes stared directly at me. They were unseeing.

"Mom!" I began to cry. "Mom, you're gone, aren't you? I'm too late."

I felt her. She was still warm. She must have died only a few seconds before I arrived.

I took her hand and held it in mine and began to cry. I laid my head on her chest and sobbed into the blanket. I didn't cry because I missed my mother or our relationship. There had never been a relationship. No, I cried for all the things that never were. For all that never was between us. For fullness and joy of life that she never knew. I cried for the pain of a small girl who stamped her foot and talked back to her pregnant mother and then never saw her again because her mother went to the hospital that night and died. I cried for a young teenager who felt she was responsible for every death in her family. I cried for a woman who lived in fear, unforgiveness, bitterness, and rage at God and never knew His love and healing and deliverance. I cried for a woman who couldn't accept her daughter's forgiveness because she was unable to forgive herself. I cried for a person who never became what God created her to be. I grieved for all that, and knew it must be what God feels about *us* when we strain and strive and get ourselves into horribly painful situations when all we need to do is turn to Him and surrender.

I looked up at her face again and stroked her hair. I cried for all the years of my life I wasn't able to touch her like that. She would never allow it.

Oddly enough, I didn't feel disappointed because I missed seeing Mother alive. Near the end of our trip to the hospital I had peace that whatever happened was God's will. I had felt His presence all the way there, and if He had wanted me to see her alive He could easily have gotten me there 60 seconds earlier. God *had* answered my prayer by giving me peace, and I knew that I had arrived right on *His* schedule.

With still no one else in the room, I did something that might have seemed disrespectful and odd. I lifted the covers to look at Mother's body. Her legs were beautiful—thin, with milky white skin, yet exquisitely formed. Her stomach was distended. I lifted her gown and put my hand on the area where I thought the liver would be located, and I felt a large, hard mass. I then touched her left breast and felt an enormous lump the size of half a grapefruit. It was just as I had suspected from Suzy's telephone description: cancer taken to its final form. I marveled at how Mother must have suffered all those years without ever allowing anyone to help her. What a horrifying, awful death. It sickened me to think of the agonizing pain she must have experienced.

I pulled her gown down, laid the covers neatly back over her, and picked up her hand again. The fingers were getting cold now. I stared at her face. Her blue eyes were extra big because of her extreme weight loss. I had always thought of her as large and ugly. Now she looked tiny, frail, and pretty.

As her body cooled and became stiff, the finality of it hit me. Suddenly my mind flashed to the little church we had attended when I was 14. I remembered how she talked about God and Jesus as if they were real to her, and how dedicated she was for those few months until she threw out the large family Bible in a fit of rage. She never spoke about God again, except to say that He knew people were trying to kill her, but wasn't able to help. Now I felt peace about her, as if God was saying, "It's okay. Your mother is with Me. She doesn't hurt anymore. She's not crazy anymore. I've got her."

Actually, it was a strangely peaceful time, unlike what I would have expected. Death didn't feel so bad. Of course it was easy for me to say that, I wasn't the one who had died. But it seemed natural—like a normal part of life.

Finally two nurses walked in, and when they realized that my mother was dead they asked me to leave the room. As I did, Michael was just coming down the hall. "She's dead, Michael," I said softly.

"Oh, no. We were too late?"

"Too late to see her alive," I nodded, "but not too late in the Lord's plan."

When Michael and I were allowed back in Mother's room, I saw that the nurses had closed her eyes, folded her arms, and straightened the sheet across her body. As we stood there silently, the doctor entered. He was a kindly man in his sixties.

"I'm very sorry about your mother," he said. "There was nothing we could do. She had cancer in her breast and liver, and possibly a brain tumor as well. Her liver was five times the size of a normal liver."

He expressed shock at how advanced the cancer had become before she permitted anyone to give her medical aid.

"Doctor, I'm grateful for all that you've done for my dad through these last five years, and I'm thankful you were able to alleviate Mother's pain in the last few hours of her life," I assured him.

"The cancer was so bad that even if your dad had brought her to me a year ago, I don't believe I could have saved her," the doctor went on. He had known fully about Mother's mental condition because my dad had frequently confided in him and sought his counsel, though no one knew she was physically ill as well. "The medical expenses would have been tremendous for your dad, and it wouldn't have made any difference anyway. That cancer had been growing in her for many years. It was really better this way."

"What happens now?" I said, at a loss for the next step.

"We need to call your dad immediately," said Michael, and he left to find a phone. Dad was unprepared for Mother's death. He had no idea she was that sick, and the shock of it put him to bed. Michael and I handled all the arrangements.

I picked out the most beautiful casket I could find and ordered large, colorful bouquets of flowers because I knew she would have thought them beautiful. I chose a burial plot under a big shade tree because she always loved trees. I also bought her new pretty underwear, and as I handed my money to the cashier, tears I had been choking back flooded down my cheeks and I began to sob. I was struck by the remembrance of all the times I had wanted to do and buy things for Mother, like I was doing and buying now, but she would never receive them from me. Now I was doing it for her funeral. The cashier gave me my change, handed me my purchase, and looked at me with great concern. She was speechless and I was glad.

My sister took Mother's death hard. I had trouble understanding why, because I never realized that they had a relationship. I made the mistake of assuming that Suzy was the same as I was—wanting the same things, experiencing the same things. But the opposite was true; there was nothing similar about us. Suzy talked back to my mother; I cowered in a corner. She got angry and showed it; I got hurt and kept my rage inside. She had a relationship with my mother; I had none. Suzy felt grief; I felt relief. Even as children, we had been raised in two completely different worlds. I never realized any of that until now.

I was happy that I had no hard feelings toward my mother— no unforgiveness, no anger, no resentment, no unsettled scores. God had cleansed it all. Everything had been accomplished before her death, and I would never have to deal with those things again.

Word of Mother's death traveled quickly among family and friends. We received many phone calls, and I was shocked when one woman mentioned how much my mother had cared about me.

"Your mother was always very proud of you," said Anita, a longtime family friend who remained loyal to us even though Mother had often treated her rudely.

"Mother was always proud of me?" I asked astonished, not believing what I had just heard.

"When you starred in your high school play, she was very pleased. And she was proud of all your television shows. She never attended any of them because she thought the people who were trying to kill her might want to kill you too."

"I can't believe what you're saying, Anita. Why didn't she ever give me even the slightest indication that she felt that way?"

"You know your mother, Stormie. She had very strange ideas. She believed that if she were ever to tell you *anything* good about yourself, you would be spoiled."

"Spoiled?" I said in amazement. "She thought if she said something nice to me I would be spoiled?"

"I'm sorry you never knew your mother when she was younger. She was a lovely woman, she really was. The mental disease took over her life and disguised anything recognizable of her good qualities."

Unsuccessfully choking back tears I said, "Thank you, Anita. It means a lot to hear what you just said."

I hung up the phone and cried. "Mother, why couldn't you just once have said you were proud of me?"

After Mother's funeral, we stayed a number of days to help Dad and then drove up every weekend for many months. His house was dirty, dark, and depressing because Mother never allowed anyone in to clean or paint. Her room was filled with thick cobwebs that hung down just like in an old horror movie. The bed was backed up to the closet so that the headboard covered the doors, preventing them from being opened. Inside, the closet was filled to the ceiling with dirty clothes and every canceled check, receipt, letter, and magazine clipping she had ever possessed.

Dad asked me to sort through her things. I didn't blame him— he'd been through too much to do it himself. The sorting was far beyond what I anticipated. I found in the house and the adjacent shed nearly every dress, coat, shoe, or purse that I, my sister, and my mother had ever owned. It was like reliving my past to see it all. I knew she never threw anything away, but I had never imagined the extent of her hoarding. It was another sign of her mental sickness and fear.

Michael and I decided that it was crucial to my dad's health

that the house have a "face-lift," and the job was too monumental for any of us. So we hired people to paint it inside and out
and to install new carpets, drapes, and bedspreads. With each
step I could feel my dad's spirit lift. The unhappy memories faded,
the place felt new, and so did Dad.

Amid the cleaning I found that old green diary of mine that
I wrote in when I was 14. I had thrown it out, but Mother had
obviously found it in the trash and retrieved it. Over the next
few days I read it from cover to cover. My life back then was
far worse than I even remembered. I was shocked at my ignorance; I knew nothing of the right way to live. As I finished
reading the diary, I thanked God for the reminder of how far
He had brought me. Time and much healing had dimmed the
pain in my memory.

I gazed out the window to the yard, where Dad was pushing
little Amanda in the swing he had constructed for her in the large
willow tree. She giggled and chirped, "Higher, Gampa, higher!"

Over the past few weeks of cleaning and sorting, it was Dad
who had basically taken care of Amanda. She went with him to
feed the cows and pick the oranges, and he attended to her every
need. Their mutual love was apparent. Now that Mother was
gone, we were at liberty to visit Dad anytime, and he was free
to be himself. As he blossomed, so did our relationship. He had
always been a social individual, but a shadow of fear that he
would say something wrong in front of my mother and set her
off had shrouded his every word. Now all that was gone.

For years he had been hard-of-hearing. After Mother's death
I suddenly noticed one day that his hearing was normal. Could
it be that in order to cope with her he had stopped listening? Was
his poor hearing an act of survival? Maybe that's why he didn't
suspect she was dying. She had complained for so long that he
had partially tuned her out. I used to be impatient with Dad's
hesitant speech and poor hearing. Could it be that all these years
I blamed him for things that were just a part of his coping with
Mother? God knows we all learned to cope with her in our own
way. How cruel to blame someone for surviving the only way
he knows how!

My eyes were opened like never before, and I saw what a great man my father really was. Even though Mother had been heartlessly cruel to him, he still took good care of her until she died. Most other men would have left years ago. Once he developed a painful case of shingles and was so sick he couldn't get out of bed. Mother made a huge dinner and refused to give him anything to eat. In spite of that, he brought her every meal in bed during the three weeks before she died, and he harbored no ill feeling toward her. He never even said a critical word about her after she died. His example of forgiveness was greater than any other I had ever seen.

"You can't hold a grudge. You gotta forgive and forget," he said over and over. Mother's death brought no regret to him. He had given above and beyond the call of duty. He was clean.

As I continued watching through the window, there was fulfillment in seeing my own daughter being swept up in Grandpa's arms to go out and feed the cows. I suddenly saw myself in her, as if that was how it might have been for me years ago. My eyes filled with tears and my heart filled with gratitude to God as I thanked Him for not giving up on me until my healing was complete.

# CHAPTER SEVENTEEN

## Stormie

# COUNTING FOR SOMETHING

The last of the three sets of large steel doors slammed shut with a finality that made me shudder as I entered the women's prison in Oregon. All my earthly possessions were left outside, and I carried nothing in with me but one necessary piece of paper.

As I walked down the long, sterile corridor with the prison chaplain on one side and a female guard on the other, the heels of my shoes clicked against the hard floor and echoed throughout that wing of the prison. My hands and forehead perspired, my heart pounded, and my legs were so weak and shaky that I was concerned I might fall. The dryness of my mouth made it difficult to swallow, and waves of nausea came up into my throat. I wondered why I had made certain choices that caused me to end up in this place.

"What's going to happen to me here?" I thought. "What if the inmates hate me? I'm really afraid, God. You've got to help me through this." As I prayed, I remembered His words: "I will never leave you or forsake you." I repeated them over and over to myself, thanking Him that He always means what He says.

We entered a large room with a low ceiling and many metal folding chairs set up in a loose formation of rows, facing the front.

"This is it," said the chaplain.

"This is it?" I questioned, trying to mask my disappointment that the conditions weren't a little more inviting.

"Yes, we're very proud of the fact that we have a new tape deck in this room. You'll be able to play your background tapes on it. Do you want to use the bathroom before the inmates arrive? You have ten minutes.''

"Yes. Yes, I do," I said eagerly. Long having used the bathroom as a place of solace where I could pull myself together, I went around the corner with the guard, who unbolted the door with one of her many keys and waited for me just outside. Inside, I locked myself in one of the stalls, got down on my knees beside the toilet, and prayed, "Lord, help me. I need Your strength, Your power, and Your words. Be Lord over this prison tonight.''

When I walked back to the large room, I met the lady who had been instrumental in bringing me into the prison. It had taken her over a year to get the necessary clearance from those in authority, allowing me and several others to be there for three days to speak with the inmates.

"How do you feel?" she asked.

"In Jesus' name I feel great," I said positively. "In my flesh I feel sick," I confessed.

She laughed and agreed that this was how she felt too.

"Okay, the inmates are on their way," the chaplain informed us. "Take your seats along the side wall up front.''

We sat down and waited tensely as one-by-one the inmates filed in. They started filling in the chairs at the back of the room first, and then worked their way reluctantly toward the front. They moved as if they were not thrilled to be there.

"I didn't know they were letting the male prisoners in tonight," I gasped to myself as I observed the ones in work jeans, black leather jackets, heavy black boots, short greasy hair pulled straight back on the sides, and cigarettes hanging out of the corner of their mouths. They looked tough, hard, and angry, as if someone had given them a choice of going into this room or cleaning toilets all night.

Then I looked closer. "Those aren't men at all; they're women!" I whispered to myself in disbelief.

I had been praying all along, but now my prayer rate nearly doubled. "God, do I have to speak here? Maybe it's not too late to call this whole thing off. God, please, I don't think I can do this.''

"I am a Redeemer," I heard Him say to my heart once again. "I redeem all things. I make all things new. I can take all the hurt, the pain, and the scars, and I can not only heal them, but I can make them count for something."

"Yes, Lord, I know. I know You want me to tell them that, but I'm afraid if I open my mouth nothing will come out. Help me to speak, Lord, and make what I say come alive in their hearts. And God, forgive me for trying to find a means of escape when You've sent me with such an important message to those You love."

I glanced down at the paper in my hands that contained the notes of what I planned to say. I had copied them so neatly on the plane, but as I looked up at the prisoners staring at me suspiciously with their arms folded across their chests, I knew right then that these prisoners didn't need my notes. They needed my heart. They also needed my love, and they needed to know that God was waiting with open arms for them to turn to Him. I put my paper aside and decided that if I ever lost eye contact with them, it was all over.

The room filled with inmates at the same rate it filled with smoke. Nonsmokers were definitely a minority here. As I was being introduced, I prayed to God that I wouldn't start coughing. I also thanked God that I had chosen to wear my leather pants and boots as opposed to one of the pretty silk speaking dresses I use for churches. I needed all the credibility I could get.

Finally it was time to speak. I got up, looked each inmate directly in the eye, and in my best street language began to tell my story. I described how I was abused as a child and grew up feeling rejected and unloved. I told them of my search for acceptance and the way it led me to make wrong choices that got me into trouble. I mentioned the drugs, the abortions, the suicide attempt, and how my life finally collapsed. I described the day God met me where I was and I came to know Jesus. They listened intently as I graphically revealed the hell I'd known and contrasted it with the peace and wholeness I had found.

When I came to the end of my alloted time, I said to them, "There was a point soon after I came to know Jesus when I looked over my life and I saw it scattered into a million pieces. I grieved over that because I couldn't see how it could ever be put back together again. But God spoke to my heart and said, 'I'm a Redeemer. I redeem *all* things. It doesn't matter what you've done, it doesn't matter what's happened to you. I can take all the hurt, the pain, the scars, and I can not only heal them, but I can make them count for something.' "

Then I told them of the song I wrote that day God spoke those words to me. I closed my eyes, took a deep breath, and sang it to them in the slow, tender way I first heard it in my mind.

Pieces...pieces,
So many pieces to my life.
Scattered all around
And some of them are gone,
And I know that I can't ever
Put them back together again.

Pieces...pieces,
So many pieces to my life.
A puzzle left unfinished,
Jumbled and unformed.
Who can really ever
Fit it all together again?

In a vision like a daydream
That filters through your mind,
I saw Jesus coming closer,
Holding all my dreams combined.
He spoke with great compassion
As He put one hand on me,
And in His other hand He held
What I could never see.

He said, "Pieces...pieces,
I've got all the pieces to your life,

A thousand tiny fragments
Of every single day.
I can put them all together
So they'll never fall away.
I can put them all together
And there'll never be another one who can.
No, there'll never be another one who can.''[17]

I opened my eyes on the last note of the song to see what I'll always know was a miracle. Nearly everyone in the room was crying—even some of the guards. The tough inmates that I at first thought were men were wiping away tears from their eyes. Some had Kleenex and many buried their faces in their hands and sobbed quietly. The hardness of their expressions had melted into a gentle beauty.

For one brief moment I felt the combination of all the pain in that room, and it was unbearable. "Oh, God, there is so much hurt here," I cried along with them. "Thank You, Holy Spirit, that You have come to meet the need and help these women come to know You."

The inmates began to clap, quietly at first, and then it grew into a loud cheer as they stood and applauded. I knew they were clapping for God's presence in that room. Whether or not they understood that this is what it was, no one could deny that it was there. The ice had been broken, the walls penetrated, the defenses laid to waste. God's love had broken through.

Over the next three days, nearly half the women in attendance received Jesus, and many were healed of past hurts. Every life was touched that weekend, and many, including mine, were changed forever.

All the way home on the plane I cried and praised God that He had used me as one of His instruments. "Lord, I can't believe what You've done. You've taken my broken life, and You've not only restored it but You're using it to restore others too."

God had kept His promise: My life had meaning and purpose now. But it didn't happen overnight. In fact, it took 14 years. Yet during those years there was ongoing healing and deliverance, a layer at a time. No, it certainly didn't happen overnight, but it *did* happen. God took all my pain and scars, and He not only healed them but made them count for something. *That* is God's total restoration!

# ALL MY LIFE

STORMIE OMARTIAN                                    MICHAEL OMARTIAN

All my life,
Never knowing what I was reaching
    for.
Never could I find any reason for
Always feeling somehow there must
    be more.

Then there came a light
Searching out my heart in the
    blackest night,
Touching me with love that I
    knew was right.
Lord of all filling all my life.
All my life.

Looking back,
Jesus, through my life You were
    everywhere,
Picking up the pieces I'd scattered
    there,
Holding them for me 'til my heart could
    care.

You gave me life,
You made my spirit new,
Now I give all my life to You.

Yes, my Lord,
You were everything I was searching
    for.
You were every dream I had dreamed
    before.
Now every day of life is worth so much
    more.

You gave me life,
You made my spirit new,
Now I give all my life to You.[18]

# NOTES

1. Isaiah 47:13,14 NIV.
2. Deuteronomy 18:10-12 NIV.
3. Isaiah 40:2 NIV.
4. 2 Timothy 1:7 NKJV.
5. Luke 6:46 NKJV.
6. John 14:23 NIV.
7. 2 Timothy 2:5 NIV.
8. Deuteronomy 7:26 NIV.
9. 1 John 4:18 NIV.
10. 1 John 2:5 NIV.
11. 2 Corinthians 3:18 NKJV.
12. Psalm 84:7 NKJV.
13. "Half Past Three" Lyrics by Stormie Omartian, Music by Michael Omartian, Copyright © 1980 by See This House Music and Word Music (A Div. of WORD, INC.). All Rights Reserved. International Copyright Secured. Used by Permission.
14. Psalm 3:8 NIV.
15. 2 Corinthians 3:17 NIV.
16. Psalm 72:12 NIV.
17. "Pieces" Lyrics by Stormie Omartian, Music by Michael Omartian, Copyright © 1980 by See This House Music and Word Music (A Div. of WORD, INC.). All Rights Reserved. International Copyright Secured. Used by Permission.
18. "All My Life" Lyrics by Stormie Omartian, Music by Michael Omartian, Copyright © 1980 by See This House Music (A Div. of WORD, INC.). All Rights Reserved. International Copyright Secured. Used by Permission.

# Just Enough LIGHT for the Step I'm On

## Stormie OMARTIAN

HARVEST HOUSE PUBLISHERS

EUGENE, OREGON

**JUST ENOUGH LIGHT FOR THE STEP I'M ON**

Copyright © 1999 by Stormie Omartian
Published by Harvest House Publishers
Eugene, Oregon 97402

2 in 1  ISBN 0-7394-5141-3

**Printed in the United States of America.**

# Acknowledgments

With special thanks:

- to my husband, Michael, for believing so strongly in me and in this book.

- to my children, Mandy, Chris, and John, for your love and support.

- to my prayer partners and dear friends, Susan Martinez, Katie Stewart, Donna Summer Sudano, Roz Thompson, and Jan Williamson, for your prayers and encouragement.

- to my wonderful secretary, sister, and friend, Susan Martinez, for blessing my life in so many ways.

- to Bob Hawkins, Jr., Carolyn McCready, Bill Jensen, Julie McKinney, Teresa Evenson, Ruth Samsel, Barb Sherrill, Janna Walkup, and Betty Fletcher for catching the vision for this book and making it all happen. You are the best!

- to Patrick Raffy Frantz for your inspiring photographs, my favorite of which appears in the beginning of this book.

# Contents

# Introduction

More and more, God is teaching me to trust Him for every step I take. He constantly calls me to stretch beyond what's comfortable. To walk through new territory when I would rather stay with the familiar. To face difficult physical, mental, and emotional challenges. To do things I know I can't achieve by myself without His power. Each time something is required of me that I'm certain I am unable to accomplish in my own strength, I see a picture of just one or two steps being illuminated, while those before and after are engulfed in darkness and cannot be seen. This describes my walk with God. I trust Him for each day of life, grateful for every breath, determined to look for the blessing in the moment, no matter what the circumstances. I follow His lead—even when I can't see where I'm going, even when it scares me to do so—because deep within my spirit I know that these simple steps of faith are preparing me for eternity.

—Stormie Omartian

... come and let us walk in
the light of the LORD.

*Isaiah 2:5*

# Just Enough Light

Sometimes only the step I'm on,
   or the very next one ahead,
      is all that is illuminated for me.
God gives just the amount of light I need
   for the exact moment I need it.
At those times I walk in surrender to faith,
   unable to see the future
   and not fully comprehending the past.
And because it is God who has given me
   what light I have,
      I know I must reject the fear and
      doubt that threaten to overtake me.
I must determine to be content where
   I am, and allow God to get me where I
   need to go.
I walk forward,
     one step at a time,
        fully trusting that
          the light God sheds
            is absolutely sufficient.

Life is a walk.
Each day we take
steps. Our tomorrow
is determined by
the steps we
take today.

# ONE

# Learning to Walk

Life is a walk. Each day we take steps. Our tomorrow is determined by the steps we take today.

When both of my children learned to walk, they didn't get very far without falling. They fared much better if they reached up and took my hand. Or their father's hand. We were able to guide them away from danger and get them safely where they needed to go. But sometimes they quickly headed off without our help. My son would end up falling down and hurting himself, or my daughter would wander off to someplace she wasn't supposed to go and get into trouble. Occasionally we *allowed* those things to happen because we wanted them to eventually learn to walk *without* our assistance. Of course, we did step in and protect them when we saw danger. But our goal was always to prepare them for the day when they would no longer need our help. And we were thrilled when we saw them experience that joy of freedom for the first time.

Learning to walk with our Heavenly Father is somewhat different. He wants us to reach up and take His hand, but He doesn't want us to *ever* let go. In fact, His desire is that we become *more* and *more* dependent upon Him for every step. That's because He wants to take us to places we've never been. To heights we can't even imagine. In order to do that, we have to go through the low valleys, treacherous mountains, rough terrain, and narrow paths of life—places where we could easily get lost or off the track. And there is definitely no way we can just head off on our own and expect to arrive safely in the place He has planned for us. And, quite opposite of the way we teach our children, we will *never* know the joy of *true* freedom until we understand we cannot take a single step without His help.

But it's up to us to take the first step. If we don't, we will never learn to walk with Him. We can be so afraid of taking a wrong step that we fail to take any step at all. God didn't part the waters of the Jordan River for the Israelites until they first put their feet in the water (Joshua 3:15-16). That's because God always requires the first step to be ours. In order to take that first step, we must look into the face of God, reach up to take His hand, and say, "Lead me in the path You have for me, Lord. From this day on I want to walk with You. I take this step of faith and I trust You to meet me here. Align my heart with Yours."

Once you've taken *that* first step, God will show you other steps to take. He will teach you how to walk in the light of His truth, revelation, and love. You'll discover ways to avoid the things that separate you from Him and all He has for you. You'll learn to walk away from fear, depression, condemnation, loneliness, loss, unforgiveness, and disappointment. You'll understand what it means to walk through the dark times of your life with the comfort of His presence as your only light.

I know what it's like to walk without His light. In my teens and twenties, I wandered around in a confusion of drugs, alcohol, occult practices, eastern religions, and unhealthy relationships, trying to find an escape from the emotional pain I endured daily. I was desperately struggling to live, but was moving closer to death with every decision I made and step I took. I experienced it all, but nothing worked and I became desperate. As I carefully planned my suicide, I knew I didn't really want to die. But I couldn't live with the pain anymore, and I had no other way to stop it.

When a close friend saw my hopelessness and took me to meet her pastor, I found what I had been searching for all along. Pastor Jack Hayford showed me that I had been crying out for love, acceptance, purpose, fulfillment, peace, and joy, and that these things could only be found in one place. When I prayed, "Jesus, come into my heart. Forgive me for not living Your way and lead me on the path You have for me," I knew I had found that place. It was at His feet. I felt hope for the very first time. It was the initial and pivotal step on a journey that would transform my life.

*No matter how far away from God you've gone, when you surrender your life to the Lord, a path is carved from where you are to where you are supposed to be, and He puts you on it.*

This is the miracle of His power. If the path you've been on is crooked, He will make it straight. If you are headed in the wrong direction, He will turn you around. If you have come to a standstill, He will get you moving. If you are going around in circles, He will correct your course and cause you to arrive at your destination. The simple act of giving your

Love, acceptance, purpose, fulfillment, peace, and joy, can be found in only one place.

life to Him will immediately put you on the correct path and aim you in the right direction.

*As you take one step at a time, holding God's hand and letting Him lead, He will get you where you need to go.*

The moment I made that decision, I felt a major course-correction happen. I didn't know where I was headed, but I saw a light at the end of the long, dark tunnel of my life and I started going toward it, away from the life I had known. Away from the ungodly friends, the destructive habits, the self-promotion. Away from hopelessness, depression, and futility. The road was not smooth and I fell a number of times, not because God let go of me, but because I let go of Him. But every time I reached out for His hand, He was always there to help me get back up and on the path again.

I have now been walking with the Lord for nearly thirty years. When I look back, I see that I was a different person then and living a whole other life. I know that I would never want to return to the way things were. Yet I occasionally find myself reverting to the old habit of trying to do things my own way. I sometimes forget that I need to depend on Him for every step.

Pastor Jack told me a story of a man who prayed, "Lord, I haven't done anything wrong today. I have not made any mistakes, spoken any wrong words, or thought any bad thoughts. I've done everything right so far. But I'm really going to be depending on You now, Lord, because I'm about to get out of bed."

Haven't we all felt like that sometimes? But that's the way God wants us to feel. He doesn't want us to just depend on Him as a last resort when we have a medical emergency or a financial crisis. He wants us to depend on Him for every breath we take. And, quite opposite of the way it may seem, that kind of dependent life is not stifling. It's liberating!

Learning to walk with God is a process. And just when we think we have it all figured out, God leads us into a new place where our old tricks won't work. In fact, it may seem like we're learning how to walk all over again. And in a way we are. We enter unfamiliar territory and are soon reminded that, on our own, we stumble. Yet when we take His hand, we fly. God wants us to soar far above the limitations of our lives and ourselves. He wants to take us to a place we have never been before and can't get to from where we are without His help.

When God used Moses to lead the Israelites out of Egypt, they had to learn to depend on the Lord for every step of their journey to the Promised Land. When they did not do that, they got into trouble. It's the same for us today. God moves us out on a path to someplace we've never been before, and we believe we're failing if we have to depend on Him to get there. We try to make it on our own because we think that dependency is a sign of weakness, instead of understanding that it signals our willingness to allow God to be strong in us.

If you are at a place in your life where you feel like you can't take one step without the Lord's help, be glad. He has you where He wants you. If you're wondering, "Have I done something wrong?" the answer is most likely, "No, you've done something right." God has you on this path, no matter how difficult and impossible it may seem right now, because you are willing to follow Him. He wants to accomplish great things through you that can only come out of a life of faith. He wants your undivided attention because you can't do these

*God moves us out on a path to someplace we've never been before, and we believe we're failing if we have to depend on Him to get there.*

things on your own. The path is not a punishment; it's a privilege. It's not a restriction; it's a reward.

*God loves us so much that He allows us to get into difficult places in our lives so we will realize how dependent upon Him we must be.*

If you have been walking with God for some time and you suddenly feel like your life has come to a halt, don't be alarmed. Most likely, God is adjusting your way. Having God correct your course doesn't necessarily mean the one you were on was incorrect. But it does mean that something needs to change to get you headed in the direction God wants to take you. And it doesn't matter how young or old you are. As long as you are breathing, God will have new paths for you to take and exciting things for you to do. It's best to trust His leading and get on with it. This is what a walk of faith is all about.

Abraham was walking by faith when God led him out of all that was familiar to him to a place he had never been. He knew God had called him from where he was, but he didn't know where God was leading. And Abraham's is one of the greatest stories in the Bible in regard to walking in faith: ". . . he went out, not knowing where he was going" (Hebrews 11:8).

How often have we felt like that? We go out because God is leading us, but we don't really know where we're headed.

Pastor Jack Hayford says, "It's a more certain proposition to follow the Lord, not knowing where you're going, than to think you know where you're going and you're not following the Lord."[1]

How true!

You might want to read the above quote several more times. It will be a great comfort to you on those days when you wonder if you're actually going *anywhere*. Don't worry,

## *Footlights*

O LORD, I know the way of man
is not in himself; it is not in man who
walks to direct his own steps.

JEREMIAH 10:23

You will show me the path of life;
In Your presence is fullness of joy;
At Your right hand are pleasures forevermore.

PSALM 16:11

A man's heart plans his way,
But the LORD directs his steps.

PROVERBS 16:9

The steps of a good man are
ordered by the LORD,
And He delights in his way.

PSALM 37:23

Come, and let us go up to the mountain of the LORD,
To the house of the God of Jacob;
He will teach us His ways,
And we shall walk in His paths.

MICAH 4:2

# TWO

# Beginning to See the Light

Our lives are touched by many different kinds of light.

Sunlight and moonlight. Stoplights and spotlights. Firelight, city lights, candlelight, and lamplight. Headlights, night-lights, neon lights, and streetlights. Glittering and blinding lights. Confusing and deceiving lights.

All of these lights have one thing in common. They eventually go out. They're not reliable. They can never be the light we need to illuminate the path of our life. There is only one light that never goes out. It comes from God.

It *is* God.

God's light is the true light. His light makes clear. All other light confuses. His light *reveals* the truth. All other light obscures it. His light brings us out of our blindness, and helps us see in a way we've never been able to see before. He says, "I will bring the blind by a way they did not know; I will lead them in paths they have not known. I will make darkness light before them, and crooked places straight. These things I will do for them, and not forsake them" (Isaiah 42:16). God's light penetrates darkness, and darkness cannot put it out.

*Unless we follow the true light, we are being led into darkness.*

In the years before I had a personal relationship with God, I walked in a thick darkness of depression, fear, anxiety, and despair. Everything I experimented with was a desperate search for something to light up my life. But I never found anything lasting. When I received the Lord I was not suddenly flooded with light, as some people have described it. The light I saw was a glimmer of hope. I compare it to sleeping in a dark room with a pinhole of light entering through the curtain and shining brightly in your eyes. It's a small light, but noticeably bright enough to awaken you if you've grown accustomed to the blackness of the room. The light of the Lord was that unmistakable to me because of the contrasting darkness of my life. Any more light would have been blinding. But because of my own bondage, the light was dim at the beginning of my walk compared to what was to come.

From that day on, I walked toward the light. There were times when I took a wrong turn and fell into sudden darkness, but I found it so shocking and repulsive that I quickly got back on track. The more I walked in the light of the Lord, the brighter it became until it lit up every part of my being.

I have heard people talk about near-death experiences where they saw a bright light. I don't doubt that they saw it. But I know that when we who believe in the Lord die, we won't see *a* light. We will see *the* light. We will see Jesus who is the light of the world. The best way to make sure we see His light after we die is to follow His light as long as we're alive.

*We begin to see the light when we begin to see the Lord.*

The way to keep from following the wrong light is to not follow any light except for the light of Jesus. The world wants us to follow *its* light. The devil wants us to follow *his* light. "For Satan himself transforms himself into an angel of light" (2 Corinthians 11:14). We will encounter people who fancy themselves to be our savior and will want us to follow *their* light. But God does not have us follow a light. He has us follow *Him*. And He becomes our light. The more faithfully we follow Him, the more of His light we will have shining on our path. "In Him was life, and the life was the light of men" (John 1:4).

God's light is constant because *He* is constant. He is without change. His light doesn't grow dim or go out. If it appears to, it's because we have stepped out of the light of His presence. Although God is omnipresent, we must remember that there are degrees of the fullness of His presence we can enjoy and experience. He gives us as much of His presence as we are able to receive. Although His light never goes out, we sometimes do things that separate us from the fullness of His life and cause His light to appear dim in our lives.

King David was a man who went through some very dark times. Some of them were his fault (his immoral relationship with Bathsheba), and some of them weren't (his volatile relationship with the jealous King Saul). In either case, David always knew that the light on his path came from God. He was still God's anointed no matter how dark it got. Even when he made bad choices, he had a heart for the Lord. And God never allowed him to be destroyed.

It's the same with those of us who love God. His light is always

ᗕ

*G*od does not have us follow a light. He has us follow *Him*. And *He* becomes our light.

ᗕ

available to us. No matter how badly we think we've blown it in our lives, we are never truly in darkness when we look to Him.

Our problem is that when we enter into a dark time, we don't always realize that we have a light within us which never goes out. Jesus said, "I am the light of the world. He who follows Me shall not walk in darkness, but have the light of life" (John 8:12). If we don't understand what that verse means, we can get confused and begin to doubt. We see darkness and run after a light that is unreliable, instead of opening our eyes to follow the true light that cannot be extinguished.

During my first year as a new believer, every time anything went wrong I thought God had abandoned me. I felt like I was moving backward. I didn't realize that the layers of darkness I had lived a lifetime with needed to be stripped away so I could be free of them. In order to do that, I should have turned to God each time they surfaced. Instead, when the darkness of depression descended upon me as it had so many times in the past, I thought God was not there for me and so I sought out the old familiar comforts of ungodly relationships and alcohol. I became sidetracked and wasted precious time. None of this would have happened if I had made a strong effort to walk in the light every day, no matter what was going on in my life.

> ∾
>
> *N*o matter how badly we think we've blown it in our lives, we are never truly in darkness when we look to Him.
>
> ∾

I have electricity in my home, but if I don't plug into it, I don't see the light. I have Jesus in my heart, but if I don't plug into Him daily, I won't see His light either, even though it is there. I have to connect with Him. Talk to Him. Worship Him. Spend time with Him. Bask in His radiance like bathing in the sun. Become so familiar with *His* illumination of my soul that I immediately recognize any counterfeit.

I remember a conversation I had with a man who works as a night watchman. He described how he always looked intensely for the first sign of morning light, because that meant he and the property he had been guarding were out of danger and he could be relieved from the burden. God wants us to look for *His* light in our lives even "more than those who watch for the morning" (Psalm 130:6). That means we don't rest until we know we see it.

Whenever we go through difficult times, we anticipate the coming moment when all the pressure is off, the worry has subsided, the healing has manifested, the sadness has lifted, and the pain is gone. We continuously look for God to take away the discomfort we are experiencing. But God wants us to know that even as we wait for those changes to happen, His light is there *all* the time shining into our darkness. He wants us to trust that, and open our eyes to see it.

No matter how dark things seem in your life, when you walk with God you will find an abundance of His light right where you are. You will never be without it because you have the source of true and everlasting light within you. "The city had no need of the sun or of the moon to shine in it, for the glory of God illuminated it. The Lamb is its light" (Revelation 21:23). When God is your light, you have no need of any other.

So don't worry about seeing or understanding what the future holds. God wants you to trust Him as He leads you, even though you can't see clearly ahead. And don't be overly concerned about fully comprehending the past. Only He knows the whole truth about it, anyway. You have *Him* now. *He* is your light. And that's all that matters.

## *Prayer Light*

L ord, You are the light of my life. You illuminate my path, and I will follow wherever You lead. Shield me from being lured by the light of the world. Keep me from being deceived by the light of evil. Protect me from being blinded by the light that confuses. Help me to always identify the counterfeit. I depend on You to lift up the light of Your countenance upon me (Psalm 4:6). Thank You, Lord, that because You never change, Your light is constant in my life no matter what is going on around me. Shine Your light through me as I walk with my hand in Yours. I give this day to You and trust that the light You give me is just the amount I need for the step I'm on.

## *Footlights*

This is the message which we have heard
from Him and declare to you, that
God is light and in Him is
no darkness at all.

If we say that we have fellowship
with Him, and walk in darkness,
we lie and do not practice the truth.

But if we walk in the light as He is in the
light, we have fellowship with one another,
and the blood of Jesus Christ His Son
cleanses us from all sin.

1 JOHN 1:5-7

That was the true Light which gives light to
every man coming into the world.

JOHN 1:9

While you have the light, believe in the light,
that you may become sons of light.

JOHN 12:36

The path of the just is like the shining sun,
That shines ever brighter unto the perfect day.

PROVERBS 4:18

God is the LORD,
And He has given us light . . .

PSALM 118:27

# THREE

# Refusing to Be Afraid of the Dark

Darkness is the absence of light. Everything is dark until light is brought into it. If we don't have the true light, we live in darkness. If we have the light in us that cannot be extinguished, then we can never be in total darkness.

There are different kinds of darkness, however, and we need to be able to discern one from the other. There is spiritual darkness that happens when we refuse to let God enter into our lives. There is the darkness of negative emotions like ignorance, pride, jealousy, anger, or hatred. There is the darkness we experience when we make selfish demands that satisfy our flesh at the expense of others. There is the darkness of living in disobedience to God's ways.

All of these kinds of darkness come about because of our own choices. "Those who sat in darkness and in the shadow of death, bound in affliction and irons—because they rebelled against the words of God, and despised the counsel of the Most High . . ." (Psalm 107:10-11).

Yet as damaging as our mistakes can be, God gives us a way out of the darkness we get ourselves into. "Then they cried out to the LORD in their trouble, and He saved them out of their distresses. He brought them out of darkness and the shadow of death, and broke their chains in pieces" (Psalm 107:13-14). When we return to Him, He restores us to the full light. Even if we foolishly create our own darkness, as long as we have a personal relationship with the Lord, His light *in* us cannot be put out.

When I gave birth to my first baby, the doctor told me, "You have a boy." I didn't forget that information and have to keep asking him over and over "What was my baby?" I did not wake up in the hospital the next morning and say to the nurse, "Tell me again what I had." I didn't call my best friend the following week and wonder, "Do you happen to remember whether I gave birth to a boy or girl?" The minute I heard I had a son, no one had to tell me again. From that moment, I knew. An entire vision for my child's future was in place the second I was told the truth.

This experience is the same for every mother and every father. Or anyone who receives lifechanging good news.

God wants you to have that same certainty about Him.

*God wants you to be so convinced of His presence in your life that even when you can't feel it, sense it, or see it, you know He is there.*

He wants you to be so convinced of His presence in your life that even when you can't feel it, sense it, or see it, you know He is there. He wants you to be completely sure that the light of His Spirit *in* you will never be put out. You don't have to keep looking for it. You don't have to doubt it. No circumstance can dim it. It is there for now and all eternity.

One of the ways God makes us certain of His light is by allowing us to test it in the darkness. But this darkness is not to be dreaded. It is the darkness God has created for His purposes. "I form the light and create darkness . . ." (Isaiah 45:7). God sometimes allows things to get very dark in our lives in order to grow us up and teach us about Himself. And some things that we accomplish in darkness cannot happen in any other setting.

Think about what it's like when the power goes out in your home at night. You can barely function in the dark. You walk carefully, one step at a time, reaching out for familiar things to steady and guide you until you can find a flashlight, candle, or generator switch. If someone is holding a source of light, you reach out and take their hand so you can move together. You don't take a step until you're certain that both of you are going in the same direction.

That's exactly how God uses darkness in our lives. We're in the dark until we see *His* light in it. He wants us to reach out for *Him* so we can walk together in the same direction. He desires that we draw close so that we sense His presence at all times.

This is not like the darkness of evil, which you can clearly sense. Or the darkness of our own disobedience, which we know in our hearts. This is a different kind of darkness, and God says there are treasures to be found there. "I will give you the treasures of darkness and hidden riches of secret places, that you may know that I, the LORD, who calls you by your name, am the God of Israel" (Isaiah 45:3).

*The treasure we find in the darkness is Him.*

I have gone through dark times with my children, my marriage, my health, my work, and my relationships, and for many years I didn't realize that God was using these situations to increase my knowledge of Him. Now that I look back, I realize these were the very times that I had the greatest sense of His presence in my life. The more serious the difficulty, the more fervently I reached out to Him. As a result, my perception of who God is grew deeper and deeper. I discovered the amazing largeness of His love and grace toward those who walk closely with Him. Some things we only learn in the dark.

I'm not saying that God causes bad things to happen in our lives. He doesn't. We live in a fallen world and bad things happen. But God works in the midst of even the deepest darkness. His presence and His light are there for those who open their eyes to see it, and He brings good out of every situation.

If God desires to teach us things about Himself that we will only learn in the dark—when we are walking closely with Him and He has our undivided attention—then we will be the losers if we resist Him or our circumstances during this time. He wants to share His secrets with us. "He reveals deep and secret things; He knows what is in the darkness, and light dwells with Him" (Daniel 2:22). The biggest mistake we can make during this dark time is to be angry with God because we are in it. "'Woe to him who strives with his Maker!'" (Isaiah 45:9).

When I was pregnant with my second child, I was extremely sick. Month after month I went in and out of the hospital, so ill with nausea and pain that I could barely function. I felt like I was dying and truly didn't know if I could carry my child to full term. During this very dark time, I couldn't understand why God didn't heal me or at least give me some sign of relief. Anyone who has walked through the dark night of physical suffering knows what I am talking about.

One morning in the midst of deep despair, I bitterly asked God what I had done to deserve this agony. At nearly that same moment I received a call from Pastor Jack wanting to know if my husband and I would become leaders in a new area of ministry at our church. It was a position that required great trust and—in view of my recent attitude of striving with my maker—I felt especially unworthy. When I hung up the telephone, I was deeply repentant.

My experience taught me that even in the darkest times, we should never doubt God. Even when it may *appear* like our life is over and He has forgotten us, He is actually growing us into our future.

*Sometimes what seems like the darkest step we've ever been on comes just before the brightest light we've ever experienced.*

That's why we can't be angry about being in the dark. People who doubt God in the midst of darkness and blame Him for their discomfort don't really know Him. If they really knew Him, they would never feel that way.

Obviously I didn't know Him as well as I thought I did. But I came to know Him in a much deeper way through that experience. Eventually I was healed of my sickness, I gave birth to a healthy baby girl, doors of opportunity opened for my writing, and our family was blessed in countless ways. I am embarrassed to think that I had doubted God's goodness. In the darkness of the situation I had given up hope, and here He was about to do something great. I had doubted His light was there for me, but it had never changed because *He* will never change.

Often when we find ourselves in the midst of a dark situation, we immediately believe we must be out of the will of God. That might be true, but if we've been living in obedience to the Lord to the best of our ability, we are more likely right in the *center* of God's will. In fact, God's will can lead us into some very dark circumstances. Oswald Chambers

> ∾
>
> *O*ften when we find ourselves in the midst of a dark situation, we immediately believe we must be out of the will of God.
>
> ∾

said, "Let it be understood that the darkness our Lord speaks of is not darkness caused by sin or disobedience, but rather darkness caused by excess light. . . . Such times of darkness come as a discipline to the character and as the means of fuller knowledge of the Lord." [1]

When we find ourself in the dark, we must *stop* what we're doing, *look* for His light, and *listen* for His voice. If He is directing us, yet we ignore it, fail to see it, refuse to do it, run from it, don't comprehend it, or deliberately disobey it, we will be miserably lost. We have to be still and know that He is God. We have to reach out to Him and He will give us a sense that He is there.

When my son was a small child, every evening I read a bedtime story to him, put him in his crib, and turned out the light. Then sometimes I would lie down on the floor beside his bed with a pillow under my head. It had a calming effect on both of us. We would occasionally sing little songs, but usually we simply lay quietly there together. Whenever I reached up my hand in the dark, his tiny hand always found mine and held on. It was one of those precious moments you like to remember when your children become teenagers.

I think it is even more precious to our Heavenly Father when we reach out in the dark and find *His* hand waiting for us. So many times I felt alone and afraid in the darkness of my circumstances, yet when I reached out to God I always found His presence there, calming, reassuring, protecting, and loving me. I know to expect it now. I am certain that even in my darkest times, when I can't see anything, God is there and will not forsake me. He wants us to trust Him so completely that He can take us on a journey where *His* light is our *only* light. Then when we take His hand, He can lead us anywhere.

The unknown can be frightening, but when we immerse ourselves in the presence of the Lord, we can know *Him* in it. His love takes away our fear. When we take a step, His light is with us. When we take the next step, His light is with us still. Sometimes we stumble around faithlessly in the dark and don't even recognize His light when we have it. I did that when I questioned God during my difficult pregnancy. I was walking in the light and thought I was in the dark. In the dark season of my own soul, I failed to see that His light had never left me. "The light shines in the darkness, and the darkness did not comprehend it" (John 1:5).

*When we walk with the Lord, the dark is actually a place we can never fully be.*

The unknown is not so frightening when we realize that our all-knowing God is in it. We know *Him.* And once we experience His light in the midst of darkness, our darkness will never be the same.

If you feel like you're in a dark place in your circumstances right now, know that God has not abandoned you. You are not wandering aimlessly. He sees the path you are on. "For the ways of man are before the eyes of the LORD, and He ponders all his paths" (Proverbs 5:21). He is there with you in great power and wants you to realize how much He loves you. If you're in darkness as a result of your own choices, confess that to Him and He will lead you out of it. If it is a darkness He has created to grow your faith, be joyful. There are awesome treasures of His presence ahead for you.

Don't be afraid of the dark. Instead of seeing the darkness as frightening, view it as a precious and wonderful place to be. When everything around you gets darker, the light inside you will grow brighter. God will speak to you and give you illumination right where you are. He wants you to reach up, take His hand, and walk every step with Him. He wants you to rest in the knowledge that the light He gives you, His light that is in you, is enough light to keep you securely on the path.

*Prayer Light*

ord, thank You that because I walk with You I don't have to fear the dark. Even in the blackest night, You are there. In the darkest times, You have treasures for me. No matter what I am going through, Your presence and grace are my comfort and my light. Your Word says, ". . . if one walks in the night, he stumbles, because the light is not in him" (John 11:9-10). But I know Your light *is* in me. Jesus, You have come as a light into the world so that whoever believes in You should not abide in darkness (John 12:46). I believe in You and know that You have lifted me out of the darkness of hopelessness, futility, and fear. I refuse to be afraid. I confess any time I have chosen to walk in the darkness of doubt, disobedience, or blaming You for my circumstances. Forgive me. I give my hand to You, Lord. Take hold of it and lead me. Thank You that as I take each step, the light You give me will be all I need.

# Footlights

Who walks in darkness and has no light?
Let him trust in the name of the LORD
And rely upon his God.

ISAIAH 50:10

They need no lamp nor light of the sun,
for the Lord God gives them light.

REVELATION 22:5

Even the night shall be light about me;
Indeed, the darkness shall not hide from You,
But the night shines as the day; The darkness and
the light are both alike to You.

PSALM 139:11-12

For You will light my lamp;
The LORD my God will enlighten my darkness.

PSALM 18:28

The people who sat in darkness have seen a
great light, and upon those who sat in the
region and shadow of death
light has dawned.

MATTHEW 4:16

# FOUR

# Embracing the Moment

None of us like pain, uncertainty, strife, or frustration. We want things to run along smoothly. But the challenging and miserable times are not without their aspect of good. Things happen to us during those times that are as precious as diamonds. For it is then that we have the opportunity to experience the Lord's presence in a deeper way. If we embrace the moment, we see Him in it.

The first winter after my family and I moved to Tennessee from sunny Southern California, we found ourselves in the middle of an ice storm. Living in California, I didn't really know what an ice storm was, and I was later told this one was the worst Tennessee had seen in a hundred years. The temperature was well below zero and *everything* was covered with ice—every tree limb, every house, every bit of ground including our driveway and all the streets beyond. Everything! It looked like a sparkling fairyland. It felt like Siberia.

The weight of the ice on the trees caused big branches to break off and land on the power lines, knocking electricity out all over the city. We had no lights, no heat, and no phone. Coming from California, where anything below fifty degrees is considered life threatening, I seriously thought we might die there with the temperature well below zero.

We couldn't go anywhere, so we built a fire in the fireplace, huddled around it, and waited for the power and the telephone to come back on. They didn't that day. Nor the next. Or the next. And in that coldness, the fireplace didn't offer enough heat for us to move more than a few feet away from it without becoming painfully cold. On that first night, I stirred hot soup in a big pot that sat right on the fire and prayed, "Lord, help us. We need to know You're here."

I immediately sensed that instead of despairing over the misery of the situation, I was to embrace the experience and find His goodness in it. As I did, the results surprised me. I thanked God that He had kept us together as a family, instead of having someone stranded elsewhere and not knowing if they were safe. I was grateful that He had prepared us with a good supply of food and bottled water. I appreciated our fireplace and warm clothes that kept us from freezing. Though I might *feel* like a Siberian prisoner, I knew that I wasn't one. And I thought of the many people who experience this kind of existence as a way of life, only without the house, the food, the warm clothes, and the family. But most of all, I sensed God's presence there with us, and I praised Him for that. Our bodies were cold, but our hearts were warmed by the light He gave our souls.

Walking step by step with God requires embracing the moment for all it's worth. When you are tempted to become fearful, frustrated, uncertain, or panicked about what is happening in your life, stop and see that God is in it. And with Him, you have everything you need for this moment. Here and now.

It's amazing that when we open our eyes to the whole picture, we have a different perspective. The Bible says, "Open your eyes, and you will be satisfied with bread" (Proverbs 20:13). When we embrace Him, we see the blessings that are right in front of us. We can be content right where we are no matter what state we are in—literally or figuratively—because *He* is there (see Philippians 4:11).

Regardless of what your situation is at this moment, God has an abundance of blessings for you. Right where you are, God is working powerfully in your life. He wants you to close your eyes, call out His name, and say, "Lord, show me Your hand in my life." He wants you to sense His presence. He wants you to trust that when you are afraid, you can turn to Him and find His peace. When you are weary, you will find His strength. When you are empty, you will find His fullness. When you are sad, you will find His joy. And when you are in the middle of a raging storm, you will find His shelter and provision. But so often we become blinded by our circumstances, afraid of what's happening, easily discouraged, drawn toward bitterness, or quick to complain. And our first instinct is not to look for God in the midst of our circumstances.

*"Why can't I have all the light I need right now, Lord?"* we cry.

However, God knows that too much light can be hard to take. It can blind and confuse us. He prefers to give us just enough to keep us dependent on Him. In that way, He can teach us to take bigger steps of faith in order to prepare for what He is calling us to in the future.

When we have a deep and personal relationship with the Lord, our

*Regardless of what your situation is at this moment, God has an abundance of blessings for you.*

difficult times are not the same as they are for people who don't have Him. For unbelievers, their dark and troubled times are without hope. Even for believers who don't understand all that God has for them, their difficult experiences are filled with fear and doubt instead of a sense of God's sustaining presence.

My friend Bill thought he knew the Lord well, but he actually had only a passing acquaintance with Him. Every Sunday morning he needed to get reacquainted with God because he had neglected to nurture that relationship on a daily basis. He didn't realize it was the most significant and life-transforming relationship he would ever have, so it didn't have a priority in his life. As a result, when he went through difficult times, his inability to hear God's voice and see His hand in the situation left him feeling powerless and defeated.

What would a marriage relationship be like if the husband and wife only saw each other for an hour each week? It would be shallow and inferior. It would be hopeless. It would probably not last. But many people have a similar relationship with God because they don't spend quality time with Him. They don't bring Him into their daily life and experiences. They don't look for Him in the midst of their difficulty and need.

I remember one particular time of great need in my life when I felt deeply lonely. It was the kind of loneliness that is so severe it brings physical pain as well as emotional agony. Because my lonely childhood had turned into a lonely adulthood, I always feared that loneliness would become a way of life for me. Even after I became a believer and experienced healing for the layers of emotional pain I had, it never occurred to me to ask God to heal my aloneness. Actually, I thought it could only be taken away by the right person. One night, however, I was so overwhelmed that I turned to God. I lifted my arms and cried, "Lord, why must I always be lonely? What can I do to get rid of this pain? You have promised to supply all my needs, and I need You to take this loneliness away."

The moment I prayed, I felt the arms of God surround me in an unmistakable way. I know that may sound strange. It would have sounded strange to me, too, had I not experienced it. But even more amazing is the fact that I have never felt loneliness like that since, even though I have been every bit as alone at times.

I now see any sign of loneliness as a call from God beckoning me to spend time with Him. I know He is not *causing* my loneliness. Nor is He *ignoring* it. He *sees* it and wants to fill the empty places of my heart with His love. As I embrace Him in the moment, He is always there.

*When you take the first step to embrace God in your circumstances, He will go the distance to embrace you.*

No matter what is going on in your life, embrace the moment. Instead of becoming upset when things go wrong or something doesn't happen the way you planned, look for God in the situation. You'll see He hasn't forsaken you. You'll understand that you won't be suffering forever. When you embrace the heart of God in the nitty-gritty details of your life, you will find a oneness with Him you never dreamed possible. And you'll sense that He is in control and will not let you get off course. Whenever you feel angry, sad, depressed, or fearful, say, "God, reveal Yourself to me in this moment. What are You doing in my life that I am not seeing? If all things work together for good, then show me the good." When you're determined to see the good, you will find it.

> ⏶
>
> *W*hen you embrace the heart of God in the nitty-gritty details of your life, you will find a oneness with Him you never dreamed possible.
>
> ⏶

If God knows your thoughts (Psalm 94:11), your heart (1 Samuel 16:7), when you stand up and sit down (Psalm 139:2), and how many hairs you have on your head (Matthew 10:30), then He knows where you are at any given moment. He sees your circumstances. Just because *you* can't see anything ahead doesn't mean *He* can't. He *can* and *does*. He knows where you've been. He knows where you're headed. He knows where you are supposed to be going. And He knows how to get you there. If you have light for just the moment in which you find yourself, it is enough. It *must* be enough. For you have Him, and He is all you need.

## Prayer Light

Lord, You are everything to me. Thank You that I can walk each moment with You and not have to figure life out on my own. And when I come to a dark time, I can put my hand in Yours and depend on You as we walk through it together. I know that "the upright shall dwell in Your presence" (Psalm 140:13), and that's where I want to live. For in Your presence I will find healing, deliverance, love, peace, joy, and hope. Lord, help me to embrace the moments of my life that are hard to get my arms around. Enable my eyes to see You in them. Help me to always acknowledge the abundance of Your goodness to me. I lift to You the deepest struggles in my life. I trust You to open my eyes to see all You have for me in them. Reveal to me the fullness of it all. Thank You that I can be filled with the joy of Your presence in every step I take, because You have given me the light I need for whatever step I am on.

*Footlights*

For our light affliction, which is but for a moment,
is working for us a far more exceeding and
eternal weight of glory, while we do not look
at the things which are seen, but at the things
which are not seen. For the things which are
seen are temporary, but the things which
are not seen are eternal.

2 CORINTHIANS 4:17-18

In the day when I cried out, You
answered me, and made me bold
with strength in my soul.

PSALM 138:3

You know my sitting down and my rising up;
You understand my thought afar off.
You comprehend my path and my lying
down, and are acquainted
with all my ways.

PSALM 139:2-3

Though I walk in the midst of trouble,
You will revive me; You will stretch
out Your hand against the wrath
of my enemies, and Your right
hand will save me.

PSALM 138:7

# FIVE

# Dancing in the Footlights

We would never dream of hiking up a treacherous mountain path in the dark, with deep cliffs on one side that drop straight down for hundreds of feet and dangerous scorpions, snakes, wild animals, and patches of quicksand on the other. Why then would we even consider going through life that way?

Walking through each day without a clear guide, an accurate map, and a consistent light source is hazardous to your well-being. Fortunately, God's Word provides us with the tools and help that we need.

*Unless the light of God's Word is shining on your steps, you are walking in dangerous territory.*

After I came to know the Lord, I experienced times when it seemed like everything in my life was falling apart and I was walking blindly in darkness and confusion. But after only a few minutes of reading God's Word, clarity came to my mind. Confusion disappeared like fog in the presence of the sun. I gained a new perspective. Fear and anxiety left and peace took their place. God's voice spoke to my heart and I found clear direction again. It never failed!

That still happens every time I read the Scriptures.

People who say the Bible isn't relevant today obviously don't know the Author. They read it like a storybook or a history lesson, having no idea of the power behind it. They don't hear the Shepherd's voice because they have not become one of His sheep. But those of us who immerse ourselves in it, who press in deeper and deeper, know its power. We love His Word like a love letter that we read over and over because we desire to be close to the one who wrote it. We long to connect with and remember everything about that person. We want to understand how he thinks. We yearn to hear his voice again in our mind. We crave his touch. When we hunger for those same things from God, we learn to appreciate His love letter—the Bible—in that exact way.

Of course, if we don't love the person who sent us the love letter, it is meaningless. It holds no life for us. The key to receiving the full message in God's love letter is to love God. Because I love Him, I hear His voice speaking to me when I read His Word. If I read it often, the words find residence in my heart and bring me life.

>
>
> *T*hose of us who immerse ourselves in God's Word, who press in deeper and deeper, know its power. We love His Word like a love letter we read over and over.
>
> ∾

## God's Love Letters Are a Guide

In the theater, lights at the front of the stage that are level with the performer's feet are called footlights. They act as a guide to help the actors know where to go and keep them from falling into the orchestra pit. God has provided footlights for us, too—to guide us as we walk and to keep us from falling into the pit.

When we read God's Word, it lights our path and keeps us surefooted. "Thy Word is a lamp unto my feet, and a light unto my path" (Psalm 119:105 KJV) is more than just a line from a nice worship song. It is a way of life. Walking step by step with God can only be done successfully if we have God's footlights showing us the way.

Those of us who have read the Bible many times from cover to cover have to be careful not to fall into the trap of thinking that the light we had last year, last month, last week, or even yesterday is enough to keep us safely on the path today. I have done enough public speaking to know that most of my preparation has to be done in prayer and in the Word of God. On my own, I am not able to speak words that will transform anyone's life. Only the anointing power of God attending those words can bring them alive in the hearts of the people listening. If I believe that I can rely on last week's anointing and don't have to prepare in the Word of God for next week's talk, I will find my message lacking in the very thing people want to experience— the Lord's touch. And that means I don't just read the Bible to prepare for the message. I also must feed on God's Word to prepare my soul and spirit.

A miner will never go down into a dark mine without checking to make sure the light on his cap has sufficient power to last the entire time he's down there. We need to be that diligent about God's Word. We can't just read it once from cover to cover and then be finished like we can with any other book. The light we receive from God's Word must be renewed, revitalized, and solidly reestablished daily. When God's truth is renewed in us each day, it becomes like *our* miner's light. As we look in the direction God is leading us, we are better able to see where we are going. "The law of his God is in his heart; none of his steps shall slide" (Psalm 37:31). In order to take it in so deeply that it becomes a part of us, we have to open the Bible and say, "Lord, speak to me today and show me what I need to know." Then we must read until our light is recharged.

*God can speak to you from any page of His Word.*

## God's Love Letter Is a Weapon

When Satan came to tempt Jesus in the wilderness, Jesus spoke the Word of God to refute everything Satan said. Jesus told him that we live "by every word that proceeds from the mouth of God" (Matthew 4:4). If God's own Son refuted the devil in that way, shouldn't we do the same? Who among us are not susceptible to lies and temptations? Who does not get blinded by his or her own prejudices? Who never faces a battle and doesn't need a spiritual sword with which to slay the enemy? Only God's Word in our mind, on our heart, and out of our lips will burn away the darkness of untruth and arm us with a double-edged sword more powerful than any weapon the opposition can use against us. Who does not need that?

> ∾
>
> *Only God's Word in our mind, on our heart, and out of our lips will burn away the darkness of untruth and arm us with a double-edged sword more powerful than any weapon the opposition can use against us.*
>
> ∾

During times of great anxiety I have quoted passages from God's Word that dissolved my fear immediately. I liberally sprinkle Scriptures throughout my prayers for others, and I see them bolster faith like nothing else can. When I'm aware that my children are being threatened by an evil influence, I will speak the Word of God over them in prayer to see them released. There are no strongholds of the enemy that can prevail against God's Word.

## God's Love Letter Is a Message of Hope

There are no times so hopeless in our lives that God's Word will not shed light on the situation and bring us comfort. I've known many parents who have used the Word of God to combat the hopelessness they felt about the actions of their teenagers. They went into the child's room and simply read Scriptures out loud. Not only did hope rise in their own hearts, but they saw changes in their children happen soon after—even if the child was not there to hear it.

If you find yourself struggling with hopelessness, loss, sickness, or temptation, make God's Word an ongoing presence in your life. Hook up to it like an IV and let it flow continuously through your spiritual veins. Its light will burn hopelessness out of your life. "Whatever things were written before were written for our learning, that we through the patience and comfort of the Scriptures might have hope" (Romans 15:4). Don't let yourself even consider constructing a life without using God's Word as a power tool. In fact, make it your very foundation.

Anytime you feel like you are in the dark or on shaky ground, ask God to shed the light of His Word in your heart. Say, "send out Your light and Your truth! Let them lead me; let them bring me to Your holy hill" (Psalm 43:3). If you want to figure out how life works, read His instruction book. When you need to know where you're supposed to be going, His truth will aim you in the right direction, illuminate your way, and keep you from getting off the path.

Hunger for God's Word like food. Thirst for it like water. Soak in it like a jacuzzi. Put it on like a garment. Weave it into your soul so that it becomes part of the fabric of your life. When you do, you won't just be trudging up the trail. You will be dancing in the footlights.

*Prayer Light*

*L*ord, shine the light of Your Word on the path of my life today. Make it a lamp for my feet so that I do not stumble. Bring it alive in my spirit so that it illuminates my mind and soul. Let it be a guide for every decision I make, every step I take. Keep me from turning to the right or the left so that I will stay on the narrow path that leads to life. Help me daily to carve out time to be alone with You and to feed on Your Truth. "Oh, how I love Your law! It is my meditation all the day" (Psalm 119:97). Open my eyes to see new treasure every time I read or hear it. Speak to me and comfort my heart. Make Your Word come alive in me and use it to nourish my soul and spirit like food does for my body. Align my heart with Yours and give me revelation and guidance so that I may know Your will for my life. Shine the lamp of Your truth where I am right now and show me the next step to take.

## Footlights

The entrance of Your words gives light;
It gives understanding to the simple.

Psalm 119:130

Great peace have those who love Your law,
And nothing causes them to stumble.

Psalm 119:165

For the commandment is a lamp,
And the law a light;
Reproofs of instruction
are the way of life.

Proverbs 6:23

Direct my steps by Your Word,
And let no iniquity have dominion over me.

Psalm 119:133

For the word of God is living and powerful,
and sharper than any two-edged sword,
piercing even to the division of soul
and spirit, and of joints and marrow,
and is a discerner of the thoughts and
intents of the heart.

Hebrews 4:12

# SIX

# Paying Your Light Bill

When your light bill arrives, you might be able to come up with at least four reasons for not paying it:

1. "I don't have what it takes."
2. "I don't want to."
3. "I didn't know I had to."
4. "I forgot."

Which one of these do you think the electric company will accept as a legitimate excuse for not paying?

You guessed it!  None of the above.

Which one of these same four reasons does *God* accept as a good excuse for not living in obedience to His ways?

Right again!  None of the above.

It doesn't matter if we forget to do the right thing, don't know what the right thing is to do, openly rebel, or feel like we just don't have it in us to accomplish it. The consequence is still the same—*darkness*.

*Often we find ourselves walking in the dark simply because we are not willing to pay the price for having the light.*

The price God requires for enjoying the fullness of His light is living His way. Whenever we don't live the way God asks us to live, or do not do what He has specifically told us to do, we forfeit the abundance of what He has for us. We won't experience the awesomeness of God's power in our lives if we are not willing to meet His conditions for plugging into it.

Receiving God's salvation doesn't cost us anything. He paid the price for that. His love and grace, among other things, are free as well. But receiving *all* He has for us does not happen without meeting certain requirements on our part. When we don't meet them, we end up being like "those who leave the paths of uprightness to walk in the ways of darkness" (Proverbs 2:13). In order to enjoy the *fullness* of His light, we have to walk in obedience to His ways. Usually we know when we are rebelling against God's laws. But sometimes our disobedience happens with such subtlety that we're not even aware of it.

When I was fourteen, I lived not far from the ocean in Southern California. One day I went to the beach with my friend and her family. Because my friend and I were both good swimmers, no one was concerned when she and I ventured out in a little deeper water. Our peaceful floating was interrupted by a riptide, which began as a subtle undercurrent that we could not see or feel. In fact, we didn't notice it at all until we looked to shore and realized we were dangerously far out. We immediately tried to swim back, but the more effort we put forth, the further away from the beach we were carried. The

> ∾
>
> *W*e won't experience the awesomeness of God's power in our lives if we are not willing to meet His conditions for plugging into it.
>
> ∾

tide was way too strong for us to swim against, and our sense of powerlessness was frightening.

Fortunately, there was a very long pier somewhat nearby, and as we were carried out beyond it we signaled to a fisherman standing on the end. He understood that we needed help and ran to tell the lifeguards. By that time we could see my friend's parents standing in the distance at water's edge, waving frantically for us to come back to shore.

The lifeguards arrived not a moment too soon for our pounding hearts and brought us safely back, where we fell in an exhausted heap on the sand. From our perspective on the shore, we were utterly amazed that we had been carried so far into dangerous territory without even realizing what was happening.

That's the way our lives are. The cares of the world, the influence of the ungodly, laziness, busyness, obsessions, ignorance of God's ways, or our own unsubmitted hearts, can be like a subtle riptide that carries us off course until one day we find that we are so far away from where we should be that we can't get back without help. Failure to be alert to the direction we are moving in is dangerous. And we don't have to be in open rebellion to get off course. All it takes is neglect in one small area of obedience and a subtle drift begins without our even noticing.

The Bible says that people who do *not* love God and who willfully do things their own way, for their own pleasure and with no regard for what it does to others or what God says about it, are called wicked and will find themselves in utter darkness. To them, what light they have is even dark. "The light of the wicked indeed goes out, and the flame of his fire does not shine" (Job 18:5). God withholds light from people who do not love or obey Him, but His light is placed in the path of those who live rightly. "Light is sown for the righteous . . ." (Psalm 97:11).

You and I are not the wicked God speaks of in His Word. But when we don't live the way He asks us to, we sacrifice much of the light we could enjoy. We don't experience the degree of His protection, guidance, and answers to prayer that we otherwise would. We forfeit certain blessings when we are not willing to do the things that must precede them.

## When We Obey God, We Are Protected

Noah was called to build the ark because God said, "I have seen that you are righteous" (Genesis 7:1). Noah's righteousness ultimately saved him and his family from destruction. We can end up in the most wonderful places in our lives, places we wouldn't have thought to go on our own, simply because God sees our heart to live His way. When we love Him enough to obey what He asks, we come under the covering of His protection. When we don't, we come *out* from under it and drift further and further away from the shores of safety and blessing.

We can find ourselves in the wrong place at the wrong time simply because we didn't do what God was telling us to do, or we neglected to ask Him what we were supposed to be doing before we made decisions. Or perhaps we asked Him, but we failed to wait for an answer before we went ahead and did what we wanted to do. So much grief can be avoided by living God's way.

## When We Obey God, We Hear His Voice

The more we obey God, the clearer we hear Him speaking to our heart. The more we hear God speaking to our heart, the more we want to obey Him. The more we obey, the more He can teach us of His ways, His truth, and

His nature. "His secret counsel is with the upright" (Proverbs 3:32).

After I became a Christian, I was not able to clearly hear God's direction for my life until I cleaned out my house of all the occultic books, magazines, music, and artifacts I had collected before I became a believer. I had stopped all occult practices, but had unwittingly neglected specific directions in God's Word until one day I read, "Do not bring a detestable thing into your house, or you, like it, will be set apart for destruction" (Deuteronomy 7:26 NIV). Suddenly my eyes were opened to what should have been obvious, and I got rid of everything that was offensive to God. I wanted to separate myself from anything that separated me from Him, and when I did I was able to hear His voice speaking to my heart.

*God reveals Himself to us in greater dimensions when we are doing what He has asked us to do.*

Pastor Jack Hayford says, "Obedience is not a work that *earns* something from God. Obedience is a willingness to *learn* something from God. We need to ask God, "Where do I need to obey You, Lord? What do I need to learn today?"

When we are walking in obedience, we don't miss God's direction for our lives.

## When We Obey God, We See Answers to Our Prayers

If you find you are not enjoying answers to your prayers, ask God to show you if you have neglected to be obedient to His ways in some area of your life. For the longest time I did not see any answers to my prayers

*If* you find you are not enjoying answers to your prayers, ask God to show you if you have neglected to be obedient to His ways in some area of your life.

concerning my marriage. As a result, my husband and I went through some very dark times. When I finally realized that I had unforgiveness in my heart, I confessed it as God requires us to do and asked Him to set me free of it. After that, I prayed with a right heart, and I saw major answers to prayer that I had only dreamed about before. The light of God's restoration shined down on our relationship and brought much-needed healing.

The Bible says, ". . . whatever we ask we receive from Him, because we keep His commandments and do those things that are pleasing in His sight" (1 John 3:22). There is a direct correlation between obedience and answered prayer. Oswald Chambers says, "Intellectual darkness comes through ignorance; spiritual darkness comes because of something I do not intend to obey." [1]

## When We Obey God, We Can Be Led by Him

Whatever we are passionately devoted to in our life will mold and control us. Whether it be the dictates of a trend-setting magazine or the catalogues of the rich, if the lust of our flesh or the pride of life is more important to us than obeying God, we will be overly influenced by the things we want or the image of who we want to be.

There are ways that are right and ways that are not and we cannot confuse the two. "Woe to those who call evil good, and good evil; who put darkness for light, and light for darkness . . ." (Isaiah 5:20). The voices of false gods, no matter how dressed up, popular, or politically correct their message appears to be, will get us so far off the path that we will never be able to find it again without God's intervention. If we obey Him, He will give us the light of His revelation and get us where we need to go. If we don't, how will He be able to lead us?

God is not trying to be a dictator. He simply wants to show us how life works best. When we don't live His way, confusion enters in and disturbing things happen that otherwise wouldn't. God is saying to us, "If you will do this, I will do that." In whatever area He is asking us to obey, we can be sure He is trying to teach us something that will be for our benefit.

Obedience is not legalism. It does not discount God's grace. Legalism says, "You have to do it perfectly on your own." God's grace says, "You need to do it to make your life better, but God will help you and pick you up if you fall."

Ask God to show you if there are certain steps of obedience He wants you to take. He'll tell you. You can depend on it. When you come to a place where you trust Him so thoroughly that you will obey whatever He says, you'll find that obedience won't be a gut-wrenching misery; it will be a privilege. You'll obey because the rewards are great. You'll obey out of the desire to have nothing come between you and God. You'll obey because you'll pay any price to not have your light shut off.

———————— *Prayer Light* ————————

Lord, I thank You that You have given me all the light I need for this day. I want to experience everything You have for me, and I am willing to pay the price of obedience for it. So if there is any area in my life where I am not walking in full obedience to Your ways, show me. If You want me to do something that I am not doing, make me understand and enable me to accomplish it. Don't let me drift away. Pull me out of deep waters and rescue me from all that takes me from

You. I lay down my will and surrender to Yours. I turn away from selfish claims to my own life in order to heed Your direction. Take any rebellion in me and expose it with Your truth. "Search me, O God, and know my heart; try me, and know my anxieties; and see if there is any wicked way in me, and lead me in the way everlasting" (Psalm 139:23-24). Lord, I choose this day to obey You because I know my life works best when I do. In the areas where obedience is hard for me, walk me through step by step. I don't want to do anything that would dim the light You have for my path.

## *Footlights*

Unto the upright there arises light in the darkness;
He is gracious, and full of compassion, and righteous.

PSALM 112:4

He shall bring forth your righteousness as the light,
And your justice as the noonday.

PSALM 37:6

For everyone practicing evil hates the light
and does not come to the light, lest
his deeds should be exposed. But he
who does the truth comes to the light,
that his deeds may be clearly seen,
that they have been done in God."

JOHN 3:20-21

. . . Your judgments are like light that goes forth.

HOSEA 6:5

"Enter by the narrow gate; for wide is the
gate and broad is the way that leads to
destruction, and there are many who go in by it.
Because narrow is the gate and
difficult is the way which leads to life, and
there are few who find it."

MATTHEW 7:13-14

# SEVEN

# Standing in the Line of Fire

If we go running into enemy territory and get shot at, we're not exactly being attacked. If we open ourselves up to the consequences of not living God's way, we shouldn't be surprised if enemy arrows pierce our lives. We've gotten out from the safety of God's covering.

On the other hand, if we are on our home turf minding our own business and doing what we know is right in God's sight, and from out of nowhere we are shot at, then we know our enemy has targeted us. We are in his line of fire, and he has mounted an attack on us. When that happens, we must immediately draw near to God. Oswald Chambers says of those dark times of enemy attack, "The thing that preserves a man from panic is his relationship to God." [1]

When we consistently live close to God, we have the peace and confidence of knowing who is our enemy and Who is our Defender. That doesn't mean that going through the battle is easy. But the closer you walk with God, the easier it becomes. We always hope that God will lift us *above* our circumstances. And sometimes He does. But much of the time He walks us *through* them so we can learn a new dimension of His power.

When the Israelites were delivered out of Egypt by the mighty hand of God and set on a journey of many miracles, they were doing what God had directed them to do. Still, they found themselves backed into an inescapable corner, with the Red Sea before them and the entire Egyptian army thundering up behind. They cried out to Moses in fear, and he assured them that the dangers they saw facing them would not be seen again. "'Stand still, and see the salvation of the LORD, which He will accomplish for you today. . . . The LORD will fight for you, and you shall hold your peace'" (Exodus 14:13-14). Not only did God fight the battle for them by parting the waters of the Red Sea so the Israelites could walk across the bottom, He also took them across on dry land.

Dry land!

*When God does a miracle, He does a complete work.*

Even when the Egyptian soldiers followed the Israelites into the riverbed to attack them, the sea closed and drowned the entire army. The Israelites "did not gain possession of the land by their own sword, nor did their own arm save them; but it was Your right hand, Your arm, and the light of Your countenance, because You favored them" (Psalm 44:3).

*When God goes to battle for someone, He doesn't stop until the enemy is destroyed.*

God will do the same for us today. When we are up against a wall and, in our eyes, the enemy is giving us no means of escape, the Lord will open up a way out. God will fight the battle for us. Even if we lose all strength in the face of it, *His* strength will be manifested as He wipes out the threat and works complete deliverance. But because any opposition we face from the enemy has spiritual power behind it, the battle must first be fought in the spirit before victory will be seen in the flesh. That means we need to pray.

I remember one morning when an article appeared in a prominent newspaper that misrepresented my husband, Michael. The story cast him in a very bad light by associating him with a recording artist who was living a seriously ungodly lifestyle. It said that Michael, who is a record producer, had a close association with this person, and the implications were that Michael condoned the immoral choices that this artist had made. Neither of these things were true. Michael and I were very concerned, so we prayed about the situation, contacted the newspaper, and then began calling everyone we could think of who might be hurt by such lies.

We talked to a number of people, including the writer of the article, but soon realized there was no way we could possibly reach everyone we needed to in order to preserve Michael's reputation. So we began to battle in prayer. We declared that Satan could not destroy what God had built. We would stand with the Lord and watch Him fight the battle for us, just as Jehoshaphat had done in the Old Testament.

When Jehoshaphat realized that "a great multitude" was coming against him, he set himself to seek God. He stood in the middle of the believers and said, "O LORD God of our fathers, are You not God in heaven, and do You not rule over all the kingdoms of the nations, and in Your hand is there not power and might, so that no one is able to

*Because any opposition we face from the enemy has spiritual power behind it, the battle must first be fought in the spirit before victory will be seen in the flesh.*

withstand You? . . . 'If disaster comes upon us—sword, judgment, pestilence, or famine—we will stand before this temple and in Your presence . . . and cry out to You in our affliction, and You will hear and save'" (2 Chronicles 20:6,9).

Jehoshaphat didn't say these things to remind God what He was capable of doing in case He had forgotten. He wanted to proclaim his own faith and inspire faith to rise up in the people. He knew that if they were reminded of the good things the Lord had done for them, they would be better equipped to believe God could save them.

Once the people humbly declared their dependence upon God, He spoke to them and said, "Do not be afraid nor dismayed because of this great multitude, for the battle is not yours, but God's" (2 Chronicles 20:15). God told them He would fight the battle for them. As Jehoshaphat and the people sang praise to the Lord, they won the battle *and* came away with more than they had before.

That's basically what happened to us in this situation with the newspaper article. We went to God, declared our dependence upon Him, reminded ourselves of His power and goodness, took a stance of faith in God's Word, and praised Him as we watched Him fight the battle for us. God miraculously shined the light of His grace and favor upon us and the entire matter dissipated. Of the countless people who read the article, no one to our knowledge ever gave it any credence. And we were left with a greater sense of God's power than we ever had before.

At the first sign of an enemy attack, go to the Lord and listen to what He tells you to do. He will guide you. No matter how dark it gets, He promises that "the light of the moon will be as the light of the sun, and the light of the sun will be sevenfold, as the light of seven days" (Isaiah 30:26). In other words, the light you have will be *magnified*.

Do you hear what He is saying?

*In the midst of the battle, the light you have will not only never be put out, it will be brighter than it otherwise would have been.*

That same passage of Scripture goes on to say, "You shall have a song as in the night when a holy festival is kept . . ." (Isaiah 30:29). That means that in the midst of what you are facing, your heart will have so much joy it's as if you are celebrating. You will have such a sense of His awesome presence that your soul will sing!

Much of the misery of being in a battle is thinking that we are all alone in it. I recall many times when I felt alone and afraid as I stood in the line of enemy fire, thinking I would surely be overcome by the waters of destruction swirling around me. But when I cried out to God and refused to doubt His goodness, He brought me through on dry ground and gave me peace and strength. The light I had was magnified, and He put a song in my heart. He will do that for you, too. No matter what your circumstances are, you can be sure that the Lord will be with you and help you successfully stand against whatever opposes you. When you walk with Him in the battle, you're never alone.

The hardest part about letting God fight your battle is that He sometimes waits until the eleventh hour so you will have no doubt of where the power is coming from. If that happens to you, hide yourself in Him and refuse to lose faith in His ability to come to your defense. "In returning and rest you shall be saved; in quietness and confidence shall be your strength" (Isaiah 30:15). Rest in the security of your Heavenly Father's

*M*uch of the misery of being in a battle is thinking that we are alone in it . . . but you can be sure that the Lord will be with you and help you stand against whatever opposes you.

arms until you see His power transform your circumstances.

The moment you realize you are standing in the line of fire, recognize who your enemy is and run to your Protector. Take His hand and He will show you moment by moment what you are to do. Put on the armor of God—prayer, praise, obedience, perseverance, peace, and faith. Throw a party in the Lord's presence and celebrate the victory He has for you, even before you see its manifestation. Let the song of praise and deliverance rise in your heart and sing it on the mountaintop of your soul as you watch the power of God defeat the enemy on your behalf. No matter how dark the night of your circumstances gets, remember that you still have a light. It comes from Him. It's in you and no enemy can ever put it out.

## *Prayer Light*

Thank You, Lord, that You are my defender. You are more powerful than any plan the enemy has against me. Thank You that You will never leave or forsake me, and that You are always strong in my behalf. "I will lift up my eyes to the hills—from whence comes my help? My help comes from the LORD, who made heaven and earth" (Psalm 121:1-2). No matter what happens, I will look to You to deliver me from the hand of all that opposes me. I know that because I put my trust in You, You will be my shield (Proverbs 30:5). And I will not fear what man can do to me. "Lead me, O LORD, in Your righteousness because of my enemies; make Your way straight before my face" (Psalm 5:8).

In myself I don't have what it takes to establish a formidable defense. I cannot protect myself and all I care about from the weapons of the enemy. But the enemy's strength is nothing to You. And no weapon formed against me shall prosper (Isaiah 54:17). I know You have armed me with strength for the battle and will keep me safe (Psalm 18:39). Help me to "cast off the works of darkness, and . . . put on the armor of light" (Romans 13:12). Cause a song of deliverance to rise in my heart and I will sing praise to Your glory as You fight the battle for me. I will walk with You through the enemy's attack, knowing that Your light on my path signals my certain victory.

*Footlights*

Do not rejoice over me, my enemy;
When I fall, I will arise;
When I sit in darkness,
The LORD will be a light to me.

MICAH 7:8

. . . be strong in the Lord and in the power of His might.
Put on the whole armor of God, that you may be
able to stand against the wiles of the devil. For
we do not wrestle against flesh and blood,
but against principalities, against powers,
against the rulers of the darkness of this age,
against spiritual hosts of wickedness in the
heavenly places. Therefore take up the whole
armor of God, that you may be able to withstand in the evil day, and having
done all, to stand.

EPHESIANS 6:10-13

Keep me as the apple of Your eye;
Hide me under the shadow of Your wings,
From the wicked who oppress me,
From my deadly enemies who surround me.

PSALM 17:8-9

## EIGHT

# Seeing What's Right with This Picture

Have you ever found yourself angry, upset, or devastated when things didn't turn out as you'd hoped or planned? Next time that happens, look deeply into the situation and ask God to give you a new perspective.

We can usually find another way to view our situation beyond how we initially see it. Because we walk in the light of the Lord, blessings abound for us in each moment. Sometimes, though, we have to deliberately look for them. God's light does not blind us, but we can be blind to God's light. We don't always see the *whole* truth. Sometimes we see everything *but* the truth.

My daughter, Mandy, and I have developed a plan for seeing the truth whenever something goes wrong. We look at the situation and ask, "What's *right* with this picture?" We pray for God to show us how what we think of as a negative situation is actually a positive one. We take even the smallest issue and reverse it. We examine the flip side. This process can become funny as we stretch to find every positive aspect, but it keeps us protected from the cynical, hopeless, and bitter attitudes that can creep into our personalities.

For example, Mandy had a car accident when she was sixteen. Fortunately, the lady who hit her apologized and admitted to the police and the insurance company that she was entirely to blame. As the cars were towed away, I asked my very shaken daughter what was right with this picture.

"Well, no one was hurt," she replied.

"Yes, that's the best thing," I said. "But there is another good thing. This accident is going to make you a better driver because now you realize that even when you're doing everything right, bad things can still happen. You'll be extra aware of other drivers and how important it is to pray for God's protection as you travel. What you have learned from this might be the very thing that saves your life some day."

This is not just positive thinking or trying to make good things happen with your thoughts. This is seeing things from God's perspective and letting Him show you the truth. That means *finding* the light in what seems to be a dark situation. It's knowing that, because you have invited God into every step of your life, you can find His light there no matter how dark it seems.

> ∾
>
> Seeing things from God's perspective and letting Him show you the truth means finding the light in what seems to be a dark situation.
>
> ∾

"Embracing the moment" is embracing God and finding Him in the moment. "Seeing what's right with this picture," on the other hand, is searching for the truth and seeing reality from God's perspective. It's being willing to let go of our determination to see things through our own tunnel vision.

Have you ever known people who are so set on believing something bad about another person that they refuse to hear anything good? They make a case against that person and everything that person says or does is twisted to support the case. Nothing will change their minds. Not reason. Not God. This is the same kind of hard-nosed narrow-mindedness that feeds prejudice, gossip, jealousy, and hatred. Seeing what's right with this picture counteracts that tendency. It may be a lighthearted way of approaching a very dark-spirited issue, but it's a good place to start.

Let me give you some more examples. When my family and I were on a plane coming home from vacation, we flew through severe turbulence. The plane rocked and shook so violently that everyone on board was afraid. After it was over and people could actually talk again, we looked to find what was good about the situation. We decided that the best part, of course, was that we landed safely. Another good thing was that it forced all of us who were believers on the flight—and probably non-believers as well—to pray fervently. (Actually, *desperately* might be a more accurate word choice.) When we found out later that the turbulence we flew through was the edge of a serious tornado that hit Alabama, we realized that if we had not been praying at that very time for God to calm the storm, there might have been even more damage and fatalities on the ground than there were.

In another instance, I spoke to a young man named Mark who had always disdained his father's success because he only saw it as something he had to live up to. In Mark's mind, it had become such an impossible task that he felt defeated by it. When he was able to flip the picture over and see what was good about the situation, Mark gained a completely different perspective. He saw the advantages of having a father who was respected and gave his family a good name. He saw the benefits of the good schooling his father was able to provide. He recognized the positives of having a hardworking father for a role model. Together, we found many more positives than negatives. This exercise changed Mark's whole attitude, which led to great healing in his relationship with his dad.

In yet another example, a friend of ours named Jonathan was laid off from work and was initially feeling very defeated about it. But instead of letting his frustration turn into bitterness, he looked to see what was right with this picture. Jonathan gradually recognized it as an opportunity to help his wife, Lisa, establish a new business she had been wanting to start now that their children were grown. Instead of falling into depression, he worked hard for her. The business soon took off and became one of the most successful companies of its kind in town. Lisa would never have been able to do what she did without Jonathan's help. What seemed like a disaster at first actually was a blessing. What appeared to be a dark time became a time flooded with light. If Jonathan had complained and blamed God, refusing to see the situation from His perspective, things probably would have turned out quite differently.

This may be a big shock to you—I know it was to me— but often when we think something unfortunate is happening to us, it's actually an answer to a prayer we have prayed. Only the answer didn't manifest the way we thought it should, so we failed to recognize it. That's why seeing what's right is entirely a matter of having God's perspective.

Jennifer had been praying faithfully for her troubled relationship with her husband, David. When the company David had been working for was downsized, he found himself without employment for what turned out to be ten months. This kind of a turn could have destroyed an already ailing marriage. But instead of sinking into despair, Jennifer asked God to show her the truth about the situation. God revealed it was *not* true that her husband's career, as well as their marriage, was finished as they had both feared. The truth was that God had a great path ahead for them, but they couldn't walk it if they were crippled by a broken marriage. God was giving them time together to repair it.

Instead of letting this situation become a disaster that ripped them apart, David and Jennifer wisely took advantage of the opportunity to seek Christian counsel, be with godly friends, and spend time together doing the things they never had time to do before. Their marriage healed miraculously, and David eventually found more fulfilling work than he had ever had before.

*Often we pray for something and don't even recognize the answer to our own prayers when we receive it, because it does not happen the way we thought it would.*

When I read about God leading the Israelites out of Egypt after many unmistakable miracles, I was amazed at how they continually grumbled and complained and failed to see how God was taking care of them.

*What is the matter with these people that they can't see the answers to their own prayers?* I thought.

Then I realized we are all just like them. God is in the middle doing something great for us and, because we are not as comfortable as we'd like to be, we don't recognize the good things He has put in our lap. "Eyes they have, but they do not see" (Psalm 115:5).

*How many blessings must we have forfeited because we resisted God when we should have been thanking Him?*

*God is in the middle of doing something great for us and, because we are not as comfortable as we'd like to be, we don't recognize the good things He has put in our lap.*

Look at your life right now. Is there anything that worries or upsets you? If so, say, "Lord, show me what's right with this picture. What is the truth in this moment? Help me to see it from Your perspective." You'll be amazed at what God reveals.

If your attitude is one of gratefully searching for God's truth and goodness in any situation, it will change your life. You'll never see things the same way again. No matter what happens, you'll be able to say, "This was the LORD's doing; it is marvelous in our eyes" (Psalm 118:23). What we're really talking about here is an issue of trust. It's basically believing that God is good and he desires the best for you. "Oh, taste and see that the LORD is good; blessed is the man who trusts in Him!" (Psalm 34:8). Give God the benefit of your trust and you'll see that you are standing in more light than you ever dreamed possible.

---

*Prayer Light*

*L*ord, I lift to You the situations of my life that concern me. I lay my worries before You and ask for Your mighty intervention to show me what's right when I can only see what's wrong. I am determined to see the good, so help me not to be blinded by my own fears, doubts, wants, and preconceived ideas. I ask You to reveal to me Your truth in every situation. Give me Your perspective. Bless me with the ability to understand the bigger picture and to distinguish the valuable from the unimportant. When something seems to go wrong, help me not to jump to negative conclusions. Enable me to recognize the answers to my own prayers. I trust You to help me see the light in every situation.

## Footlights

And we know that all things work together
for good to those who love God,
to those who are the called
according to His purpose.

ROMANS 8:28

I would have lost heart, unless I had believed
That I would see the goodness of the LORD
In the land of the living.

PSALM 27:13

Turn away my eyes from looking at worthless things,
And revive me in Your way.

PSALM 119:37

Open my eyes, that I may see
Wondrous things from Your law.

PSALM 119:18

This is the day the LORD has made;
We will rejoice and be glad in it.

PSALM 118:24

# NINE

# Testing, One, Two, Three

Remember how each time you took a test in school you had to study hard so you'd know the material and be able to pass the test? The purpose of the test was for the teacher to determine how much you knew and, consequently, what grade you would receive. The more you knew, the better your grade.

God's tests are not like school tests. First of all, He already knows how much we know. The test is not for Him. It's for us. God's test helps us clearly see what we're made of. It teaches us about ourselves and about God. The test itself is part of our learning process.

The results of the tests God gives us, depending on our attitude in the midst of the testing, will determine whether we are refined like gold by the process or become cold and hard like steel. It won't necessarily be how much we know that counts, but what we do with the knowledge we've got. It's *how* we take the test.

In the tests that God gives us, we receive no grade. We will either pass, or we'll have to keep taking it until we get it right. We have two choices with regard to God's tests. We can resist God, have a bad attitude, and try to run from it. Or we can embrace *Him* in it and welcome His perfecting hand in our lives. Our reaction will determine the outcome.

The most miserable times in my life as a believer have been during what I see now were periods of testing. And they came just before the most significant breakthrough of God's light. The good news is that the more challenging the test, the more monumental the reward waiting for us on the other side of it—*if* we react to it in the right way.

*We are often put to our most difficult test just before the greatest work of God in our lives is about to be accomplished.*

I remember one particular time when my husband and I were going through a serious financial crunch and it looked like we would have to sell our house. I was pregnant and seriously ill and did not see how I could possibly find another place to live, make the move, and still live through it. My husband and I were before God daily trying to determine if this was an enemy attack, or if we had done something wrong, or if we were being put to the test. The only answer we received was to be still and know that the Lord was God.

Although the crisis seemed to go on forever, it actually lasted only a few months. During that period God showed us how to not do anything but praise Him in the midst of what was happening. When we submitted fully to the Lord, even though it wasn't our first reaction, we clearly saw how utterly dependent we were upon Him. It was exactly what we needed to learn in order to navigate the waters that were ahead for us in the coming years. Our financial crisis was resolved when people who owed my husband money for work he had done finally paid him. We were able to keep our house, and the Lord poured blessings upon us that I doubt we would have enjoyed had we not gone through that time of testing. We knew the rewards were from Him.

The Bible's story of Job is important because the magnitude of Job's suffering in his time of testing is unimaginable. It is the worst case scenario. He lost everything, including his children and his health. Although he suffered such agony, he never doubted or turned against God. His reward for faithfulness was that "the LORD blessed the latter days of Job more than his beginning" (Job 42:12).

I know that most of us feel we would just as soon not be quite so blessed in our latter days and forget the whole testing thing. But we aren't given that choice. God decides the time, place, and manner of testing. No matter what the test entails, God wants us to have unflinching faith in the midst of it, just like Job had.

After God performed so many miracles to deliver the Israelites from the hand of their enemies and they still continued to doubt Him, He then took them into the wilderness and there He tested them (Exodus 15:25). He let them go without water for three days. Now God knew they needed water and could have easily provided it for them. But they didn't ask. They didn't pray. They complained. And that was part of the test. God wanted them to ask. He wanted them to be dependent on Him for everything. When Moses cried out to God on their behalf, God said that if the people would listen to Him and do what He commanded, He would meet all their needs. So they listened, and obeyed. They got their water. And were content. That is, until the next crisis.

*God* decides the time, place, and manner of testing. No matter what the test entails, God wants us to have unflinching faith in the midst of it.

Instead of learning something from the water situation, the Israelites complained again about their lack of food. God was not trying to starve them. He knew they needed food, and He wanted to provide it for them. Only He wanted them to come to Him and rely on *Him* for it. Once more, Moses prayed and God provided. But this time, God provided only what was needed for that day. He desired that they trust Him for everything, each day that they needed it. He wanted them to learn to walk with just enough light for the step they were on.

Does this sound at all familiar? Can you think of anyone who wants to get to the Promised Land, but doesn't want to do what's necessary to make the trip? Are you aware of a person who desires to have everything he needs, but is not willing to give up anything to get it? Can you imagine someone who believes she should have already arrived without having to trust God for every step to get there? Can you think of anyone who would even consider trying to pass a test without having taken it? So can I. I think we all can.

God puts us through different kinds of tests. But He gives us three major tests that we will all have to take at one time or another.

### Test One: God Tests Our Heart

"I know also, my God, that You test the heart and have pleasure in uprightness" (1 Chronicles 29:17).

The famous fall that pride always goes before is something God allows in order to purify us from our inclination to be full of ourselves. Just when we have enough arrogance to think we can live one moment without Him, God searches our heart for humility. If found wanting, He allows us to hit rock bottom and gain a new perspective. Looking up. And this is exactly what we need if we've been looking down for too long. God doesn't give this kind of test to torture us. He does it so our hearts can be purified and we can see *Him*. "Blessed are the pure in heart, for they shall see God" (Matthew 5:8).

Six years ago, I had a serious fall that broke two bones in my ankle and tore the ligaments on both sides. As I lay in bed for weeks, unable to put pressure on my foot even in a cast, I had plenty of time to pray and listen. I soon realized that God had been trying to get my attention for some time in order to make certain major changes in my life, but until I was flat on my back in pain I didn't want to listen. It was in this predicament that God showed me clearly we were to move from Los Angeles to Tennessee. My heart had to be tested in the fire and it was painful. Would I do what God wanted, or what I wanted? Ultimately, God's purposes were accomplished and we ended up in the right place at the right time.

### Test Two: God Tests Our Faith

". . . count it all joy when you fall into various trials, knowing that the testing of your faith produces patience" (James 1:2-3).

One of the most profound times our faith is tested is when we are struggling with our finances. Few things are more upsetting than the prospect of losing your home, not having enough food, or not being able to pay your bills. This is especially frightening when it involves a family with dependent children. But learning to walk in the provision God gives us for the day in which we find ourselves opens our eyes to see how we must depend on Him for everything. It forces us to live in God's presence in a deeper way as we look to Him to work daily miracles on our behalf.

When our faith is tested during these times, our response to it is revealing. Do we trust Him to provide, or do we get angry and take it out on others? Do we view this as a time that God wants us to draw closer to Him, or do we see it as the termination of our future? Do we understand that God is testing us in order to prepare us for what He is going to do in our lives, or do we believe He is forsaking us? Will we lose patience in this time, or will we grow in faith? The answers we give to these questions are the keys to passing the test.

### Test Three: God Tests Our Obedience

"'In this way I will test them and see whether they will follow my instructions'" (Exodus 16:4 NIV).

My own children have always determined the amount of privileges they enjoyed by how obedient they were to the rules we laid down in our home. If they didn't obey the rules, we didn't extend the rewards. Of course, we were committed to feed, clothe, educate, shelter, and love them no matter what they did. But the extra blessings they enjoyed over and above those things depended on their obedience. For example, when they were teenagers we asked them to do their own laundry and clean their rooms. If they didn't obey, we knew they were therefore not responsible enough to drive a car. Of course they could live without driving a car, but their joy would certainly not be as full.

God views us much the same way. He requires specific things of us and tests us to see if we will do them. If we don't, He doesn't withhold His love, provision, and protection from us. But He wants to bless us in so many more ways, and He can't unless we are completely submitted to Him. Moses told the Israelite people, "'God has come to test you, so that the fear of God will be with you to keep you from sinning'" (Exodus 20:20 NIV). God also says that "fire will test the quality of each man's work" (1 Corinthians 3:13 NIV). None of us want to go through the fire of being tested, but we can eliminate much of our misery by being quick to respond to what God asks us to do.

A frequent question we all have is, *How do I know if what I am going through is an enemy attack, a result of my own disobedience, or one of God's tests?* The way to determine the answer is to ask God, "Lord, is this from the enemy?" If He doesn't show us that it is, then we should not automatically blame everything on the devil and thereby absolve ourselves of any responsibility. We're still made of flesh no matter how spiritual we get. We can all be tempted to think, say, or do things that are not right in the sight of God. That's why we must also say, "Lord, have I done anything to cause this?" He will reveal it to you if you have. God doesn't keep our sins secret from us. If you still don't have an answer, say, "Lord, are You putting me to the test? If so, show me what I need to learn. Create in me a clean heart and a right spirit."

Don't fear the time of testing God takes you through. It doesn't have to be miserable. Think of it as a refining that will reveal anything amiss in your life and show you where changes need to be made. The only way God can lead you to where you've never been, and can't get to without Him, is to call you to a new place in your life that requires more purity of heart, more faith, and more obedience than you've ever known. Your reaction during this period will be revealing. Will you love Him above all else? Will you believe He is who He says He is and trust Him to provide for your needs? Will you do what He tells you to do? If you are fearful and bitter during the process, you delay the blessings God is waiting to rain on you. That's what the Israelites did, and they wandered around for forty years on a journey that should have taken just a few weeks. You don't want to do that.

Walking with just enough light for the step you're on in a time of testing is God's way of preparing you for the great things He has ahead. Ask Him to help you learn your lesson well.

──────────── *Prayer Light* ────────────

*L*ord, grow me up in Your ways and lead me in Your will. Help me to become so strong in You that I will not waver or doubt. Make me to understand Your Word and Your directions to me. "Test me, O LORD, and try me, examine my heart and my mind; for your love is ever before me and I walk continually in your truth" (Psalm 26:2-3 NIV). I want to pass successfully through any time of testing You bring me to so that I might be refined. I don't want to wander around in the wilderness, going over and over the same territory because I haven't learned the lesson. I pray that I will always have a teachable heart that recognizes Your hand in my life and soaks up Your instruction. Help me to trust Your timing. Establish in me an unwavering faith so I will know that when I walk with You, even the refining fire provides the perfect light for the step I'm on.

## Footlights

You have tested my heart;
You have visited me in the night;
You have tried me and have found nothing;
I have purposed that my mouth
shall not transgress.

PSALM 17:3

. . . You, O LORD, know me;
You have seen me,
And You have tested my
heart toward You.

JEREMIAH 12:3

Praise our God, O peoples,
Let the sound of his praise be heard;
He has preserved our lives
And kept our feet from slipping.
For you, O God, tested us;
You refined us like silver.

PSALM 66:8-10 (NIV)

. . . I have refined you, but not as silver;
I have tested you in the furnace of affliction.

ISAIAH 48:10

I will bring the one-third through the fire,
Will refine them as silver is refined,
And test them as gold is tested.
They will call on My name,
And I will answer them.
I will say, 'This is My people';
And each one will say,
"The LORD is my God."

ZECHARIAH 13:9

# TEN

# Knowing How to Pack for the Wilderness

When God is taking us to a place we've never been before, we envision that it's going to be better than where we are. And ultimately, that's true. But often we have to go through a wilderness to get there.

God has a purpose for the wilderness, but it's hard to see it when we're in it. It can be frightening if we don't know what to expect. The most frightening thing about it is the thought that this may be our final destination.

When God called my husband and me to leave Los Angeles and move to Tennessee, it was one of the most difficult things I had ever done in my life. I had to leave what I loved and what was familiar to me to go where everything seemed foreign. Not that one culture was better or worse than the other, but they were so different from each other—and from the rest of the world. It was like going from Mars to the moon. I hope that none of the good people of California and Tennessee will take offense to my analogy, but in *my* particular experience on this journey that God was taking *me* through, California was Egypt and Tennessee was the wilderness.

Even though there was a lot I did not miss about Los Angeles, there were many things I couldn't let go of. And even though Tennessee is probably one of the most beautiful places in the world and home to the kindest of people, so much was missing for me. I felt like an alien. And, just like the Israelites did when God led them out of Egypt, I grumbled and complained.

"Oh, for the meat and bread of Egypt!" the Israelites cried.

"Oh, for the fruits and vegetables of California!" I lamented.

"Oh, for some fish and a new pair of shoes like we had back home!" they complained.

"Oh, for the restaurants, amusement parks, and beaches I used to go to!" I moaned.

I knew God had clearly led us to Tennessee, so I was completely surprised to find myself this miserable. I thought that when God flies you out of Egypt, you touch down in the Promised Land. *Of course* I knew that the Israelites had to go through the wilderness, but they were a bunch of ungrateful complainers, weren't they?

"Lord, why did you bring me here to the middle of nowhere?" I grumbled. "I had a life in L.A."

I didn't know then that although the wilderness may seem like nowhere at the time, it is *somewhere* if that's where God wants you. For it's there He will prepare you for the good thing He is about to do in your life. It's there you will be thoroughly convinced that you won't get anywhere or accomplish anything lasting without Him.

*It's not where we are in life that matters, but Who is with us.*

The wilderness is where we are forced to leave behind the familiar, the comfortable, the past successes, the accomplishments, and the old bag of tricks that always worked before. The wilderness is where God takes us when He wants to get Egypt out of our hearts. He wants to separate us from all that we crave, so that all we crave is Him. Just as God wanted to get the taste for Egypt out of the Israelites' mouths, He wants to get the lust for certain comforts out of our appetites, too. It's not that He doesn't want us to ever be comfortable. It's just that He doesn't want us to *depend* on the comfortable. He wants us to depend on *Him*. He doesn't want us to love the comforts more than we love *Him*. When God aims us in a new direction, we have to let go of what we've known, be willing to embrace the unfamiliar, and trust that He will sustain us on the journey.

All great people of faith have traveled into the unknown at some point in their lives. How must Noah have felt when he gathered his family on board the ark before the floods came? Nothing like it had ever been built before. He didn't even know for sure that it would float. He had to leave all that was familiar to him, and he certainly did not know where he would end up. I'm sure his hand was in God's when the rains came and the fountains of the deep were released. Who could imagine the magnitude of such a flood? I'm certain Noah took each step clinging to God's every word of revelation. He knew God was in control of his life and had put him in the right place at the right time.

That's exactly the place we want to be. That's the kind of assurance

>
> *W*hen God aims us in a new direction, we have to let go of what we've known, be willing to embrace the unfamiliar, and trust that He will sustain us on the journey.
>
> ∾

we must have. We need to be walking so close to the Lord that we hear His voice in the midst of any upheaval in our lives. We have to trust Him so thoroughly that we will follow Him wherever He leads us. We must walk perfectly within the revealed light God has given us, not running ahead, not lagging behind, not striving to go somewhere else.

When traveling in the wilderness, there is a good possibility that God will not reveal our final destination. He has a number of reasons for this. For one thing, if He did reveal where we were going, it wouldn't be such a walk of faith. Another reason is that the full magnitude of what's ahead is often too much for us to comprehend. We might get in God's way by thinking too small, or delay the process if we become doubtful. We also might have so many questions that we become paralyzed with fear waiting for the answers.

God took the Israelites through the wilderness because taking them the direct route meant they would have to fight the Philistines. "Then it came to pass, when Pharaoh had let the people go, that God did not lead them by way of the land of the Philistines, although that was near; for God said, 'Lest perhaps the people change their minds when they see war, and return to Egypt'" (Exodus 13:17). God knew that the Israelites would have been too afraid at that point to trust Him to fight their battles for them, so He took them on a different route.

Their wilderness experience could have been a much shorter one had their response to it been one of obedience and submission. But they wandered in the wilderness for years because they didn't get it. You and I won't have to do that because we *do* get it. We now understand that the reason God takes us through these wilderness times is because He wants us to learn a walk of faith whereby we trust Him for every step. We recognize that the wilderness is a place where God calls us to forsake what's comfortable and move into the unknown so He can guide us where we need to go.

The bread that God fed the Israelites in the wilderness was called manna. Every day they had to look for it and gather it. We, too, have to daily gather the manna God has for us. We have to seek God's presence and find the strength, joy, peace, and rest that nourishes and feeds our souls. We have to understand that in a place where there appears to be nothing, God will provide everything we need. The knowledge that all this is there for us in the wilderness is liberating. It frees us from having to be discontent. It frees us from striving to get out of the wilderness before it's time to leave. It frees us from trying to make things different than they are. It liberates us to allow God to do a new thing in us as He wills.

Just as God wanted the Israelite's allegiance, He wants yours, too. He also wants your attention, your trust, your mind, your soul, your body, and your obedience. In a word, He wants *you*. Don't deny Him that pleasure. Embrace the wilderness and say, "I want to be with You, Lord, even if that means staying in the wilderness until You're ready to bring me out." As Moses said, "'If Your Presence does not go with us, do not bring us up from here'" (Exodus 33:15).

God had the Israelites fill one jar with manna to keep in order to show future generations how He provided for them in the wilderness. Once

> ∾
>
> We have to understand that in a place where there appears to be nothing, God will provide everything we need. The knowledge that all this is there for us in the wilderness is liberating.
>
> ∾

you are out of the wilderness, don't forget it. Remember and talk about the goodness God showed you there, and how He sustained you and how you trust He will continue to do so. It will strengthen your faith and the faith of those around you.

My husband and I and our children frequently remind ourselves of how our lives have been blessed in Tennessee. Our wilderness time is over now and we're enjoying the milk and honey of the Promised Land. We love L.A., but don't long for it anymore. We know the wilderness is not a place; it's a spiritual growth process. In our case it was actually an answer to our own prayers. We followed the Lord, made it through the wilderness, and now the wilderness will always be a part of us because we don't ever want to let go of the priceless knowledge of God's goodness we gained there.

If you ever find that God is leading you into some kind of wilderness, my advice is to forget Egypt as quickly as you can. The comforts you once knew will not be there, so don't expect them. And don't lament over what you're missing or think you're lacking. Give yourself five minutes of grief over them, then let them go so you can enjoy the journey. Be happy where God has you. No one ever gets out of the wilderness as quickly as they would like to anyway, so refuse to feel deprived.

When traveling in the wilderness, learn to seek the abundance of the moment. Ask God to open your eyes to all the blessings He has for you there. As you see each one, let them become a refreshing spring. Soak them into the dry pores of your soul, drink them into the parched areas of your spirit, praise Him for every one, and feel that solid ground at the center of His will. Oh, and remember to pack lightly. I'd say take the Word of God, a measure of patience, a garment of praise, a pair of knee pads for those fervent prayer times, and an open vessel to hold the living water God is going to pour out on you. That's all you can manage on that path, anyway—especially in the kind of light you're going to have.

——————— *Prayer Light* ———————

*L*ord, I am at home wherever You are. If you call me into the wilderness, I will embrace it because You are there with me. Help me to not walk in fear or doubt, but in faith. Shine Your light on the path You have for me to travel, for I know that all my days are in Your hands. Forgive me when I grumble or have less than a grateful heart about where I am right now. I realize that my attitude will have a direct bearing on whether I wander around in circles, coming back to the same place over and over, or whether I get through to the Promised Land You have for me. Help me to trust You for every step. Enable me to see all the blessings that are right here in this moment. I trust that Your grace is sufficient for this day, and each day that follows.

*Footlights*

"If anyone serves Me, let him follow Me;
and where I am, there My servant will be also.
If anyone serves Me, him My Father will honor."

JOHN 12:26

"Whoever desires to come after Me,
let him deny himself,
and take up his cross,
and follow Me."

MARK 8:34

"My Presence will go with you,
and I will give you rest."

EXODUS 33:14

"My sheep hear My voice,
and I know them,
and they follow Me."

JOHN 10:27

Blessed are the people who know the joyful sound!
They walk, O LORD, in the light
of Your countenance.

PSALM 89:15

# ELEVEN

# Surrendering Your Dreams

Most of us have experienced a time when our lives appear to be standing still. No matter how hard we work, it seems like every door is closed and no new ones are opening. Often that's because we have an image in our mind of what we *want* to be happening, and when we see that it isn't we think *nothing* is happening.

*We can end up in a stagnant wilderness of frustration and confusion if we have made idols out of our dreams.*

God wants us to dream. He puts dreams in our heart for His purposes. But in our dreaming, He doesn't want us to exclude *Him*. God's Word says we will perish if we don't have a vision, but the vision we have must be His. If we don't have a vision from *Him*, then we don't have a vision that will ever be realized.

I know a young man who had a dream of the girl he wanted to marry. He had her every detail figured out, from the way she looked to the way she talked and thought. However, he could never find anyone who lived up to his dream. And I didn't have the heart to tell him that there was no girl on earth who could. Or would want to, for that matter. After years of frustrated searching, he was finally led to the feet of the Lord where he surrendered that dream to God. Right after he did, he met his future wife and married her within that year. When I met her, I found it amusing that she was nothing like the dream girl he had previously described to me. But she was perfect for him because she was the one God had chosen.

God wants us to surrender our dreams because we can't be led by Him if we are chasing after a dream of our own making. And He wants us to surrender *all* of them. That way He can tell us which of them are from Him and in line with *His* will, and which of them are ours and born out of *our* will. If they are only our dreams and visions and not His, we will experience a lifetime of unfulfillment and strife trying to make them happen. Even if the dream in your heart *is* from God, you still won't see it fulfilled until you give it to Him. The dream has to be realized *His* way.

Every fall in California we would cut our rosebushes back to nearly nothing. For about four months they looked like pathetic little dead sticks from which nothing could ever possibly grow again. But when spring came, they blossomed and bloomed profusely. First they grew hundreds of little buds. Then one by one they opened and burst into all shades of pink, purple, yellow, burgundy, and white. Abundant, fragrant, breathtaking, life-giving flowers that people driving or walking by would stop to admire. That's what God wants to do with us. He wants us to be His rose garden. He wants us to have beauty and purpose, and to give out a lifegiving fragrance to those around us. But first comes the pruning. First comes the period of dead-looking sticks.

When God wants to make changes in our lives, and we're willing to let Him, He starts by cutting away all that is unnecessary. In this process, He strips from us everything that could hinder our future growth, in order to prepare us to bring forth good fruit. Our life may look barren during that time, but God is actually freeing us from anything that does not bring forth life. This process of surrendering all to the Lord, especially our dreams and desires, is called pruning.

My husband, who has been a successful musician for thirty years, once knew that God was asking him to lay down his music for a time. He was twenty years old and already a professional piano player and writer when the Lord made it clear to Him that music was an idol in his life. He had to surrender his dream of ever playing or writing again. After two years of not doing anything in the music field—he didn't even practice the piano during that time—God gave him back the dream because it now had a different place in his heart. He went through the test, he endured the wilderness, he surrendered his dream, and he saw it resurrected. I don't believe his success would have been as far-reaching, or have had the longevity it has had, if he hadn't surrendered his dream years ago.

God puts dreams in our hearts to give us vision and inspiration and to guide us to the right path. That's why we have to make sure the dreams we have are not from our own flesh. The only way to be sure of that is to lay all of our dreams at His feet and let them die. And we must also die to them. The ones that are not from Him will be buried forever. The ones that *are* from Him will be given new life.

> ❧
>
> *W*e don't want to be just wishful thinkers. We want to live with confidence that our hopes, dreams, and expectations are based on God-given certainty that He is behind them.
>
> ❧

We don't want to be just wishful thinkers, always living in a dreamworld and never seeing anything of significance materialize. We don't want to be continually chasing after something God is not blessing. We want to live with confidence that our hopes, dreams, and expectations are based on God-given certainty that He is behind them. We want the hope that comes from God alone and is built on a foundation of His promises to us and His revealed purposes in us. This kind of hope is an anchor to the soul.

When my husband and I were first dating, I released Michael to the Lord every day. As much as I loved him, I did not want to manipulate a relationship to happen that was not meant to be. I had done that far too often in my past. I did it in my first marriage before I became a believer, and it ended in divorce less then two years later. As much as I wanted Michael, I desired what God had for me even more. Every day I sat at the feet of God and said, "Lord, I thank You that Michael is in my life. But if he is not the man you have to be my husband, I release him to you. Take him out of my life if we are not to be together. Close the door on this relationship if it is not of You. I'm walking step by step with You because I do not want to make another mistake."

When that door did not close, Michael and I were married and I knew it was God's will.

As the difficult times came in our marriage, I never wondered if God had really put us together. That issue had been settled long before when I fully surrendered the relationship to God. In the same year we celebrated our twenty-fifth wedding anniversary, my husband and I wrote a song called, "When the Dream Never Dies." One of the verses says,

> Isn't it just like the Lord to invite me
> To put all my dreams in His hands
> Forever releasing the grip that once held them
> Forever surrendering my plans

And then when He's certain it's not born of men
He calls for the fire to rekindle again
And asks me to know in my heart what's not
    seen with my eyes.
So the dream never dies.

Dying to our dreams is not fun. It's painful. Especially if our identity is wrapped up in them. But we have to do what God asks of us. And we must have a right attitude in the process or it's meaningless. The Bible says that if I "surrender my body to the flames, but have not love, I gain nothing" (1 Corinthians 13:3 NIV). Doing the right thing with a bad attitude does not work. Standing with our hands on our hips saying, "Okay, God, if you want to ruin me, go ahead," is not surrendering our dreams. It will definitely get God's attention, but it won't be the kind of attention we want.

The greatest breakthroughs in my life always came after a time of surrendering everything to God. I literally prostrated myself before Him with my face in the carpet and said, "God, I release everything to you and I freely give you permission to take out of my life what is not of You." I've done that with my children, my relatives, my friends, my work, my possessions, and my aspirations. It's difficult to say those words and mean them, but when we do the rewards are great.

Ask God if there are dreams in you that need to be laid down. If He says yes, this doesn't mean you have been doing anything wrong, or that you are out of the will of God. You

*O*ften God has us surrender our dreams because our dreams are usually for *us.* God wants our dreams to be for *Him.*

might be right in the *center* of God's will. The dream you have may be the one God wants you to have. But often God has us surrender our dreams because our dreams usually are for *us*. We want to do something that feels good and right to *us*. God wants our dreams to be for *Him*. He wants us to do what we do for *His* glory.

*Even if you are certain God has given you a vision or dream for your future, He will still ask you to surrender it to Him so thoroughly that you will think it's as good as dead.*

God doesn't want any part of you to be unsurrendered, not even the dreams He has put in your heart. If you give Him *all* of your dreams, then you will see which ones are born of His Spirit. Pursuing the ones that aren't will only lead to misery, frustration, and unfulfillment. Dying to your dreams is difficult, but if you reach up and take your Heavenly Father's hand, He will shine His light on the situation and walk you through the process step by step.

*Prayer Light*

Lord, I release all my hopes and dreams to You this day. If there is anything that I am longing for that is not to be a part of my life, I ask You to take away the desire for it so that what *should* be in my life will be released to me. I realize how dangerous it is to make idols of my dreams—to try and force my life to be what I have envisioned for myself. I lift up to you all that I desire, and I declare this day that I desire *You* more. I want the desires of my heart to line up with the desires of *Your* heart. As hard as it is for me to let go of the hopes and dreams I have for my life, I lay them all at Your feet. I know that as I die to them, You will either bury them forever or resurrect them to life. I accept Your decision and fully submit to it. Lead me in Your path, Lord. I don't want to speak a vision of my own heart (Jeremiah 23:16). You never said life would be easy. You said You would be with me. I now take each step with the light of Your presence as my guide.

## *Footlights*

Where there is no vision, the people perish.

PROVERBS 29:18 (NIV)

This evil people, who refuse to hear My words,
who follow the dictates of their hearts, and walk
after other gods to serve them and worship them,
shall be just like this sash which is profitable
for nothing.

JEREMIAH 13:10

. . . if we hope for what we do not see,
we eagerly wait for it with perseverance.

ROMANS 8:25

Hear now My words:
If there is a prophet among you,
I, the LORD, make Myself known to him in
a vision; I speak to him in a dream.

NUMBERS 12:6

Beloved, now we are children of God; and it
has not yet been revealed what
we shall be, but we know that when
He is revealed, we shall be like Him,
for we shall see Him as He is.

1 JOHN 3:2

# TWELVE

## Waiting in the Wings

Has it ever seemed like you are waiting in the wings for the next scene of your life to start? The stage is dark and you're expecting the lights to go up and the curtain to rise. The first act may or may not have gone smoothly, but by now you've been on an extended intermission and you're beginning to wonder if the second act will ever begin.

How many times in our lives have we found ourselves waiting like that? Waiting for things to change. Waiting for something to happen. Waiting for life to get back to normal. Waiting for more time or more money. Waiting for the relationship to get better. Waiting for the right door to open. Waiting for the right person to come along. Waiting for somebody to notice. Waiting, waiting, waiting.

We don't like waiting. We want action. But God says waiting can be good, because that's how we learn patience. We respond that there's nothing wrong with patience, but we want it now!

We can't have patience, however, without the waiting. And God says we need patience because it will ultimately make us complete. That's because patience is one of the attributes of God. When we are patient, we are like Him. When we are being tested, walking in the wilderness, surrendering our dreams, or standing in the line of fire, part of what we are learning is to be patient.

I've found that it's best to view these waiting times by thinking of them as times of waiting on the Lord. Try it. You'll see. It's much easier to think about waiting on God than it is to be patient with your circumstances. Waiting on the Lord gives you the sense that something is going on— only you just can't see it. You are waiting in eager anticipation of what God is going to do next.

I remember shortly after I became a believer and surrendered my dreams to the Lord, I felt like my life was turned upside down and shaken and everything that wasn't supposed to be in it came flying out—including my acting career. As the doors to that dream closed, I went through a time of waiting. I certainly had not yet learned to welcome a waiting period as an opportunity to develop patience. I was used to fulfilling my own destiny. It took months of impatient misery before I finally said to God, "What do you want me to do, Lord?"

I clearly understood Him to say that I was to completely give up any thought of an acting career. Instead I was to wait on Him and write. From the time I was old enough to hold a pencil, I had written stories, poems, songs, articles, skits, and plays. It was something I just did—like breathing. But I wanted to perform, so people would love me and I wouldn't have to feel bad about myself. Acting was a dream I had for *me*. But once I laid it down, I knew I had heard from God.

As a step of faith I bought a desk. (Waiting doesn't mean doing nothing.) I had never owned a desk in my life, but I bought an antique rolltop and filled it full of writing supplies. I sat down each day with a pen and empty sheets of paper and waited on the Lord to tell me what I should write. I didn't have a specific assignment; I simply wrote. I wrote about what I knew, what I felt, what God was teaching me, what I hoped, what I dreamed, what I had lived, what I had learned, and what I observed. I was still waiting, only now I was writing about waiting.

It seemed like I was going to wait forever for that curtain to go up on the next scene of my life, but it was only a matter of months until the waiting period was over. Just like a violent thunderstorm that suddenly stops and the sun comes out, my waiting ended. Writing opportunities opened up to me, and I was set on a new path, walking step by step with God. That was eight books, sixty magazine articles, and hundreds of song lyrics ago. I've never looked back or missed what God took out of my life, nor did I regret the time of waiting.

*Going through a waiting period doesn't mean there is nothing happening, because when you are waiting on the Lord, He is always moving in your life.*

Even though it may not seem like it, as long as you are walking with the Lord you are going from "glory to glory" and "strength to strength." You are always going somewhere in God's plan. And His purpose for you is constantly being realized. But you have to be patient and wait for Him to accomplish it His way and in His time.

I performed in live theater for years. The dialogue and stage directions were set, so all of us in the cast would do the same thing over and over, night after night. Same costumes, same words, same props, same actions. It could have been a

*Even though it may not seem like it, as long as you are walking with the Lord you are going from "glory to glory" and "strength to strength."*

boring experience where we ended up just going through the motions waiting for the play to be over. But we didn't, for one good reason. The audience was different every time. We performed it for new ears and new eyes each night, and that kept the play fresh for us as well.

If you ever feel like you are just going through the motions in your own life, don't let yourself become frustrated over it. Know that God's mercies to you are new every morning and as a result, God freshly hears your words spoken to Him as well. There is no such thing as the same old prayer. Each prayer you pray, even if it's about the same thing, has new life to it every time you pray it. Every day you have another opportunity to affect your future with the words you speak to God. Even though you may not see results as soon as you would like, much is happening in the spirit realm that you don't see. Each prayer sets something in motion.

Besides praying, there are other things you can do to keep your season of waiting on the Lord from turning into a dark time. Stay in God's Word and keep learning about Him. Ask the Lord to show you the talents and abilities He has given you and how you should develop them. Ask Him to reveal anything you need to start or stop doing. Perhaps He is waiting on *you*.

If you continue to walk with God and take the steps you know are right, you will get where you need to go. It may seem like forever, but don't be discouraged. God has been known to do a quick work for which He has been preparing a long time. Let Him sustain you in the interim. Tell yourself that you will "Rest in the LORD, and wait patiently for Him . . ." (Psalm 37:7).

*E*very day you have another opportunity to affect your future with the words you speak to God. Each prayer sets something in motion.

Patience is not resignation. It's joyful anticipation of the glory that is before you. Actors use that time before the curtain goes up to get focused and prepare for what's ahead. As you wait for the next scene of your life to begin, center yourself in the Lord, tell Him you are content to wait for His perfect timing, and ask Him to keep you from stumbling into any bad lighting.

───────────── *Prayer Light* ─────────────

Lord, I wait upon You this day. I put my hope in Your Word and ask that You would fill me afresh with Your Holy Spirit and wash away all anxiety or doubt. Shine Your spotlight into any dark corner of my soul that needs to be exposed. I don't want my impatience or lack of trust to stand in the way of all You desire to do in me. I realize that even when my life seems to be standing still, as long as I cling to You I am moving forward on the path You have for me. As I wait on You, help me to grow in my understanding of Your ways, and not succumb to impatience or discouragement because my timetable does not coincide with Yours. Strengthen my faith to depend on Your perfect timing for my life. Help me to rest in You and be content with the step I'm on and the light You have given me.

*Footlights*

. . . those who wait on the LORD
Shall renew their strength;
They shall mount up with wings like eagles,
They shall run and not be weary,
They shall walk and not faint.

ISAIAH 40:31

I wait for the LORD, my soul waits,
And in His Word I do hope.
My soul waits for the LORD
More than those who watch for the morning.

PSALM 130:5-6

Count it all joy when you fall into various trials,
knowing that the testing of your faith produces
patience. But let patience have its perfect work,
that you may be perfect and complete,
lacking nothing.

JAMES 1:2-4

The LORD is good to those who wait for Him,
To the soul who seeks Him.
It is good that one should
hope and wait quietly
For the salvation of the LORD.

LAMENTATIONS 3:25-26

Wait on the LORD;
Be of good courage,
And He shall strengthen
your heart.

PSALM 27:14

# THIRTEEN

# Expecting a Call

God has a great purpose for each one of us. There is a call from God on your life and mine. The question is, will we listen to find out what it is?

*We can be in the dark about the call of God on our lives for two reasons: either we have not heard God's call and we're living as though we have, or we have heard God's call and we're living as though we have not.*

I've seen many people who were too busy, too drugged out, too tired, too preoccupied, or too in pursuit of riches and fame to hear God calling them. Others were afraid they might be called to insignificance and so they didn't want to know about it. I've known others still who clearly heard the call of God and ran away from it. The direct line from heaven was ringing and they turned up the volume on their lives so they wouldn't have to hear God and answer. I've also known people with such a low opinion of themselves that they didn't believe God had them destined for anything great. So when the call came, they thought it must be for somebody else and didn't respond.

*The only reason it appears that some people are "more called" by God than others is that they were expecting the call and answered it.*

In the early days of telephones, people had party lines. Several households were on the same phone line and anyone in any of those households could pick up the phone and listen in on your conversation. This meant that by afternoon there might be many different opinions and interpretations of the conversation you had that morning. Receiving God's call does not happen that way. God's line to you is not a party line. You won't hear conflicting opinions. His call is entirely personal and private, and He will speak directly to you.

I'm not saying that God won't speak to someone else about you as well, because confirmation of His call is important. But true confirmation will only come from a person with a direct line to God themselves, who seeks to know God's will on your behalf. It will be someone with God-given authority in your life such as a parent, pastor, counselor, or mentor. But it won't be that only *they* hear and you don't. And do not ever think that you have strayed so far away from God that you've forever missed your call.

God will find you wherever you are. You can never be in so remote a place that He cannot bring you into all He has planned for you.

It never entered my mind that I had a life's calling until I was in my early thirties, and then I thought about it with deep regret. I was certain that by this late in life, I had passed up any opportunities for God to do something significant through me. Having lived far away from Him for so long, I despaired over what I considered an unredeemable loss. It wasn't until I understood that

> ∾
>
> *G*od is a Redeemer who redeems *all* things—even our past. Therefore, we can never be such a lost cause that His call on our lives is not longer applicable.
>
> ∾

God is a Redeemer who redeems *all* things—even our past—that I began to have hope. The Bible says that "the gifts and the calling of God are irrevocable" (Romans 11:29). When God issues a call, He doesn't take it back. He only waits for us to move into it. Therefore, we can never be such a lost cause that His call on our lives is no longer applicable.

Everyone shares certain calls on their life. For example, we are all called to partake of His divine nature (2 Peter 1:3-4), we are called to His eternal glory (1 Peter 5:10), and we are called to bless others (1 Peter 3:9). But we are individually called according to His own purpose. In other words, He has a specific calling for each one of us.

Many people know their calling, but can't see how it will ever be realized in the details of their lives. That's because they are trying to accomplish it in their own strength. But God doesn't say, "Here's what I want you to do with your life, now go do it." He first gives a vision and then says, "Walk step by step with Me and *I'll* do it through you."

Also, the whole of our call does not suddenly drop in our laps. We grow into it a step at a time, and it is realized gradually. For example, I know that I'm called to help people who are hurting, discouraged, or unfulfilled find a way out of their pain and frustration and see Jesus as the answer for every area of their lives. But I didn't just start doing that one day.

First, I asked God what I was to do with my life. Then when I began to hear, I didn't understand exactly what it was I was hearing. I had to surrender my dreams and watch the doors to what I thought was opportunity close. During the quietness of the waiting period that followed, I felt a tug on my heart that I would never have otherwise noticed in the noisy fast lane where I had been traveling. I sensed what

God wanted me to do, but I still didn't see how it could ever come about. I knew there was no way I could make it happen on my own.

Having a sense of God's call on my life forced me to declare my complete dependence upon Him more fervently than ever before. I was convinced that the only way anything of lasting significance would ever happen through me was if He accomplished it. As I waited for Him to do that, there were times I doubted whether I had even heard Him correctly. But eventually doors opened and as I walked through them the Lord blessed the outcome. When opportunities came my way that were not in line with my calling, I knew it. In certain moments of insecurity, I did accept a couple of offers that were outside of what I understood to be God's purpose for my life. The results brought emptiness, and I knew I was doing something that fell far below what God had called me to do.

If you feel called to something better than what you are doing now, let me assure you that it is probably because you are. If you have never sought God about His plans and purposes for your life, do that now. If you have already done that, then there must be a purpose for what you are doing at this moment that you cannot see. Or perhaps you have unsurrendered dreams. In any case, know that He will not leave you where you are forever.

This doesn't mean you have to accept everything that comes your way as the will of God. Far from it. Ask Him about it. Say, "Lord, is what I am doing consistent with Your purpose in my life? If it is Your will, I submit to it and embrace You in it. If it isn't, then make me what You created me to be." As long as you are consistently praying about it, God will either take you where you're supposed to be, or give you grace to remain where you are until He says it's time to move on.

Keep in mind that once you hear God's call on your life, it doesn't mean that things will start happening immediately. You will most likely experience a time of waiting until He decides you are ready. So don't let the waiting period turn into a dark time that causes you to doubt whether you've heard God at all. Keep in mind that in this time He wants you to forget any plans you might have for accomplishing your purpose on your own. He wants you to be totally convinced it won't happen without Him.

*God's call on all of us is to be a light to those who are in darkness, but sometimes He has to take us through our own darkness so we will learn to depend totally on His light.*

Oswald Chambers said, "If I am going to approach the holy ground, I must get into the right frame of mind—the excellency of a broken heart."[1] Our hearts break when we think we have missed our destiny. We suffer over unfulfilled purpose. But God perfects our hearts when we suffer. He makes us humble and compassionate, and these are two traits we must have for success in the call He has for us.

Don't be afraid of the perfecting process that prepares you to move into God's call on your life. It will establish, strengthen, and settle you (1 Peter 5:10). Just stand strong through the fire and you will be purified, molded, humbled, and made ready for what He has for you to do. If you walk step by step with God, you'll come out of that time with a sense of His presence and power that will make it all worthwhile. It will set you on the path to greatness.

*T*oo often when people think of greatness, it stirs up images in their minds of having great talent, riches, fame, or accomplishments. But greatness is not about *us;* it's about *His* greatness *in* us.

Let me clarify the meaning of greatness. Too often when people think of greatness, it stirs up images in their minds of having great talent, great riches, great fame, great influence, great power, or great accomplishments. They mistakenly believe that greatness comes about because of something they are or something they have. But greatness is not about *us*; it's about *His* greatness *in* us.

*God's idea of greatness is having a heart, soul, and spirit so full of His greatness that it manifests through us.*

In the Bible, the word "great" is nearly always used to describe who God is: "For the LORD is great and greatly to be praised . . ." (1 Chronicles 16:25). Or what God has done: "The LORD has done great things for us, and we are glad" (Psalm 126:3). A great person is one who obeys God: "Whoever therefore breaks one of the least of these commandments, and teaches men so, shall be called least in the kingdom of heaven; but whoever does and teaches them, he shall be called great in the kingdom of heaven" (Matthew 5:19). A great person is one who is a servant: "Yet it shall not be so among you; but whoever desires to become great among you, let him be your servant" (Matthew 20:26).

When we acknowledge God's greatness through our worship of Him, we invite His greatness to dwell *in* us. When we obey God and serve Him, then He does great things *through* us. This is the kind of greatness God has called us to in our lives.

If you heard God's call to greatness years ago and have been following it faithfully, that doesn't mean you won't hear a fresh, new call now. Or maybe God will newly define the old one. Whichever it is, you need ears to hear. If your heart is not quickened with anticipation over what God is going to do through you, perhaps your listening has become dulled by the processes of life. Find time to get away with the Lord and let Him speak to you again.

Remember that in order to hear God's call, you must be expecting a call. You need faith that He *will* speak to you, that you *can* hear Him, and that it *will* be good news. Say, "I have set the Lord always before me" (Psalm 16:8), and expect to hear His voice. When an encounter with the living God is your greatest desire, you can be sure you will have it.

If you have not heard anything from God, may I politely suggest that there *is* a person-to-person call on line one for you. You'd better take it. It's God wanting to cast a definitive light on your path.

─────────── *Prayer Light* ───────────

Lord, I know You have great purpose for me and a plan for my life. Open my ears to hear Your voice leading me into all You have for me. Align my heart with Yours and prepare me to understand where You would have me to go and what You would have me to do. Help me to hear Your call. If my expectations and plans are out of alignment with Your will for me, I surrender them to You. I let my desires for myself die. I would rather endure the suffering of that than the pain of never realizing what You made me to be. Because I want to hear Your voice say, "Well done, my good and faithful servant," when I meet You face to face, I will listen for Your voice now. I don't want to be unfruitful and unfulfilled because I never clearly heard Your call. I want You to fill me with Your greatness so that I may do great things for others as You have called me to do. I commit to walking this road step by step with You so that I may fully become all that You have made me to be.

## Footlights

. . . you are a chosen generation, a royal priesthood,
a holy nation, His own special people, that you
may proclaim the praises of Him who called you
out of darkness into His marvelous light. . . .

1 PETER 2:9

. . . whom He predestined, these He also called;
whom He called, these He also justified; and whom
He justified, these He also glorified.

ROMANS 8:30

. . . the God of our Lord Jesus Christ, the Father of
glory, may give to you the spirit of wisdom and
revelation in the knowledge of Him, the eyes of
your understanding being enlightened;
that you may know what is the hope of His calling,
what are the riches of the glory of His inheritance in
the saints, and what is the exceeding greatness of His
power toward us who believe, according to the
working of His mighty power. . . .

EPHESIANS 1:17-19

"You are the light of the world.
A city that is set on a hill cannot be hidden.
. . . Let your light so shine before men,
that they may see your good works
and glorify your Father in heaven."

MATTHEW 5:14, 16

# FOURTEEN

# Believing It's Not Over Till It's Over

You might be too young to appreciate this now, but there may come a time in your life when it feels like you have outlived your usefulness and purpose. You fear that God and everyone else is through with you and you're no longer relevant. You start to believe that although you may have *had* a call on your life, it's over now. You're being put out to pasture.

The enemy of your soul wants you to believe that you have no purpose so that you can actually become all those things you fear becoming. It's one of his most common deceptions. But the truth is, God is *never* through with you. He *always* has a plan for your life. There is no time limit on His call or what He wants to do in and through you. God will use you for His purposes until the day you go to be with Him. And don't let yourself be convinced otherwise.

What *may* be true about what you are experiencing is that life as you have known it is changing. What existed *before* may be over, but what is *ahead* for you is as great or perhaps much greater. Just when you suspect things may be winding down in your life, God will do something new. He may call you to rework the details of your present walk, or He might set you out on a completely new path. God will call you to a new time, a new assignment, and a new work of His grace. That is, of course, if you are open to letting Him do what He wants. This is where staying attentive to His leading and being willing to move accordingly is important.

I know a man who owned a successful business for years. In his late fifties, he experienced some health problems that forced him to retire. At first He was discouraged and thought his life was over. But he and his wife began to sense a leading from God to move to a more favorable climate and adopt a less stressful lifestyle in order to develop a successful ministry to troubled or runaway teenage girls. It was a service they had always enjoyed volunteering part-time for at their church, but now they were able to devote themselves to it full-time. They are presently more fulfilled than they have ever been.

*We are such creatures of habit and so resistant to change that God sometimes has to shut off the way things were in our lives so He can bring us into the way He wants us to be.*

When my husband and I made our move from California to Tennessee the transition was very difficult physically, mentally, and emotionally. Moving is upsetting anyway, but relocating from one part of the country that was so completely different from the other at age fifty was too much, and I let God know it.

"Lord, don't you realize we're too old for this? We don't have it in us to

*God* will call you to a new time, a new assignment, and a new work of His grace. That is, of course, if you are open to letting Him do what He wants.

start all over again. It's too hard. Are you putting us out to pasture?"

We knew that we had followed the leading of the Lord, but it wasn't until our California home was destroyed in the Northridge earthquake a few months after we moved that we stopped questioning Him. That was answer enough. We were certain we had made the right decision. We even knew why we had never been able to sell the house. Anyone living in it surely would have been seriously injured or even killed.

Over the years that we've been here, many opportunities and blessings for Michael and me and each of our children have come along that would not have been available to us had we stayed in California. What originally seemed like the end became a new beginning. But new beginnings don't happen without something ending.

Major life changes can be scary. But if we don't cling desperately to the old life, the new experiences can be exciting as well. Trying to keep things from changing only makes the process miserable. It's far less upsetting to just let the old go and walk step by step with God into the new life He has for us.

Many of the greatest people of the Bible achieved their most significant accomplishments in their later years, at a time when they thought their productivity was coming to a close. Noah was a very old man when God called him to build the ark. "Noah was six hundred years old when the floodwaters were on the earth" (Genesis 7:6). If people can live to be ninety years old today, Noah was the equivalent of a sixty-year-old man when he and his family gave up life as they had always known it and got on board the ark. His experience was not that of a young man dreaming a young man's dream. Noah was definitely beyond the time of midlife crisis when God called him to do his greatest work.

Even Moses, just before He led the Israelites out of Egypt, thought his life was over in terms of ever doing anything significant for the Lord. Though he always had a passion in his heart to free his people from their enslavement—which was God's call on his life—it only made matters worse when he tried to help them *his* way. It was not until he had been thoroughly pruned, seasoned, literally put out to pasture, and trained to follow the Lord step by step that God used him powerfully.

Abraham was one hundred years old and his wife, Sarah, was ninety when God touched their lives and she finally became pregnant and gave birth to their first child. They thought they were too old for that to ever happen, but God was just beginning a new time in their lives. It fulfilled God's call on them and it affected the entire world and all of history.

I wonder where would we be if Noah, Moses, Abraham, Sarah, or any of the other great men and women of the Bible had listened to the voice that said, "You're too old to do anything significant." What if Noah had responded to God by saying, "Me? Build a boat? I'm too over the hill." Or if Moses had insisted, "Pharaoh is never going to listen to an old geezer like me." Or if Abraham and Sarah had looked at each other and said, "Forget it." None of us would even be here had they not seen a vision of what God had for their future and allowed Him to walk them step by step into a new time in their lives.

>
> God may call you and me to do our greatest work in our fifties, sixties, seventies, or even eighties and beyond. What a wonderful thing to look forward to!

God may call you and me to do our greatest work in our fifties, sixties, seventies, or even eighties and beyond. What a wonderful thing to look forward to! God does not devalue people over a certain age like society does. Big business may tell a man in his fifties or sixties that he is too old to do the work he has done all his life. Or that he cannot be hired because of his advanced age, even though he may be every bit as capable as someone younger. But God does not put a lifetime of experience and knowledge into you and then put you out to pasture. Your life is never over until it's over. And that's when God calls you home to be with Him.

If the job you've been doing ends, or the provision you've known shuts off, or the fulfillment level of your work and activities ceases, or something major happens to change the status of your life, don't be alarmed. These could be signs of a change God is doing in your life. He may be getting you ready to enter into a new and exciting season. God's Word says that those who love Him and live His way will bear fruit into old age and always be fresh and flourishing.

*If life as you have known it and the path that you have walked seem to be ending, draw especially close to God and He will reveal what your next step is to be.*

Although God has promised we will bear fruit into old age, remember that fruit is seasonal. We won't necessarily bear fruit constantly. We will have seasons of rest so the soil of our lives won't be depleted. When God wants to produce a fresh new crop through you, don't strive against what is intended to be a time of plowing up and preparing the soil. It doesn't mean you are going to wither. God promises that you will be filled with living water, bring forth new life, and prosper in all you do. Trust Him. He has never been closer. Become more dependent upon the Lord than ever. Lose yourself completely in Him so that He becomes everything. Follow Him so closely that you will not miss the harvest He has for you.

No matter what age you are, God has a path for you. It will undoubtedly take you someplace you've not been before.

Be willing to let Him prepare you as He sees fit. Follow the leading of the Lord as you place your hand in His, and trust that the light that is in you can never be put out.

—————————— *Prayer Light* ——————————

*L*ord, thank You that my life is never over here on this earth until You say it is. And when that time comes, I will see You face to face and dwell in Your presence. Thank You that You never give up on me, even when I have given up on myself. I am so happy that no matter what age I am, I will always have purpose because You have great things for me to do. When it's time for me to do something different, help me not to cling to the past or be afraid to move into the future You have for me. My times are in Your hands, and I know that I am secure as long as I can walk through them all with You. Give me strength, courage, health, wisdom, revelation, and faith for the journey. I trust You to keep me on the right path and to continue giving me the light I need for the step I'm on.

## Footlights

Those who are planted in the house of the LORD
Shall flourish in the courts of our God.
They shall still bear fruit in old age;
They shall be fresh and flourishing.

PSALM 92:13-14

Listen to counsel and receive instruction,
That you may be wise in your latter days.

PROVERBS 19:20

Even to your old age, I am He,
And even to gray hairs I will carry you!
I have made, and I will bear;
Even I will carry, and will deliver you.

ISAIAH 46:4

You will show me the path of life;
In Your presence is fullness of joy;
At Your right hand are pleasures forevermore.

PSALM 16:11

. . . when I am old and gray-headed,
O God, do not forsake me,
Until I declare Your strength to this generation,
Your power to everyone who is to come.

PSALM 71:18

# FIFTEEN

# Surviving Disappointment

Disappointment is inevitable. That's because life can never consistently live up to our expectations.

When my friend Marcie's husband chose another woman to be with instead of her, the disappointment she felt was engulfing. She could have turned to alcohol, bitterness, revenge, or another man's arms, but she turned instead to the Comforter. She drew closer to the Lord and let Him provide relief from her complex feelings of guilt, resentment, failure, and depression. She relied on His unfailing love and steady hand through the dark times of struggle as she carved out a new life for herself and her children. She declined to sit in the darkness of unforgiveness, but instead walked a step at a time in the light of the Lord. She refused to allow her disappointment with the way things turned out to shadow her life for years to come. Eventually she was able to find happiness again.

Life certainly doesn't always turn out the way we imagine it will. When it doesn't, how can we survive the disappointment?  How can we get through those dark times?

Often our greatest times of disappointment come when someone fails us, or we at least *feel* that they have. People can hurt us deeply. Sometimes they know what they are doing, while other times they're only doing the best they know how to do with the tools they have. In either case, the level of fulfillment and happiness we experience in our lives doesn't depend on other people; it depends on God. Of course, we do rely on other people for certain things, and it's painful when they let us down. But the ultimate success or joy of our life should not depend on them. We don't have to prolong suffering over what others do or don't do to us, because ultimately our reward is in God's hands.

It's also seriously disappointing when we believe *we* have failed in some way, perhaps due to our own carelessness or in spite of our best efforts. Or we *think* we have failed when we really haven't at all. And we sit in darkness over it, torturing ourselves. The regret and condemnation pounds us down like a giant sledgehammer to our soul. "If only I hadn't . . ." "If I just would have . . ." "Why didn't I . . ." It's a weight we can't carry and were never meant to.

> ~
> *H*ow wonderful it is to know that even in a darkness of our own creation, God is still there and so is His light.
> ~

Even when we have to bear the consequences for the wrong choices we've made, God is still on our side. "When I fall, I will arise; when I sit in darkness, the LORD will be a light to me" (Micah 7:8). How wonderful it is to know that even in a darkness of our own creation, God is still there and so is His light. I think that's what makes us love Him most. His grace. We realize how little we deserve it and how far short of His glory we fall, yet He loves and accepts us anyway. Even in our greatest depth of failure, God brings good out of it as long as we reach humbly to Him.

*We make a mistake in expecting too much from ourselves, other people, and life, when our expectations should be from God.*

One time my husband was very disappointed about a big work project that fell through. Someone had promised something great that did not materialize, and the result seemed to be financial as well as personal devastation. Not being one to look on the bright side, he was very upset about it.

"This project isn't more important than God's will, is it?" I asked him.

He hesitated a little too long for my comfort, then gave a begrudging and controlled, "No."

"Then how do you know God doesn't have something far better for you?" I asked.

He gave me a look that can only be described as equal parts hope, doubt, and suppressed irritation all rolled into one facial expression. "I don't," he replied.

"Don't waste your time being upset," I encouraged him. "This is probably more of an opportunity than a disaster, and we should thank God for it."

He still was not cheered.

It seemed like a long time, but it was actually only a few weeks later that he was offered a project far greater in every respect than the one which had been cancelled. There was no way he could have done both, and he would have had to turn the better one down if he'd already been involved in the first project.

God often allows hard things to happen in our lives in order to bless us in some way. If we are willing to allow for that possibility in everything that happens, it saves us from being devastated by people and situations that are ultimately going to be used for God's glory. If we surrender our disappointment to God and say, "Be my light and lead me through this, Lord," His work will be accomplished faster. But if we wallow in the darkness of bitterness, casting blame upon God and other people, we end up suffering more.

When Moses brought the Israelites out of slavery in Egypt, they had to choose to walk God's way. In their bondage under Pharaoh, they didn't have to make choices; they only had to do what they were told. Instead of choosing to see God's hand in the moment, they blamed Moses and God for everything that disappointed them. As a result, their suffering was prolonged.

Oswald Chambers says, "The agony of a man's affliction is often necessary to put him into the right mood to face the fundamental things of life." [1]

When disappointing things happen to you, ask God to help you discern His truth about what you are experiencing. Ask *Him* to reign in the situation instead of your feelings. It's easy to go with anger or hurt, but far more rewarding to find God's blessing in the situation instead.

*It pleases God when you have faith enough in the midst of your disappointment to put your hope and expectations in Him.*

When you experience disappointment, do not run into the arms of bitterness or unforgiveness. Run to your Father's arms instead so He can hold and sustain you. If you will maintain a humble, submitted, faith-filled, expectant heart, you will see God's goodness manifest in the midst of all that's happening to you. He will use this experience to bring

>
> *I*f you will maintain a humble, submitted, faith-filled, expectant heart, you will see God's goodness manifest in the midst of all that's happening to you.

you closer to Him, and your greatest treasure will be a deep sense of His presence. He will make things right, and He is the only one who can. Remember that no matter how dark times of disappointment become, God is still your light. Walk in the light He gives you.

*——————— Prayer Light ———————*

*L*ord, You alone are my guide, my companion, my strength, and my life. I need no other to fulfill my expectations, for all my hopes and expectations are in You. In times of great disappointment, I will cling to You. I will walk through them with You. Show me what You want me to see. Teach me what You want me to learn. Reveal Your truth to me. I refuse to allow disappointment to color my mind and emotions and outlook. I put You in charge of every detail of my life, even the pain I feel in my heart. Use it to perfect me and bring glory to You. Thank You for Your endless goodness toward me. You supply all my needs. I lift my hands to You, and I trust that the light I have is sufficient for what I face this day and this moment.

## Footlights

My soul, wait silently for God alone,
For my expectation is from Him.

Psalm 62:5

They cried to you and were saved;
in you they trusted and were not disappointed.

PSALM 22:5 (NIV)

Now hope does not disappoint, because the
love of God has been poured out in our hearts
by the Holy Spirit who was given to us.

ROMANS 5:5

. . . judge nothing before the time, until the Lord
comes, who will both bring to light the hidden
things of darkness and reveal the counsels
of the hearts. Then each one's praise
will come from God.

1 CORINTHIANS 4:5

The LORD will perfect that which concerns me. . . .

PSALM 138:8

# SIXTEEN

# Traveling Through the Dark Moments of Relationships

Relationships can be difficult to navigate because of one major variable—*the other person!* Due to that great unknown, we may be going along doing the best we know how and all of a sudden find ourselves in the middle of a relationship crisis. Our darkest hours can come because of the troubled times we have with people.

Any kind of relationship can bring pain. Strife with a mother or father, a brother or sister, a husband or wife, a son or daughter, a relative, friend, pastor, boss, neighbor, boyfriend, girlfriend, or coworker can cause us to experience a knot in our stomach, a lump in our throat, and a loss of sleep. That's because whether we want to acknowledge it or not, relationships are very important to each of us. We can't live without them. Nor were we ever intended to. God never planned for us to live entirely separate from other people.

*Much of what God wants to work in us will come about as we grow in our relationships with the people God puts in our lives.*

The enemy of our soul does not want our relationships to work. He knows that as our relationships are destroyed, so too will be our strength and effectiveness. After all, how effective can we be when our marriages fall apart, we're estranged from our children, we fight with our siblings, we don't get along with our coworkers, or we have no strong friendships? If we can be convinced that these relationships are not worth the effort it takes to fight for them, then the enemy has us in darkness. Right where he wants us.

In one of the many prayer groups I have had over the past twenty years, a situation arose that I knew could easily divide the group. It would certainly have split us down the middle, with each person taking one side or the other. During one of the dark nights of my travail over the situation, I prayed, "Lord, each one of these women is far more important to me than this issue that has the potential to divide us. I know that each one sees this matter from her own perspective and believes she is right. I don't even know how to pray about this because I see it from my own perspective and I feel *I* see it right. But I am willing to let go of *my* perspective and *my* desire to be right, so that *Your* Spirit of peace will prevail. I see where this could possibly be heading and I pray that Your Spirit of unity would reign in each of us and shine light on our path. I refuse to allow the enemy to bring strife and destruction. Let there be no severing of friendships or wounding of hearts."

I released the situation into God's hands and watched His work as He walked me one step at a time through it. Over the next several

>
>
> *The* enemy of our soul does not want our relationships to work. He knows that as our relationships are destroyed, so too will be our strength and effectiveness.

weeks He powerfully transformed the entire matter and it dissipated. The love and commitment each woman had toward God and each other became the focus and made the issue at hand pale to nothing, eventually becoming a non-issue. Had any one of us insisted that we were right, the outcome would have been quite different.

Every relationship requires a sacrifice. Every sacrifice has a reward. If we knew the rewards, we wouldn't hesitate to make the sacrifices. Part of the sacrifice we must pay in a relationship is laying down our pride and our needs. We need to be loved, cared for, valued, and respected, but we never get those needs met when we demand them. We get them met when we give them up.

*Humbling ourselves and putting the other person's needs before our own can resurrect a relationship that has suffered mortal wounds.*

Marriage, especially, has the greatest potential for deep emotional injury and by far the stiffest requirements for sacrifice. That's because the person who knows us best can hurt us most. If that weren't so, we would not see such a high divorce rate. It takes too much effort to dissolve a marriage, divide up everything, and establish separate living quarters. Even more so if children are involved. No one does it lightly. No one comes out unscathed. Yet millions of people get divorced because their hurt is so great that they believe staying in the marriage will destroy them.

I do not condemn nor criticize anyone who has chosen the path of divorce. I chose it myself at one time. I was married before I became a believer, and my first marriage did not last two years. But for me it was two years of disaster, and I believed I would die if I stayed in it. When I married again, it was under very different circumstances. Both my husband and I were committed to God and to living His way. Over the past twenty-five years of marriage we have tried to relate to one another the way God designed us to, but it has not always been easy. We experienced dark times in our marriage when the selfishness of our flesh almost brought us to the brink of collapse.

On one particularly dark night of discord, I remember going before God and saying, "Lord, I can't endure the pain I feel in this marriage another day. If You don't intervene, it's over."

The Lord, without judgement, answered the cries of my heart, saying, "If you will lay down your life for My sake and reach up your hand to Me, I will guide you through these rough waters and you *will* get to the other side of this storm and walk on calmer seas than ever before."

God did not promise that my husband would ever change or that things would be any different than they were right then, but He did promise that He would go through the storm with me. He would sustain me and my greatest blessing would come from Him. But first I had to lay down my life in prayer for my husband like I had never done before. I had to give up my desire to see my needs met, and instead pray for God to work in my husband and meet *his* needs. It was a very difficult lesson to learn, but as I walked with God through those dark moments and made the sacrifice He asked me to make, I saw His resurrecting power bring life and restoration to our marriage.

Let me make one thing clear. Laying down your life for a relationship does not mean allowing someone to physically or emotionally destroy you. Abuse does *not* get better on its own. The abuser has a serious problem that must be resolved, and you are keeping that person in bondage when you permit him to continue to abuse you. It cannot lead to life for either of you. Nothing of redemption comes out of it—only bitterness and the destruction of the soul.

God has far more for you than that. Don't allow any abuse to continue!

Problems in any marriage require a special portion of God's grace and revelation for each moment. We must ask God every day to take all our hopes, expectations, dreams, and disappointments, and give us more of His love, patience, kindness, and a willingness to sacrifice. I stayed in my marriage and saw God work miraculous change, and it is better now than it has ever been. But the good did not come without my sacrifice of laying down what *I* wanted and doing what *God* wanted.

A relational crisis with our children is right next to marital strife on the misery scale. When a relationship with a child breaks down, our heart breaks as well. But when we walk step by step with God through each crisis, we will see Him do a miraculous work of transforming, restoring, and healing. When we bring God into the midst of the situation, everyone benefits.

The most difficult confrontations my husband and I have had with our children, as upsetting as they were at the time, have brought about the greatest growth and deliverance in both their lives and ours. Each instance bonded us closer together. As we prayed through many a painfully dark night for them, strongholds of the enemy that were seeking to encroach upon their lives were revealed and broken down. We stood in the line of fire, refused to be afraid of the dark, surrendered our dreams for them, survived disappointment, held on to the light God gave us, and waited for Him to move.

*W*hen we walk step by step with God through each crisis, we will see Him do a miraculous work of transforming, restoring, and healing.

Staying on the right path in *any* relationship means getting rid of excess baggage that keeps us from seeing the light. Unforgiveness and jealousy are examples of such baggage. These negative attitudes will drive a wedge into any relationship. And they are always evident to other people, even if they don't recognize exactly what it is they are observing. The dark moments of relationships can be kept to a minimum if we humble ourselves before God and ask Him to walk us step by step through every layer of unforgiveness and jealousy. It's a sacrifice that always brings a great reward.

The best way to protect all of your relationships is to make sure your primary relationship is with the Lord. Then commit each of your relationships to God and ask Him to be Lord over all of them. Cover them in prayer and seek God's hand of reconciliation where it needs to happen. Even though we can do a great deal to offer our love and forgiveness to other people, only God can soften their hearts enough for them to receive it. Ask Him to do that, too.

If you are having trouble with a particular person who is causing you to feel so much pain that it incapacitates you, release him or her to God and allow the Lord to take the relationship away if He so chooses. He may need to do that for just a season if something needs to be worked in each of you individually that can't happen when you are together. Or there may exist some unhealthy aspect of the relationship that He wants to make right. Perhaps you are unequally yoked. After all, "what communion has light with darkness?" (2 Corinthians 6:14). If that relationship is to be restored again, *He* will restore it on *His* terms. If not, you can trust that it was not meant to be a part of your life. If that person is never to have the place in your life that you want him or her to have, don't try to hang on and make it happen. Relationships only work when the Lord is in charge of them.

In ironing out the wrinkles in relationships, I find it's best to remember two things—release people and cling to God. Gaining that perspective can help you rise above the failings of flesh and elevate you to the realm of the miraculous. The stronger your relationship is with the Lord, the better your other relationships will be. The dark moments of any relationship can strengthen your walk with the Lord as you draw closer to Him. So make Him the focus of your attention, and trust Him to shine a special light at the crossroads of where your path intersects with the path of another person.

## Prayer Light

Lord, I give all my relationships to You and ask that You be in charge of them. May Your spirit of unity reign in each one. If any are not of You, take them out of my life. Concerning my relationship with (_____), I ask that Your spirit of love and peace would reign between us. I relinquish my hold and release him (her) to You. Lead him (her) in the way You would have him (her) to go. Bless him (her) and help him (her) to have a closer walk with You. Guide us both through any difficult times and help us to discern clearly the hand of the enemy when he comes to lie and destroy.

Shine Your light of revelation into every relationship I have and show me Your truth. Illuminate any darkness of unforgiveness in me and I will confess it to You as sin. Bring reconciliation and clarity in place of misunderstanding.

Where I need to humbly extend myself, enable me to make any necessary sacrifice and not cater to the cries of my flesh. Help me to lay down my life in prayer for my family, friends, and others You have put in my life. Teach me how to love the way that You do. I join my hand in Yours as I travel the path of relationships with Your unconditional love as my guiding light.

## *Footlights*

He who says he is in the light, and hates his brother,
is in darkness until now.

1 JOHN 2:9

If we say that we have fellowship with Him,
and walk in darkness, we lie and do not
practice the truth. But if we walk in the
light as He is in the light, we have
fellowship with one another, and
the blood of Jesus Christ His
Son cleanses us from all sin.

1 JOHN 1:6-7

Let nothing be done through selfish
ambition or conceit, but in lowliness of mind
let each esteem others better than himself. Let each of
you look out not only for his own interests,
but also for the interests of others.

PHILIPPIANS 2:3-4

Let all bitterness, wrath, anger, clamor, and evil
speaking be put away from you, with all malice.
And be kind to one another, tenderhearted,
forgiving one another, even as
God in Christ forgave you.

EPHESIANS 4:31-32

"Greater love has no one than this,
than to lay down one's life for his friends."

JOHN 15:13

# SEVENTEEN

# Walking in the Midst of the Overwhelming

At some point in each of our lives, we may find our world being violently shaken. Such traumatic experiences as a devastating illness, a debilitating accident, desertion by a spouse, the death of a loved one, criminal violence, financial ruin, or a natural disaster can occur with disarming suddenness. How can we be prepared to stand strong in the midst of overwhelming circumstances that come without warning?

Let me give you an example of an overwhelming circumstance. It's suddenly being awakened out of a deep sleep, in the thick, black darkness of night, to the deafening roar and violent shaking of a severe earthquake. I endured too many earthquakes like this in Los Angeles during the forty years that I lived there, and they were by far the most traumatic experiences of my life. I *never* got used to them.

Before I started walking with the Lord, each earthquake produced heart-stopping terror in me. After coming into a personal relationship with God, I still experienced the terror, but then came a reassuring sense of God's presence. I knew He was there in the midst of it.

146 ᴗ *Stormie Omartian*

I remember one particularly strong earthquake that happened when I was living alone in a first floor apartment of a three-story building. This is an especially dangerous place to be because in older apartment buildings constructed before certain codes were established, the higher floors can easily crash down upon the lowest one. Over the deafening roar I could hear glass shattering as my dishes and lamps fell violently to the floor. I leaped out of bed and tried to make my way to a doorframe for protection, but the force of the shaking knocked me violently from wall to wall. I was desperately afraid, and my one thought was to reach the phone so I could call someone and not have to die alone. When I did reach the phone, it was dead.

The next major earthquake I endured occurred a few years later, when I was walking with the Lord. In marked contrast to the earlier quake, the instant this one hit the only One I thought to call was the Lord. Over the roar, I knew He heard my voice cry out for His help even when I could not hear it myself. I realized that He was there with me and, even if I died in that violent darkness, I would never be separated from Him.

Circumstances don't have to be catastrophic to be overwhelming. We can experience things that are nowhere near as life-threatening as what I just described, but can seem every bit as frightening. Some people view public speaking as a terrifying experience. They would rather endure an earthquake. For others, confronting a difficult person, having to make a dreaded phone call, or facing the daily challenge of an eating disorder or an addiction are earth-shaking challenges. Many people are overwhelmed by raising children, handling the responsibilities of life, or dealing with a strong-willed teenager.

Sometimes the pileup of many little things—each one alone being relatively harmless—becomes more than we can handle. Such things as stress in the workplace, pressure at school, uncomfortable social situations, or anything else that brings expectations that we feel we can't live up to can fill us with overwhelming anxiety. No matter what the specifics, the key to overcoming these kinds of overwhelming circumstances is to walk step by step with God through them.

*When we set our anchor in the Lord, we will not be carried away by the storms that threaten to overtake us.*

Godly people throughout the Bible, and anyone since who has not lost touch with reality, have all gone through times of being overwhelmed and fearful. Yet being afraid doesn't mean that God is not with you, that you are out of God's will, or that you are a spiritual weakling. It *could* be a sign that you are in the wrong place, doing the wrong thing, or that something is out of order in your life. It may also be an indication of enemy attack or a warning of a threat to your safety. If fear comes upon you without any apparent reason, ask God to show you what it means and where it is coming from. It may be a signal from the Lord to pray. That has happened to me many times, always for a good reason that I didn't understand until later.

One morning I woke up at three A.M. with tremendous fear. I asked God to show me what was causing it, then felt led to pray about the safety of my home and family. As I prayed for them, I sensed an urgency to also pray for the safety of the homes and families in our neighborhood. Then I covered the next neighborhood and the next, followed by our community, and finally the whole town. I had prayed many times before for all that. Just never at three in the morning. When the fear was gone, I went back to sleep.

*Being afraid doesn't mean that God is not with you, that you are out of God's will, or that you are a spiritual weakling.*

A few hours later, I was awakened by a phone call from a close friend telling us there were severe tornado warnings and that we should get into the basement immediately. We did. And the tornadoes came. They were all around us, but we were safe in the midst of them. Even in the area not far from us where the tornadoes did the greatest amount of damage, only one death occurred. I'm sure I wasn't the only one God woke up to pray, but when He did, I asked Him to show me what my fear meant and sensed Him leading me to intercede. Never underestimate the significance of praying through any unexpected and unexplained fear.

Don't ignore your fear, but refuse to be controlled by it. Sometimes the enemy of your soul will come upon you and in a moment show you *everything* you could possibly fear. When that barrage happens, don't listen to any of it. Tune out his lies and tune in to God's Word. Ask the Lord to speak to you, and He will tell you the truth.

Any sign of fear should always be a call to prayer. The moment you feel it, draw *immediately* close to God. Get a sense of His presence and leading and allow His love to fully penetrate your situation. Perfect love casts out all fear, but thank God it's not *our* love that has to be perfect. Only *His* can.

*The deeper we press into the Lord, the more of His perfect love we experience, and the less fear we will have.*

When your whole life is shaken, when the circumstances you face are so overwhelming that you feel like an ant in the face of Mount Everest, look to God and see *His* awesome power. Stand before the mountain and say, "Lord, where I am right now I declare

*A*ny sign of fear should always be a call to prayer. The moment you feel it, draw *immediately* close to God.

to be holy ground. I invite You to reign in this situation, for You are greater than anything I am facing. 'In Your light I see light'" (Psalm 36:9). Sense that His presence is with you to give you peace. There in the darkness of your earth-shaking circumstances, reach up to God and know that His mighty hand can reach forth to yours faster than the speed of light.

*Prayer Light*

*L*ord, I can only make it through this time if I walk closely with You. My days are in Your hands. While there are many things that can happen in life that are frightening or overwhelming, I know that Your power is greater than all of them. Even when what I experience is too much for me, it is never too much for You. Anything I face is nothing alongside Your ability to redeem it. Lord, I lift to You the things that frighten me most and ask that You would protect me and the people I love from them. Specifically, I bring before You, (name of overwhelming situation) and ask that You would work Your redemption in it. I know that my enemy is the one who "has made me dwell in darkness. . . . Therefore my spirit is overwhelmed within me. . . . Cause me to know the way in which I should walk, for I lift up my soul to You" (Psalm 143:3-4,8).

Whatever I need to do to make my path one of safety and peace, show me how and enable me to do it. Give me wisdom, strength, and clarity of mind to hear what You are saying to me in the midst of any dark or overwhelming situation. May my life be a testimony of the power of Your glory manifested as I walk in the light You have given me.

## *Footlights*

Hear my cry, O God; Attend to my prayer.
From the end of the earth I will cry to You,
When my heart is overwhelmed;
Lead me to the rock that is higher than I.
For You have been a shelter for me,
A strong tower from the enemy.
I will abide in Your tabernacle forever;
I will trust in the shelter of Your wings.

PSALM 61:1-4

The LORD is my light and my salvation;
Whom shall I fear? The LORD is the strength
of my life; of whom shall I be afraid?

PSALM 27:1

In the day of my trouble I sought the Lord;
my hand was stretched out in the night
without ceasing; my soul refused
to be comforted. I remembered God,
and was troubled; I complained,
and my spirit was overwhelmed.
. . . Surely I will remember Your wonders of old.
I will also meditate on all Your work,
and talk of Your deeds.
. . . You are the God who does wonders. . . .

PSALM 77:2,3,11,12,14

There is no fear in love; but perfect
love casts out fear, because fear
involves torment. But he who fears has
not been made perfect in love.

1 JOHN 4:18

# EIGHTEEN

# Reaching for God's Hand in Times of Loss

Everyone experiences loss. It's a part of life. It's the part we don't like and wish we never had to go through. But we all will.

When our losses are severe, we feel like a light has gone out inside of us. And nothing can turn it back on except the restoration of that which is no more. It leaves a hole in our heart the size of the Grand Canyon. But even if what was lost can never be brought back, the part of our life that has died as a result *can* be made to live again. When we walk in the light of God's resurrecting power, He can soothe our pain, heal our wounds, and fill the empty places in our heart.

The worst time of loss for me was the day after my best friend's funeral. I had cried all the way through Diane's battle with breast cancer, her painful and agonizing death in the hospital, and her funeral where I tried to help her husband and eight-year-old son deal with their grief. But nothing compared to the devastation I experienced the morning after it was all over and the finality of it hit me.

It was Monday, the day Diane and I had always prayed together. It was unbearably hard to accept that we would never talk together again. Two days before that was my birthday, and it was the first time in the twenty-eight birthdays I'd had since we'd become friends in high school that I did not receive her early morning phone call telling me she was glad I was born. During some of those years, I believed she was the only one on earth who felt that way. I knew I'd never again have a friend on earth who knew me so well, and life would not be the same without her.

Before she died, I made her a promise that I would look after her son, John. So I kept busy taking care of him, along with my own two children, until his dad was able to pull their lives together and take him home to stay. When John left, I felt the loss all over again. I carried on with my life, but inside there was always a giant lump in my throat. After a couple of months, people didn't want to hear any more about it. I gathered there was an unspoken time limit for grief, after which everything had to return to normal. But I couldn't make myself follow the schedule. I stopped talking about it, not because the grief was any less, but because no one wanted to listen.

It wasn't until I finally gave up trying to deal with the grief myself and surrendered it to God that I began to find relief. As I walked step by step with Him through each day, He gave me the light I needed for that moment, that hour. He became my consolation. He led me to people who understood my loss, whose love and prayers brought healing. And my grief finally ended.

During the dark times of loss, whether it's the death of a loved one, a crippling disease or injury, divorce, a straying child, the end of a relationship, or the loss of home and finances, we grieve because someone or something we love is no longer part of us. Life as we once knew it is forever destroyed. The way we envisioned our future—with that person, with that security, with that capability—is severely shattered. These kinds of losses can bring such pain that we wonder if we will survive them, and, if we do, will we ever feel anything other than the pain? Will we hurt forever? Will life ever feel normal again?

While every act of compassion, sympathy, and love shown to us by others can be a great comfort and help to lift us out of our grief, only the healing touch of God can completely restore us again. We can't expect mere humans to say words that will make the pain go away. People don't always know the right words to say, and what words can make it better, anyway? It's the love in people's hearts, expressed however eloquently or awkwardly, that brings us comfort. If we get hung up on the words, we can miss the love behind them. When people are trying to show us love during our time of loss, we need to let them show it and not criticize them if they don't do it perfectly.

*When we have suffered a deep loss, only God can sustain us, take the pain away, and make us whole again.*

A tragic and needless death happened in my family over fifty years ago, but the wounds of those who deeply felt the loss are still as fresh today as they were then. The mere mention of that person's name immediately brings tears of grief, pain, and regret. That's because healing is still needed that only God can provide.

When we read the morning paper or watch the news on television, we hear of people suffering devastating loss and wonder how they will survive

*It's the love in people's hearts, expressed however eloquently or awkwardly, that brings us comfort. If we get hung up on the words, we can miss the love behind them.*

it. How do the mothers and fathers who lose not one, but all of their children in a tragic accident live through it? My own cousin lost his wife and their three young children in a devastating flash flood. The pain he endured was beyond what should be the limit of human suffering. Nothing could ever take that pain away, nor heal the hole in the heart of this young man and his extended family. Several years after the tragedy he came to visit me, and I deeply regretted that I was not capable of offering any adequate words of consolation to him. I see now that nothing I could have said would have made any difference. Only the healing power of God's love could do that, and I didn't know enough about God then to help him as he needed to be helped.

Often people blame God for the tragedies in their lives and close themselves off from the very One who can take their pain away. But we won't make that same mistake if we will remember two things: God is good, and Satan comes to kill and destroy. It's crucial to not confuse the two during a time of loss.

If you suffer any kind of loss, don't try to get your arms around *it*. Let God get His arms around *you*. He knows your suffering and will give you the comfort of His presence and the healing balm of His love.

*If you walk step by step with God through each day of your loss, in time this pain that seems to be without end will actually subside and you will know happiness again.*

There is no medal given for getting over loss quickly, so don't try to rush the healing process. Submit to every stage of it. Waves of grief come and go and return again when you least expect them. Even when you begin to forget, something will suddenly remind you of what you lost and you will feel the pain all over again. Don't dread those times. Embrace the Lord *in* them. All moments traveled on this road will bring about another part of the healing. Every tear will cleanse a layer of the wound. Each memory will become a salve to the soul.

When a tragedy happens, it's normal to feel that life has come to a complete standstill. But actually it's life as you *knew* it that has stopped. Your new life, *without* that which was lost, is going forward. You just can't see it yet. Even though it's hard to imagine the future being any different than it is at that moment, healing and restoration are happening. You won't always feel this way. There *will* be an end. The loss may have been sudden, but the transition to your new life must be traveled one step at a time.

In times of loss, reach up and take your Heavenly Father's hand. He wants to comfort you and shoulder your grief. He wants to walk with you and bear your burdens. Seek His steadying arm moment by moment and He will draw you closer to Him. Even if your well of tears seems to never run dry, continue to walk in the light of God's presence and you *will* make it through the river of grief to the other side. If you can't see ahead, it's okay. God will not only provide enough light for your next step, He will also enable you to take it.

## *Prayer Light*

*L*ord, only You can fill that empty place in the canyon of sorrow that has been left in my heart. You are the one constant in my life that can never be lost to me. All else is temporary and changing. I know You are a good God and Your love for me is endless. Help me to cast my whole burden of grief on You and let You carry it. Even though there are times when it feels like I can't live through the pain, I know You will sustain me. Enable me to get beyond it. I realize life must go on, and I ask You to help me take the next step I need to take today. Even though it's hard to imagine life without the pain I feel, with You all things are possible. Your healing power can restore anything—even a broken heart. Walk with me, Lord. I trust You to take my hand and lead me until I can feel Your light on my face and joy in my heart once again.

*Footlights*

"Blessed are those who mourn,
For they shall be comforted."

MATTHEW 5:4

Surely He has borne our griefs
And carried our sorrows.

ISAIAH 53:4

"The sun shall no longer be your light by day,
Nor for brightness shall the moon give light to you;
But the LORD will be to you an everlasting light,
And your God your glory.
. . . And the days of your mourning shall be ended."

ISAIAH 60:19-20

The people who walked in darkness
have seen a great light; those who dwelt
in the land of the shadow of death,
upon them a light has shined.

ISAIAH 9:2

This is my comfort in my affliction,
For Your Word has given me life.

PSALM 119:50

# NINETEEN

# Stepping Out
# of the Past

In order to live life successfully in the present and move into the future God has planned for us, we have to step out of the past. If we don't, it will color everything we see and affect all we do.

For example, if rejection has been part of your past and you haven't yet found God's healing for it, every experience you have will be interpreted through the eyes of rejection. It will be impossible to simply accept each moment for what it is without trying to read something else into it.

For the first thirty years of my life, I struggled with feeling that I would never be anything more than a failure. It was not until I entirely surrendered my past to the Lord, and walked out of it step by step, that I was able to see myself as a child of God created for *His* purposes and not a dysfunctional mistake. The biggest problem that faced me with regard to moving out of the past was unforgiveness.

*Not forgiving the people and events of our past will keep us from ever being completely free of it.*

Layers of unforgiveness began to be lifted as I forgave my mother for the abuse I suffered at her hands. She was mentally ill and coped with me by locking me in a closet during much of my early childhood. Even though she was verbally and physically abusive as well, the closet is what affected me the most.

When I became an adult, I was still locked in a closet emotionally. It wasn't until after I came to know the Lord and went to a Christian counselor for help with my depression that I was asked to acknowledge and confess the unforgiveness I had for my mother. When I did, I found freedom from the depression that had paralyzed me for years. As each layer of unforgiveness was stripped away, I became more and more liberated from the hurt and scars of the past.

In order to walk out of unforgiveness, we have to let go of everything except God's hand. This means releasing what needs to be released, and accepting what needs to be accepted. Even an incident that happened yesterday must be given to God so that it doesn't jeopardize our future. We can torture ourselves through the night with sleeplessness over something that happened only hours earlier. We can also live in so *distant* a past that we harbor unforgiveness today for people who hurt our ancestors generations ago.

*We often refuse to let go of injustice and extend forgiveness to others simply because we can't receive the grace God extends to us through His forgiveness.*

People who suffer from eating disorders, addictions, or any other destructive habits of the flesh that are rooted in the past often beat themselves up over reoccurring failure in their area of weakness. They can't forgive themselves and, as a result, the past controls their lives so much that they are unable to function successfully in the present. No matter what our past has been, it doesn't have to rule our lives today.

Beth had a serious problem with binge eating. As a result, her weight increased to a hundred pounds more than what was considered normal for her size. Even though the weight gain seriously compromised her health, she was unable to stop herself. She refused to get help because she had experienced failure in every weight loss program she had tried, and she believed that she would only fail again. It was a cycle from which she was never able to get free. Had she been able to fully receive God's love, grace, and forgiveness, her situation would have been different.

When we walk with the Lord, healing, deliverance, and growth are ongoing in our lives. That's why what may have been true for us last year will not necessarily be true for us today. Yesterday's failure may become today's success.

If there are things in your life about which you have a choice, yet you keep making the wrong choice over and over, you are probably living in the past in some way. There are no shortcuts to emotional healing, but it can happen if you get close to God and take one step at a time with Him. When you make Jesus Lord over your past and are willing to forgive yourself and everyone else associated with it, He can set you free. That means coming to Him every time you are tempted or tormented by the problem, and asking Him to help you move forward step by step.

We can get stuck in the negative complexities of the past when we

*We* can get stuck in the negative complexities of the past when we don't recognize *our* part in it. We see injustices against us, but we fail to realize that at some point we are still responsible for our own attitudes.

don't recognize *our* part in it. We see injustices against us, but we fail to realize that at some point we are still responsible for our own attitudes. If we live in fear, doubt, anger, hatred, resentment, bitterness, and unforgiveness over something that happened in the past—even if it does seem totally justified—we will suffer. We can't be in the dark about the issue of responsibility. Jesus came "to give light to those who sit in darkness and the shadow of death, to guide our feet into the way of peace" (Luke 1:79). We have to make peace with our past.

If you are in a place where you're not able to see a future for yourself, it may be because you believe the past has kept you from moving into the future God has for you. If you find yourself saying, "If only I had not done that"; "If only this had happened instead"; "If I had experienced that I would not be in this situation I am in today"; or "I have forever forfeited the kind of life that could have been mine," remember that these thoughts are not truth. The truth is that God redeems *everything*. Even our past. He meets us as we are swimming to keep our heads above the deep waters of past hurt and failure, and He brings us to the place we're supposed to be. He doesn't do it like a magic genie. He does it one step at a time as we depend on Him.

Getting free from our past doesn't happen overnight. It took me years to become completely free. After finally getting free of layer after layer of unforgiveness toward my mother, I found that I also harbored deep resentment toward my dad for never rescuing me from her insanity. That unforgiveness was so deeply buried in me that I was not even aware of it until I asked God to show me if it was there. Once I was set free of that, I came to a place of peace and productivity I had never before experienced.

Trying to come to terms with the past on your own can be difficult. That's why I advise people who have intensely hurtful pasts to seek the prayer and counsel of godly people who can help them find the healing and restoration God has for them. There is nothing wrong with asking for help. I went to counselors who knew God's truth, and had witnessed God's power, because they best understood how to pray for me. Don't hesitate to get godly counsel, but know that in the end it will be you and God together walking out of the past.

Once you step out of your past, don't look back. If you do, you may see a pattern of past failure that will color how you feel and affect the outcome of what you do today. It can make you fearful and faithless. "Let your eyes look straight ahead, and your eyelids look right before you. Ponder the path of your feet, and let all your ways be established. Do not turn to the right or the left; remove your foot from evil" (Proverbs 4:25-27).

Along with not looking back, it's not good to look too far ahead, either. Doing so may cause you to worry about where you think you *should* be, and that can be overwhelming too. Looking back, you see all that you *didn't* do. Looking too far forward, you see all you think you *can't* do. It's best to embrace the step you're on and say, "God, give me the ability to do what I have to do today."

As we resist being controlled by the negative part of our past, we should also not rely on the positives of our past. While it is right to remember the good things God has done in our lives, we are never to rest on last year's revelation and think we know it all. We need new revelation every day. Walking with God is an ongoing process. We reach plateaus along the way and God gives us a

*D*on't hesitate to get godly counsel, but know that in the end it will be you and God together walking out of the past.

sabbath, but then He gets us up and moving on the path again. He never allows us to rest on our past success. If we did, we would become stagnant, prideful, or careless, and we would not be relying on Him.

The way we step out of the past is to walk in the Spirit. We are walking in the Spirit when the guide for our life is God's Word instead of magazines, television, movies, worldly books, or ungodly people. We are walking in the Spirit when we ask God daily for direction, guidance, and revelation. We are walking in the Spirit when we commit every aspect of our life—relationships, work, decisions, thoughts, and actions—to prayer instead of leaving it all to chance. We are walking in the Spirit when we determine each morning to worship God and set our mind on the things He has called us to, and not on things that have happened in the past.

If your past is an old familiar tune you've sung so long it's turned into the theme of your life, stop the music and ask God to put a new song in your heart. Check to see if you need to confess anything. While you may not have robbed a bank, committed murder, or had an affair, perhaps you have succumbed to doubt, criticism, self-pity, complaining, anger, or lovelessness. Until you are certain that you're washed clean by God's forgiveness, you are still swimming in the muddy waters of the past.

One of the descriptions of light is revelation. That's where the old familiar saying "Shine a light on the situation" comes from. When you need God to shine a light on your situation, ask Him for revelation. He will reveal anything you need to know, and give you understanding where you did not have it. Don't sit in the darkness of the past when God has laid out a path for you to walk in the present that is illuminated with the light of His forgiveness and revelation.

*Prayer Light*

*L*ord, I release my past to You. Everything I have done and all that was done to me I lay at Your feet. I give You my bad memories and ask that You would heal me to complete wholeness so that they no longer hurt, torment, or control me. Bring me to the point where my past, even as recent as yesterday, will in no way negatively affect today. I give You my past failures in the area of (<u>name any reoccurring problem</u>). Set me free from this. Even though I may be unable to completely resist the pull of certain things on my own, I know You are able to set me free. Make me a testimony to the power of Your healing and deliverance.

I confess any unforgiveness in my heart for things that have happened in the past, and I release all persons who are associated with it. I specifically forgive (<u>name of person I need to forgive</u>). Heal all misunderstandings or hurts that have happened between us and make things right. I know that I can never be free and healed if I tie myself to others by unforgiveness, so I ask You to bring to light any unforgiveness in me of which I'm not even aware. Give me Your revelation and show me all I need to see in order to walk out of the shadow of my past and into the light You have for me today.

## *Footlights*

"Forget the former things; do not dwell on the past.
See, I am doing a new thing!
Now it springs up; do you not perceive it?
I am making a way in the desert
and streams in the wasteland."

ISAIAH 43:18-19 (NIV)

. . . the Lord will deliver me from every evil
work and preserve me for His heavenly kingdom.
To Him be glory forever and ever.

2 TIMOTHY 4:18

Therefore, if anyone is in Christ, he is a
new creation; old things have passed away;
behold, all things have become new.

2 CORINTHIANS 5:17

. . . you have delivered my soul from death.
Have You not kept my feet from falling,
that I may walk before God in the
light of the living?

PSALM 56:13

. . . put off, concerning your former conduct,
the old man which grows corrupt
according to the deceitful lusts, and be
renewed in the spirit of your mind,
and that you put on the new man which was
created according to God, in
true righteousness and holiness.

EPHESIANS 4:22-24

# TWENTY

# Maintaining a Passion for the Present

The phrase "timing is everything" is never more true than in your walk with God. However, it is most accurately stated, "*His* timing is everything."

When we come to a place where we trust that God's timing is perfect, we can be content no matter where we are because we know that God will not leave us there forever. Maintaining a passion for the present means embracing the light we have where we are at this time and trusting that it is enough.

I wrote some of this book during the early morning hours before dawn in various hotel rooms I have shared on the road with my husband or my daughter. So as not to disturb them, I used a tiny book light they gave me for my birthday. This light allows me to see only the line I'm on— the one I'm reading or the one I'm writing. In the past, I would have been very impatient with this arrangement because I didn't think I would have enough light to be able to work freely or quickly enough. But now, since I have learned to be content where I am with the light I am given,

I have patience and am grateful for the light I do have. "For who has despised the day of small things?" (Zechariah 4:10). The light I have is enough for what I'm called to do right now.

Being grateful for what we have doesn't mean we will never have more. God doesn't say, "If you're so happy where you are, I'll just leave you there." He continually keeps us growing and moving along the path. If you are not in a place you want to be right now, refuse to let that frustrate or intimidate you. Pastor Jack Hayford says, "Don't let where you are become a prophesy of where you're going to stay."

I love that!

The *good* news is that if you are in an *uncomfortable* place, God guarantees you won't stay there. It's just a matter of time before things change. The *bad* news is that if you are in a *good* place right now, it won't last forever. You'll soon be moved into stretching beyond your comfort zone. Get ready for the ride!

That's the way it is for a child of light who walks with a leading from the Lord. "For you were once darkness, but now you are light in the Lord. Walk as children of light" (Ephesians 5:8). Children of light walk with God fully in control, and their steps are established because they take them on solid ground.

People who walk with a leading from the Lord have a sense of purpose, which clearly marks the boundaries of their lives and makes their choices easy. They are more confident, more compassionate, more aware, and more in tune to what is

> ❧
>
> *P*eople who walk with a leading from the Lord have a sense of purpose, which clearly marks the boundaries of their lives and makes their choices easy.
>
> ❧

happening in the present. Too often we are so into our own lives that we don't see what is going on with someone who is right beside us. We become concerned with securing the future, and as a result we overlook the wealth of the present. But we don't want a "seat-of-our-pants" style of living where we barely make it through every aspect of our lives. We want to appreciate each stage of life and step we're on and live it fully. And that can only happen when we are led by the Spirit of God each day.

I believe the biggest midlife crisis happens when men or women lose the leading of the Lord. Or perhaps they never had it in the first place. So when they arrive at the point in their lives where they need it most, they run toward things they *think* will give them purpose, or at least disguise their lack of it, and they become lost.

When we don't have a clear leading from God, we can never be certain we are in His will. It's so much easier to be content with the step we're on if we know God has a purpose for us being there. People who are not certain about God's will for their marriage, for example, will give up and leave at the earliest indication of problems. They will never know the joy of going through the fire and getting to the glory. Too often we abandon the good in our lives for what appears to be greener pastures, all because we don't have the mind of Christ about it.

*If God wants you in the place you are right now, then there are no greener pastures.*

Walking with God means living moment by moment with Him in the present. Some people live in the past. Some people live for the future. Others give no thought to future or past, living only for the moment. We need to find a balance.

*We must live in the present as if we don't have a past, certain that the steps we take today will determine our future.*

Because our future is determined one day at a time in the present, we need to seek the leading of the Lord daily. We each have the ability to get off on our own little tangent. All it takes is a pound of presumption and a sprinkle of self-satisfaction glazed lightly with laziness, and we have the perfect recipe for missing the path.

One of the main purposes for our lives is to be extensions of God's light. He says, "Let your light so shine before men, that they may see your good works and glorify your Father in heaven" (Matthew 5:16). When we extend the light we have been given, it brings more light to our own lives. "If you extend your soul to the hungry and satisfy the afflicted soul, then your light shall dawn in the darkness, and your darkness shall be as the noonday" (Isaiah 58:10).

If I ever feel down and am tempted to wallow in the darkness of self-pity, I ask God to show me some way to extend His light to others. He always does. When I have shared such simple things as half a sandwich, an article of clothing, a ride, a phone call, a letter, a kind word, a touch, an apology, a prayer, a gift, a compliment, or a helping hand, I've seen the light on my path grow brighter each time.

Just as light from the moon is a reflection of the sun, the light we give off to others is a reflection of *God's* Son. As we look to Him, we reflect His light. When we allow God's light to shine through us, no matter how imperfectly we feel we do that, it not only shines on those around us but it illuminates our own path as well.

So let's do that! Let's free our lights to shine now—in this hour—no matter what we feel our wattage is.

> *W*hen we allow God's light to shine through us, no matter how imperfectly we feel we do that, it not only shines on those around us but it illuminates our own path as well.

Let's live in the present believing what God says. If we need healing, let us turn to the Healer. If we need provision, let us turn to the Provider. If we need wisdom, let us ask the One who is all-wise. If we need love, let us receive God's love and pass it on to those around us. Let's not wait for *life* to be perfect before we live it. Let's not wait for *us* to be perfect before we start giving of ourselves. Let's not wait for *others* to be perfect before we start loving them. The time is now.

God says you are not to be anxious about tomorrow, for there will be plenty of things to concern you when you get there. You are to walk as a child of light, knowing that your future can only be reached one step at a time today. And you are to trust that He will give you the light you need, where you are right now, to take the right step.

## Prayer Light

Lord, I want to live my life the way You want me to every day. Help me not to be stuck in my past, or so geared toward the future that I miss the richness of the present. Help me to experience the wealth in each moment. I don't desire to take a single step apart from Your presence. If You're not moving me, I'm staying here until I have a leading from You. I know I can only get to the future You have for me by walking one step at a time in Your will today. I realize there is no better time than the present to be Your light extended to those around me. Help me to get beyond myself and become an open vessel through which Your light can shine. Give me Your wisdom and revelation and show me all I need to see to keep me on the road You have for me. Enable me to step out of my past and keep an eye on the future by following Your light on my path today.

*Footlights*

The night is far spent, the day is at hand.
Therefore let us cast off the works of darkness,
and let us put on the armor of light.

ROMANS 13:12

. . . the LORD God is a sun and shield;
The LORD will give grace and glory;
No good thing will He withhold
From those who walk uprightly.

PSALM 84:11

". . . do not worry about tomorrow, for
tomorrow will worry about its own things.
Sufficient for the day is its own trouble."

MATTHEW 6:34

For I consider that the sufferings of this present
time are not worthy to be compared with the
glory which shall be revealed in us.

ROMANS 8:18

This is the day the LORD has made;
We will rejoice and be glad in it.

PSALM 118:24

# TWENTY-ONE

# Moving into Your Future

God has so much for us. We have no idea.

We look for crumbs under the table; He has prepared a feast for us in the royal banquet hall. We wonder if He remembers who we are; He has been calling our name. We wait for Him to notice our plight; He waits for us to take His hand. We see ourselves in the dark because we've done something wrong; He sees us in the light because we've done something right. He moves powerfully at our request; we don't even recognize the answers to our own prayers. We have trouble trusting Him fully with our future; the future He has for us is better than the one we dream of for ourselves. "Eye has not seen, nor ear heard, nor have entered into the heart of man the things which God has prepared for those who love Him" (1 Corinthians 2:9).

We worry so about our future because we can never be completely certain about it. A single event can change our lives. For the better, we hope. For the worse, we fear. But God says that, although we won't know everything about our future, we are still to inquire about it. "Ask Me of things to come . . ." (Isaiah 45:11), He instructs us. And when we ask, He sometimes reveals specifics. But most of the time He doesn't give us anything more than the assurance that our future is secure in His hands. He shows us that we *have* a future, and this simple knowledge must be enough for us.

The Bible says that Jerusalem's destruction came because "she did not consider her future" (Lamentations 1:9 NIV). The people did things with no thought of future consequences. We cannot do that. Living in the present doesn't mean we should not plan for what's ahead. We can and we must. We need to do whatever is necessary to plan and prepare for a child's education, next summer's vacation, a career, retirement, the weekend's activities, or our next meal. It's just that we are not to make plans without consulting God first and bringing Him into them. "A man's heart plans his way, but the Lord directs his steps" (Proverbs 16:9). W must never consider our future without first asking God to be in charge of it. And once we do that, we are to leave it in His hands and not lose sleep over it.

> *We must never consider our future without first asking God to be in charge of it. And once we do that, we are to leave it in His hands and not lose sleep over it.*

I have a steep stairway in my house, and every time I look too far ahead when I walk up or down the steps, I stumble and fall. I don't have any problem when I pay attention to the step I'm on or the one that's just ahead. It's the same for our lives. Looking too far ahead can cause us to stumble. Some people look so far ahead into their future, it makes them afraid. It forces them to try to secure it on their own, and then they end up jeopardizing it by leaving God out of the picture. If God is not in our future plans, we spin our wheels in a scheme that doesn't have the potential to get off the ground, let alone fly.

I once knew a man who dashed frantically from one job to another, not because he needed the money, but because he was trying to make something happen for himself and secure his future. His commitment to the Lord was minimal; his obsession with success was paramount. His future is no more secure today than it has ever been, and he is still chasing after something that will forever elude him.

I know another man with the same kind of talent and abilities who chose to draw close to the Lord, humble and submit himself in every way, press into God's Word, and pray fervently for God's guidance. Doors flew open for him, some of which he didn't even dream of knocking on. He didn't try to make God fit *his* vision. He fit himself into *God's* vision. He didn't just do whatever he wanted to do, then ask God to bless it. He asked what *God* wanted him to do, and when he did it God blessed him.

Noah didn't one day decide he was going to build a giant boat and then, after he was finished, ask God to do something with it that would make him go down in history. Not at all. "Noah was a just man, perfect in his generations. Noah walked with God" (Genesis 6:9). This is worth repeating—*Noah walked with God.* And God bless him.

Abraham didn't suddenly say to Sarah one day, "Let's pull up stakes and wander in the desert, and then ask God to lead us somewhere." No, Abraham walked with God, and God told him to leave his country and go to a place He would show him. And God promised, *"I will bless you"* (Genesis 12:2). And God *did* bless him.

Moses didn't just decide one day to go to Pharaoh and ask him to release a million people so they could leave town together. No, Moses was quietly minding his own flock as

God had instructed him to do, when suddenly he heard the Lord call to him from the middle of a burning bush and *tell* him to go. When Moses waited for God's instructions, the Lord blessed everything he did.

These men were walking with God in their daily lives. God spoke to them and told them what to do. They did it. And God blessed them. Can there possibly be a lesson here for us?

*You have a great future ahead and it will be reached as you move out of your past and walk step by step with God as He reveals Himself to you in the present.*

Just as you should not live in the past, resist the urge to live in the future also. Put your future in God's hands, trusting that He will never withhold anything good from you, and then stop worrying about it. This doesn't mean a trumpet will sound announcing that you are spiritually immature if you find yourself concerned about the future. God is not asking you to be perfect. He is asking you to allow *Him* to be perfect in you. God is not asking you to have your whole future figured out. He is asking you to trust that *He* has your future planned. Thinking too much about the future can keep you from fully living the life God has given you now.

This doesn't mean you can't have goals. But some people have goals that are so strong they sacrifice everything to achieve them, even their family and God. Instead of allowing the goal to come *from* God, the goal itself *becomes* god.

*Goals are not meant to be a plumb line to determine the shortest distance to success, but rather a compass to give a sense of direction.*

> ♋
>
> *G*od is not asking you to have your whole future figured out. He is asking you to trust that *He* has your future planned.
>
> ♋

If there is one goal I have for my future, it is that I will never again do what I regret having done in my past. And what I regret is every day I did not live for the Lord. I am sorry for anything I have done that has taken me away from His presence. I see it now as such a waste.

In hindsight, I realize that on every step of my life God has been there. Even when I didn't know Him. Even when I didn't realize I needed Him. Even when I was sure He couldn't possibly care. That's why I know He will be there for me in the future. And when I die, He will be there also. He will give me the light I need for that step, too. And I will weep, possibly for the times I didn't live for Him or believe what He said, but also because He didn't forget me. And He will dry my tears like He has promised to do, and I will live forever in the light of His presence.

The Lord will do the same for you. So keep your eyes on Him. Make Him your only source of light. Follow Him on that narrow pathway and you will be free. Free to trust Him for every step. Free to be all He made you to be. Free to do what He called you to do. Free to enjoy all He has for you. And you won't end up regretting the times you didn't live for Him, because there will no longer be any. You'll walk in a depth of love, peace, fulfillment, and joy you never thought possible.

You don't have to have your life all figured out; you only have to take one step at a time. God will give you just enough light for the step you're on, and every time you put your hand in His, you'll know you've got a solid hold on your future.

----------------------- *Prayer Light* -----------------------

Lord, I ask You to be in charge of my future. I don't want to dream dreams if You are not in them. I don't want to make plans that You will not bless. I don't want to work hard trying to harvest something that will never bear fruit because I did not receive the seed from You. Help me not to waste valuable time getting off the path and having to come back to the same place again. I don't want to get to the end of my life and regret the time I spent not living for You. Therefore I surrender my past, present, and future to You now.

Help me not be anxious about my future but to rest in the knowledge that my future is secure in You. I want to keep one foot in eternity by never letting go of Your hand. I want to store up so many treasures in heaven that heaven will feel familiar the moment I arrive. And when I do take that final step into my eternal future with You, I trust that You will be there for me with all the light I need for that step, too.

## Footlights

. . . I know the thoughts that I think toward
you, says the LORD, thoughts of peace and not of evil,
to give you a future and a hope.

JEREMIAH 29:11

There is surely a future hope for you,
and your hope will not be cut off.

PROVERBS 23:18 (NIV)

Mark the blameless man, and observe the upright;
For the future of that man is peace.

PSALM 37:37

. . . I am persuaded that neither death nor life,
nor angels nor principalities nor powers,
nor things present nor things to come,
nor height nor depth, nor any other created
thing, shall be able to separate us from the
love of God which is in Christ Jesus our Lord.

ROMANS 8:38-39

"Arise, shine;
For your light has come!
And the glory of the LORD is risen upon you.
For behold, the darkness shall cover the earth,
And deep darkness the people;
But the LORD will arise over you,
And His glory will be seen upon you."

ISAIAH 60:1-2

# Notes

**CHAPTER ONE**

1. Jack Hayford, *Pursuing the Will of God* (Sisters, OR: Multnomah Publishing, 1997), p. 20.

**CHAPTER THREE**

1. Oswald Chambers, *My Utmost Devotional Bible* (Nashville, TN: Thomas Nelson Publishers, 1992), p. 44

**CHAPTER SIX**

1. Oswald Chambers, *My Utmost Devotional Bible* (Nashville, TN: Thomas Nelson Publishers, 1992), p. 11

**CHAPTER SEVEN**

1. Oswald Chambers, *My Utmost Devotional Bible* (Nashville, TN: Thomas Nelson Publishers, 1992), p. 98

**CHAPTER THIRTEEN**

1. Oswald Chambers, *My Utmost Devotional Bible* (Nashville, TN: Thomas Nelson Publishers, 1992), p. 86

**CHAPTER FIFTEEN**

1. Oswald Chambers, *My Utmost Devotional Bible* (Nashville, TN: Thomas Nelson Publishers, 1992), p. 86

# Other Books by
# Stormie Omartian

## THAT'S WHAT LOVE IS FOR
by *Stormie Omartian*

*"It always protects, always trusts, always hopes, always perseveres. Love never fails."* Following the pearls of wisdom in 1 Corinthians 13, popular author Stormie Omartian creates a beautiful picture if what love is for. Through a heart-warming collection of experiences from her life, she shares personal moments when God used her and others to demonstrate tender acts of kindness. This inspiring gift book is a precious reminder of the servant love of Christ.

## THE POWER OF A PRAYING WIFE
by *Stormie Omartian*

Omartian shares how you can develop a deeper relationship with your husband by praying for him. The practical advice on praying for specific areas, including decision-making, fears, spiritual strength, and sexuality, will help you discover the fulfilling marriage God intended.

## THE POWER OF A PRAYING PARENT
by *Stormie Omartian*

Popular author and singer Stormie Omartian offers 30 easy-to-read chapters that focus on specific areas of prayers for parents. This personal, practical guide leads the way to enriched, strong prayer lives for parents.

## STORMIE
by *Stormie Omartian*

Stormie tells her compelling story of a childhood marred by physical and emotional abuse and her involvement in the occult, drugs, and tragic relationships. She reveals the healing process that brought freedom and wholeness and shares the hope and help found in Jesus.

# MY MOST
## *Used*
## *Prayers*

### STORMIE
### OMARTIAN

# My Prayer to God

*Lord,* You have said in Your Word that whoever believes in You will have rivers of living water flowing from their heart (John 7:38). I believe in You, and I long for Your living water to flow in and through me today and every day that I'm alive. I invite Your Holy Spirit to fill me afresh right now. Just as a spring is constantly being renewed with fresh water so that it stays pure, I ask You to renew me in that same way today.

Your Word says that "the Spirit also helps in our weaknesses. For we do not know what we should pray for as we ought, but the Spirit Himself makes intercession for us with groanings which cannot be uttered" (Romans 8:26). Lord, I realize I don't know how to pray as I need to, nor as often as I want to, but I invite You, Holy Spirit, to pray through me. Help me in my weakness. Teach me the things I don't know about You.

I am desperately aware of how much I need Your power to transform me and my circumstances. I don't want to live an ineffective life. I want to live in the dynamic power of Your Spirit. I don't want to be a spiritual underachiever. I want to be an overcomer. You paid a price for me so that I could be owned by You. Help me to live like it. You planned out a course for my life so that I could be defined by You. Help me to act like it. You made it possible for me to defeat my enemy. Help me not to forget it. You sent Your Holy Spirit so that I could live in power. Help me to fulfill that promise. You gave Your life for me because You loved me. Help me to do the same for You.

I put all my expectations in You, Lord. I repent of the times I have expected other people or other things to meet my needs when I should have been looking to You. I know that You are the only one who can complete me because You are everything I need. All that I have ever wanted in my life can be found in You. Help me to remember to live not in my own strength, but by the power of Your Spirit living in me. Forgive me for the times I have forgotten to do that. Enable me to grow in the things of Your kingdom so that I can become a whole, properly functioning, contributing, productive child of Yours who moves forward in Your purpose for my life.

# My Prayer to God

*Lord,* I draw close to You today, grateful that You will draw close to me as You have promised in Your Word (James 4:8). I long to dwell in Your presence, and my desire is for a deeper and more intimate relationship with You. I want to know You in every way You can be known. Teach me what I need to learn in order to know You better. I don't want to be a person who is "always learning and never able to come to the knowledge of the truth" (2 Timothy 3:7). I want to know the truth about who You are, because I know that You are near to all who call upon You in truth (Psalm 145:18).

I am open to whatever You want to do in me. I don't want to limit You by neglecting to acknowledge You in every way possible. I declare this day that You are my Healer, my Deliverer, my Redeemer, and my Comforter. Today I especially need to know You as (put in a name of the Lord). I believe You will be that to me.

God, help me to set aside time each day to meet with You alone. Enable me to resist and eliminate all that would keep me from it. Teach me to pray the way You want me to. Help me to learn more about You. Lord, you have said, "If anyone thirsts, let him come to Me and drink" (John 7:37). I thirst for more of You because I am in a dry place without You. I come to You this day and drink deeply of Your Spirit.

I know you are everywhere, but I also know that there are deeper manifestations of Your presence that I long to experience. Draw me close so that I may dwell in Your presence like never before.

# My Prayer to God

*Lord,* I pray You would give me Your wisdom and understanding in all things. I know wisdom is better than gold and understanding better than silver (Proverbs 16:16), so make me rich in wisdom and wealthy in understanding. Thank You that You give "wisdom to the wise and knowledge to those who have understanding" (Daniel 2:21). Increase my wisdom and knowledge so I can see Your truth in every situation. Give me discernment for each decision I must make.

Lord, help me to always seek godly counsel and not look to the world and ungodly people for answers. Thank You, Lord, that You will give me the counsel and instruction I need, even as I sleep. Thank You that "You will show me the path of life" (Psalm 16:7-11).

I delight in Your law and in Your Word. Help me to meditate on it day and night, to ponder it, to speak it, to memorize it, to get it into my soul and my heart. Lord, I know that whoever "trusts in his own heart is a fool, but whoever walks wisely will be delivered" (Proverbs 28:26). I don't want to trust my own heart. I want to trust Your Word and Your instruction so that I will walk wisely and never do ignorant or stupid things. Make me to be a wise person.

You said in Your Word that You store up sound wisdom for the upright (Proverbs 2:7). Help me to walk uprightly, righteously, and obediently to Your commands. May I never be wise in my own eyes, but may I always fear You. Keep me far from evil so that I can claim the health and strength Your Word promises (Proverbs 3:7-8). Give me the wisdom, knowledge, understanding, direction, and discernment I need to keep me away from the plans of evil so that I will walk safely and not stumble (Proverbs 2:10-13). Lord, I know that in You "are hidden all the treasures of wisdom and knowledge" (Colossians 2:3). Help me to discover those treasures.

# My Prayer to God

*Lord,* You are my light and my salvation. You are the strength of my life. Of whom, then, shall I be afraid? Even though an entire army may surround me and go to war against me, my heart will not fear (Psalm 27:1-3). I will be strong and of good courage, for I know that You are with me wherever I go (Joshua 1:9). Free me from all ungodly fear, for I know that fear is never of You.

Guard my heart and mind from the spirit of fear. What I am afraid of today is (name anything that causes you to have fear). Take that fear and replace it with Your perfect love. If I have any thoughts in my mind that are fueled by fear, reveal them to me. If I have gotten my mind off of You and on my circumstances, help me to reverse that process so that my mind is off my circumstances and on You. Show me where I allow fear to take root and help me to put a stop to it. Take away any fear of rejection and all fear of man from within me and replace it with the fear of the Lord.

Your Word says that You will put fear in the hearts of Your people and You will not turn away from doing them good (Jeremiah 32:40). I pray that You would do that for me. I know that You have not given me a spirit of fear, so I reject that and instead claim the power, love, and sound mind You have for me. "Oh, how great is Your goodness, which You have laid up for those who fear You" (Psalm 31:19). Because I have received a kingdom which cannot be shaken, may I have grace by which to serve You acceptably with reverence and godly fear all the days of my life (Hebrews 12:28).

Thank You that "the fear of the LORD leads to life, and he who has it will abide in satisfaction; he will not be visited with evil" (Proverbs 19:23). Help me to grow in fear and reverence of You so that I may please You and escape the plans of evil for my life. Thank You that those who fear You will never lack any good thing.

# I Give Him My Praise

Lord, I worship You and thank You that You are the God of love. Thank You for loving me before I even knew You. I praise You especially for sacrificing Your only Son for me. There is no greater love than that. Your love brings healing to me for all the times and ways I have felt unloved in my life. I know that no matter what is happening in my life or what *will* happen in my life, Your love for me will never end. Because of Your love, "I will praise You, O LORD, with my whole heart; I will tell of all Your marvelous works. I will be glad and rejoice in You; I will sing praise to Your name, O Most High" (Psalm 9:1-2).

Thank You, Lord, that "You number my wanderings" and "put my tears in Your bottle" (Psalm 56:8). They are in Your book. Thank You that "when I cry out to You, then my enemies will turn back" (verse 9). I know that You are for me. Jesus, I know that whatever I ask in Your name You will do, so that God the Father may be glorified. I ask that You would pour out Your love upon me in a way that I can feel today. I pray that I will be so filled with Your love that it overflows from me to others and can be seen by everyone around me. May Your love be greatly evident in all that I do and say. May Your grace, Your love, and Your Holy Spirit be with me always (2 Corinthians 13:14).

It is amazing that You love me so, even though I have done nothing to deserve it. "What is man, that You should exalt him, that You should set Your heart on him?" (Job 7:17). Thank You that You "see my ways and count all my steps" (Job 31:4). Thank You that Your "favor is for life" (Psalm 30:5). O Lord, "because Your lovingkindness is better than life, my lips shall praise You. Thus I will bless You while I live; I will lift up my hands in Your name" (Psalm 63:3-4). Lord, I love You with all my heart, mind, and soul, and I worship You as my God of love.

# I Give God My Praise

Lord, I worship You as the God of heaven and earth. I praise You for Your greatness and Your goodness. Thank You that You are a good God and Your mercy and grace toward me will endure forever (Psalm 118:1). May I never forget all the good You have done for me and how You have filled my life with good things.

Lord, I desire, as David did, that I may dwell in Your house all the days of my life, to behold Your beauty and to be in Your temple (Psalm 27:4). This day I will enter Your gates with thanksgiving and Your courts with praise. I bless Your name, for You are good. Your mercy is everlasting, and Your truth endures to all generations (Psalm 100:4-5). You are my God and Lord, You are loving and patient, and You abound in goodness and truth (Exodus 34:6).

Help me to trust that You are a good God no matter what is going on in my life. Help me to believe without any doubting that even if bad things are happening, Your goodness will reign in the midst of them all. Thank You that Your plans for me are for good. Thank You that the future You have for me is good. Thank You that You bring good things into my life. Reveal Your goodness to me more and more so that I may praise You for it. How great is Your goodness to those who trust and fear You (Psalm 31:19).

O Lord, how excellent is Your name in all the earth (Psalm 8:1). I am so grateful that the earth is full of Your goodness, and that Your goodness endures continually (Psalm 52:1). You are good, and all You do is good. Teach me Your ways, for I know that they are good too (Psalm 119:68). Surely Your goodness and mercy will follow me all the days of my life; and I will dwell with You forever (Psalm 23:6).

# I Give God My Praise

Lord, I worship You as my Almighty God. You are my King and Lord over all my life. I surrender everything I have to You because I recognize that every good thing I have has been given to me by You as a sign of Your goodness, mercy, and love (James 1:17). Thank You that You are my Provider and You provide everything I need.

Lord, I praise You as my Protector. Thank You for hiding me under "the shadow of Your wings, from the wicked who oppress me, from my deadly enemies who surround me" (Psalm 17:8-9). "I will render praises to You, for You have delivered my soul from death. Have You not kept my feet from falling, that I may walk before God in the light of the living?" (Psalm 56:12-13).

I love You, Lord. I know that Your provision and protection are evidence of Your great love for me. I will call upon You, for You are worthy to be praised and I will be saved from my enemies (Psalm 18:3). My hope is in You. My heart rejoices in You. I trust in Your holy name (Psalm 33:21). I rejoice in You, I trust in You, I shout for joy because You defend me. Thank You that You bless and surround me like a shield (Psalm 5:11-12).

I bow down before You in worship, my Lord and my Creator. You are my God, and I am one of Your sheep for whom You extend Your hand of protection (Psalm 95:6-7). You are my refuge and my strength in the day of trouble, and I will sing Your praises forever (Psalm 59:16-17).

# I Give God My Praise

Lord, I worship You for all that You are. You are my Lord in the good times as well as the difficult. On the mountaintop as well as in the valley. You are King of Kings on the throne of my life in the calm as well as in the storm. I praise You in times of great blessing as well as in times of great challenge. You are Almighty and all-powerful, and I find my strength in You. It is because of You that I can stand strong, even when I feel weak. For I know that when I am weakest, You show Yourself strong. I am grateful for Your salvation, deliverance, protection, goodness, and blessings in my life every day. I know that everything I have comes from You. Because of Your great strength I go from glory to glory and "strength to strength" no matter what is happening in my life (Psalm 84:7).

I want to show my love for You every day by embracing You with my worship and touching You with my praise. Teach me all I need to know about how to worship You in ways that are pleasing in Your sight. Fill my heart with such great knowledge of You that praising You becomes a way of life. Teach me to make it my first reaction to every situation, no matter what the situation is. All honor, glory, and majesty belong to You, Lord, for You are worthy to be praised.

You are holy and righteous, and I have no greater joy in life than entering into Your presence to exalt You with worship and praise every day. I know that in Your presence I will find everything I need forever.

## A Letter to Our Readers

Dear Reader:

In order that we might better contribute to your reading enjoyment, we would appreciate your taking a few minutes to respond to the following questions. When completed, please return to the following:

Andrea Doering, Editor-in-Chief
Crossings Book Club
401 Franklin Avenue, Garden City, NY 11530

You can post your review online! Go to www.crossings.com and rate this book.

Title _____ Author _____

**1   Did you enjoy reading this book?**

❏ Very much. I would like to see more books by this author!

❏ I really liked_____

❏ Moderately. I would have enjoyed it more if_____

**2   What influenced your decision to purchase this book? Check all that apply.**

      ❏ Cover
      ❏ Title
      ❏ Publicity
      ❏ Catalog description
      ❏ Friends
      ❏ Enjoyed other books by this author
      ❏ Other _____

**3   Please check your age range:**

      ❏ Under 18    ❏ 18-24
      ❏ 25-34      ❏ 35-45
      ❏ 46-55      ❏ Over 55

**4   How many hours per week do you read?** _____

**5   How would you rate this book, on a scale from 1 (poor) to 5 (superior)?**
_____

Name_____

Occupation_____

Address_____

City_____ State_____ Zip_____